WITCHES

WITCHES

The Transformative Power

of Women

Working Together

SAM GEORGE-ALLEN

Melville House
Brooklyn · London

WITCHES

First Melville House Printing: January 2020

Melville House Publishing
46 John Street
Brooklyn, NY 11201
and
Melville House UK
Suite 2000
16/18 Woodford Road
London E7 0HA

mhpbooks.com
@melvillehouse

ISBN: 978-1-61219-834-7
ISBN: 978-1-61219-835-4 (eBook)

Library of Congress Control Number: 9781612198347

Designed by Betty Lew

Printed in the United States of America
1 3 5 7 9 10 8 6 4 2

A catalog record for this book is available from
the Library of Congress

For my mother, and my sister;
for all my mothers, and all my sisters.

CONTENTS

WITCHES

INTRODUCTION

I started pulling tarot cards while writing this book. The writing was hard and I was filled with self-doubt, so I turned to the cards in the way I have always turned to the magical in times of crisis. I trusted them because I can't control them. Even when they told me bad news—failure on the horizon, friends to be lost, the Wheel of Fortune in reverse—they helped.

The germ of this book got into me in another time of turmoil. A few years ago, I found myself suddenly and furiously envious of another woman's success. It was like having an uncontrollable crush. I couldn't stop thinking about her: comparing myself to her, finding reasons to resent and dismiss her. It was very upsetting. Wasn't I supposed to be a feminist, the good kind, one who builds her sisters up rather than tearing them down? Why was my basest nature choosing this moment, as I was carving out a career writing about gender and women's work, to make itself known? I went to the cards again, and I pulled one for me, which I immediately forgot, and one for her: Justice, reversed.

It was an injustice, what I was doing, and what was happening to me. It felt unnatural to begrudge this person her happiness. It was making me miserable. I did not think I was born with these feelings in me, and when I took hold of that thread and pulled, the whole wicked tapestry started to come apart. I wasn't born with these feelings, but I had been feeling them, in one way or another, for a long time—since I was a teenager, at least. I'm still part of a society that neither likes nor trusts women, particularly when they're working together. Even though they may have changed, learned to disguise themselves, those seeds of loathing were still there.

I hate admitting it now, because it's other women who make my life what it is today: meaningful, complicated, challenging and rewarding. I have surrounded myself, by luck and by design, with women who ask a lot of me, who give a lot to me, who are willing to sit at my kitchen table and argue with me for hours until we both have straightened out how we see the world, how we think the world should be. I owe women a lot, just for the pleasure of being in their company.

In the first episode of the second season of the excellent Netflix series *GLOW*, a show that is, in many ways, about the things that women do together (and also about a bunch of female amateur wrestlers making a low-budget TV show called Gorgeous Ladies of Wrestling), there's a moment that made me reach for my pen. The women have just returned from filming a title sequence at the mall, where they'd hammed it up in character, Welfare Queen and Liberty Belle taking swipes at each other with bunches of shopping bags, Britannica and Beirut chasing each other around stands of sunglasses. They are standing in a group, laughing with one another, relaxed and excited about what they've just made. The director, Sam (played by Marc Maron at his neurotic, curmudgeonly best), approaches.

'Hey,' he says. 'I don't like when you're in a clump, whispering.' He gestures dismissively. 'Spread out so I can see you.'

I wrote it down. *Spread out so I can see you*. It's almost a joke— but not quite. Maron's character doesn't like it when women are doing stuff he doesn't know about. He finds it unnerving. A lot of people do.

For those invested in maintaining the status quo, there's a lot to be gained from preventing women from getting together. A population that is divided, distracted and economically depressed is unable to demand to be released from oppression. Isolated women are easier to sell things to, easier to control, more easily compressed into the very few ways to acceptably be a woman. All this is made even easier if that woman is inculcated into a tradition of mistrusting others like her. For a long time, we've lived in a culture that tries to spread us out so it can see us—and so we can't see each other, except from the corners of our eyes.

We're taught to enjoy female rivalry. We look for and expect it. Celebrity feuds fuel the whole tabloid industry. The ongoing success of the many iterations of Real Housewives is predicated on the same principle. Films, books and magazines aimed at women all sell the same, sorry story of women competing with one another, often for the attention of men. And we buy it. In 2016, a study by several sociologists on feminine rivalry found that their young, female subjects 'constructed comparisons and competition among women as never-ending and seemingly natural'. The narrative has become so ingrained as to appear spontaneous, immutable and as naturally occurring as the weather. It is simply the way things are.

So when women choose to align with one another, it takes

us by surprise. We look at it sideways; like GLOW's director, we are suspicious. Suspicion often goes hand in hand with derision, because if you strip a group of their credibility, you strip them of their perceived threat, too. Consider the mockery of women-only spaces on university campuses, the w dismissal of teenage fangirls, the smirking devaluation of all-girl music groups, the sneering contempt of writers and readers of romance fiction. Mothers and daughters are pitted against one another, persuaded to be jealous, to compete for the love and attention of the father/husband; sisters, similarly; friends are always kept at arm's length in case they should prove smarter, prettier, more successful; organisations of women are frumpy or frivolous, not to be associated with; artistic efforts by women are gimmicks. To be taken seriously one must be alone among men.

What is the threat that women in groups pose? There are shades in Sam's anxiety of Margaret Atwood's eternal observation—men are afraid that women will laugh at them, while women are afraid that men will kill them—but the truth is that women together are a fundamental force for change. The change has already begun; we are seeing it happen before our eyes. Beyoncé's all-woman touring band; Taylor Swift's famous girl squad; Parris Goebel's jaw-dropping dance troupe; and, of course, the many women, visible and invisible, who have become a part of the #MeToo movement, which has begun the hard—and previously impossible—work of toppling a crooked pyramid of corrupt and predatory men, a movement that represents probably the greatest and most conspicuous collaboration of women since the suffragettes. In the wake of #MeToo, it becomes clear why those who benefit from the patriarchy have been so invested in keeping women isolated from one another. And these are just some of the feminine collaborations rising in the public consciousness. When I look at them, I feel my heart leap in an unfamiliar way. I see glimpses of how the world could be.

This is a big deal for me, because it has been the greatest revelation of my life to realise that I could choose to reject the fictions being fed to me. For a long, long time, I swallowed the poison that was compulsory female rivalry, and I did it willingly, in good humour, and while cheerfully calling myself a feminist. For a long time, and against all evidence, I was convinced that I was not—and would never be—like 'other girls'. When I think about it now, I find it hard to pinpoint where this conviction came from. Was it my parents, and their persistent, low-grade denigration of 'girl' things like Disney princesses and long hair? Maybe it was the books I read, all of which seemed to feature, at best, a solitary girl among a gaggle of adventuring guys— if a girl appeared at all. It could have been the women's magazines I'd furtively pick up in the supermarket, with their detailed instructions on how to keep a man, presumably from Other Women. The bands I liked only had one woman on the line-up, if that. Wherever it came from, I took up the posture enthusiastically. Gillian Flynn immortalised the concept in her novel *Gone Girl*, where she has her protagonist bitterly expound on the 'Cool Girl': the impossibly chill, unnaturally easygoing girl who manages to be both a sex object and 'just one of the guys'.

Even as I got older, and stopped saying stupid things like 'Most of my friends are guys, girls are too much drama', I still felt the lingering effects of that childhood indoctrination: girl stuff was silly, and boy stuff was *cool*. It's a testament to the complexity of the human mind that I could simultaneously have mostly female friends, cherished individuals with whom I shared intimate, trusting and rewarding relationships, and also think, deep down, that girls kind of sucked a bit. Internalised misogyny: it's a hell of a thing.

So I started writing this book, during my crisis of comparison, as a sort of self-help exercise. I was finally trying to stitch together my feminist theory and my deeply flawed practice. I had had a revelation, and I was trying to make it stick. I don't think it's coincidence that the revelation came during my renaissance with witchcraft.

•

Being let into the boys' club is such a monumentally disappointing prize. Reminiscing with a friend recently, we were appalled to realise how much of our teen years were spent sitting silently in male friends' houses, watching them play video games. They didn't even offer us the controller. *This* was what we were rewarded with for being the 'cool girl'? What a crock of shit.

Witches, though, have never sought entry into that club. Go back to the Middle Ages, go further to Ancient Greece and Rome, further, to the magical traditions of Africa and the Americas, and you will find women doing work—healing work, birthing work, spirit work—in their own damn club. Witches have been many things throughout human history (and by no means have they always been women), but now, after centuries of Judeo-Christian culture and colonialism, the term 'witch' has come to describe a woman on the margins. During the European witch craze of the Middle Ages, a witch was any woman who challenged or alarmed the church or the community, whether by knowing how to heal people with herbs rather than leeches and prayer, or by being poor, old, disfigured or otherwise different.

If a witch is a woman on the margins, then we're all witches, because in a patriarchy all women are marginalised in one way or another. The word is still deployed as a threat, reminding us that we're all a step or two away from the stake and the flames. During the 2016 American presidential campaign, right-wing supporters delighted in sharing images on social media of Hillary Clinton as a green-skinned, broom-riding, black hat–wearing harridan; they called her the Wicked Witch of the Left. Just a few years earlier, Tony Abbott, then the Australian opposition leader, was staging press conferences about Prime Minister Julia Gillard in front of signs that read 'Ditch the Witch'. The term might seem at home lumped alongside the other choice words reserved for putting women in their place—but there's something different about 'witch'. Maybe it's the undisguisable element of power about it. Maybe that's why now, many women, young and old, are choosing to claim the title for themselves.

I went back to witchcraft spurred by that all-consuming envy that saw me pulling cards from my Rider-Waite-Smith deck, and the unnerving, overwhelming feeling that I was being acted upon by forces beyond my control. I could not get a hold of myself. It felt like magic, so I looked to magical traditions, seeking, half-jokingly, a way of making sense of it all. What I found was a tradition of women helping women. I had my revelation here. If all women are witches because they're on the margins, then groups of women—collaborators, covens—are the witchiest of all. Women in groups make the margins their home, draw their strength from being able to see clearly from the edge, and together they are deeply and earth-movingly subversive—yes, even Australia's Country Women's Association, even the Girl Scouts, even the Concerned Women for America.

Because, let's be real: how frightening is the thought of women in concert with one another? How intimidating, for those who need the patriarchy for success, to imagine a league of women for whom male approval is the last thing on their minds? How easy is it to understand the Athenians' mortal horror in the face of reports that the Amazons, the warrior woman of Classical History, might be mobilising to move on Greece? The assumption that women always inhabit objecthood, unable to exercise the subjectivity necessary to even want to work together, is turned on its head; this is the legacy of consciousness-raising, that secondwave movement of feminism among the isolated women of the First World, the movement Rebecca Solnit says broke 'through the shame that had kept them silent and alone'; here is where Audre Lorde found 'the concern and caring of all those women which gave me strength and enabled me to scrutinize the essentials of my living'.

And here the witch emerges: unnerving enough on her own, but when she's part of a coven, converting 'good women'— those who serve their families, those spread out and visible—to disciples, increasing the numbers of an unholy alliance of female agency, she becomes outright terrifying.

Of course there is a conspiracy to keep women apart from one another. As much as my issues with competitiveness are products of my own unique neuroses, many of the women I spoke to for this book, when I told them what I was writing about, had a gleam of recognition in their eyes. When I talked to Sue Middleton, former Australian Rural Woman of the Year and phenomenally successful farmer, she brought up the fact that a lot of women her age who occupied positions of power in their industries were reluctant to let other women join them at the top.

It's a recognised phenomenon, when the women who've fought hard against the current of sexism and marginalisation to get to their position then kick the door shut behind them. Jessa Crispin talks about it in her book *Why I Am Not a Feminist*, pointing out that the door-slamming often happens along lines of privilege: white women, in particular, have opened doors for other white women but refuse to do the same for non-white women, or for trans or non-binary people.

I spoke to Melbourne artist DJ Sezzo about why we felt a sense of competition only with other women and not with men. She came at it from an economic perspective: the idea persists in lots of industries, both creative and otherwise, that most roles are for men, and that the roles available to women are scarce at best, so we feel a sense of false economy and its accompanying anxiety. Believing that there are only one or two positions available to us means that we compete with members of our own gender much more than we compete with others outside that group, and it means that we absorb the ideas that women (other women) are incompetent, unworthy of admiration or aspiration, objects of suspicion.

I think she's right. Slamming the door shut behind you, competing for artificially scarce opportunities—they're both symptoms of a system that's rigged to keep us distracted from the real problem: the fact that there is a door to slam in the first place; the outrageous lie that there are only ever a few spaces available for women at the top of their game. This was the root of the all-consuming envy I felt, and it's what I needed to tear out. Fortunately the women I've spoken to in the course of writing this book are the best possible proof that there is infinite room for wise, brilliant, talented women in every industry. Ballet dancers, weightlifters, farmers, nuns—they are all doing the work, in their own ways and their own spaces, of tearing down the paper scenery and opening up the real world.

I had hoped that this book would help with that work. For the first time in my life I've intentionally put myself in positions where I can learn from other women—*only* other women. I've spent so much time listening to people's stories, letting their knowledge and experiences change me; I wanted to make something that would change other people, too. But the change I had hoped to make is already here. When I look around, I no longer see those narratives of feminine competition. I've spent enough time talking with the people featured in this book to know for sure that the natural state of women together is not rivalry. This book is a memoir of learning, and unlearning, as well as a celebration of women in collaboration with one another. Everywhere, women are doing things together—wonderful things, magical things—in spite of all the bullshit we're told about women being catty, backstabbing, untrustworthy bitches. I'm not trying to suggest that all women are kind to each other, or supportive of one another, or any one thing at all. We all know that our lives and stories are as diverse as we are; and I'm a white, cis, straight girl from a middle-class family in Australia—I know I can't be representative of all experiences. What I am trying to show is an alternative—many alternatives—to the stories we are usually told. This book is a letter to my former self, and to anyone who's ever felt like her. Look at all these women, I want to say. Look what happens when we come together. Magic, some people say, is change driven by intent. Of course we are witches.

1

TEEN GIRLS

This emotion

Outside the cinemas, like a creep, I am watching the teenagers. Here in Brisbane's South Bank, at the Cineplex, they line up for tickets in cold-shoulder tops and jeans torn from thigh to shin. I am sitting in the gloom by the arcade machines, thinking about the impenetrable fog between me and them; between me now, and me then. Every once in a while I think I can glimpse my former self, but then the time and distance snatches her away. I barely remember what it was like to be a teenage girl; all I remember is the multicoloured pounding of my huge, vicious, terrifying emotions.

•

I have never felt so strongly as I did when I was a teen. Now, as an adult, if I get flashes of that magnitude of feeling—an unexpected attraction, unanticipated rage—it makes me feel winded. How did I spend years of my life caught in the throes of that maelstrom of feeling and come out in one piece?

The mechanics of teenage emotions are a tangle of elevated

hormones and spasmodic brain growth. Oestrogen, proges-
terone and testosterone are pumping, aiding the development of
secondary sex characteristics and in the process creating greater
emotional peaks and troughs than anyone should have to deal
with. Meanwhile, the frontal lobes of our brains, where all our
higher functions like impulse control, language, social fluency
and imagination live, are developing at a far slower rate than
our chaotic bodies. It's a volatile combination of recklessness
and profound feeling. And, thanks to gendered social attitudes,
girls' profundity of feeling and recklessness have few channels
of outlet. They're sexualised young and immediately shamed for
that sexuality; they're encouraged to take on responsibilities like
chores and childcare before their brothers; they're policed more
on what to wear and who they should and shouldn't spend time
with.

Compressed on all sides by social convention, parental expectation, educational boundaries, media scolding, scorn and
ridicule, and unutterable powerlessness, all that emotion has to
go somewhere. Throughout the twentieth century, that feeling
burst out in fads, fanaticism and obsession that drove entire industries and elevated musicians and actors to billionaire deities.
Now, thrillingly, teen girls are wielding that intensity of emotion
with more and more consciousness, using it to lift one another
up, spread their message and change the world. As dark and
uncharted as the woods of youth in an age of social media may
be, girls are picking a path through them, finding their way to a
better world on the other side. Teenage girls' force of feeling is
a force of change.

The concept of the teenager is a fairly new one. For much of
human history, a girl was a woman as soon as she hit puberty;

setting aside the teen years as a special, separate period of life didn't come about until the 1920s. Industrialisation and the burgeoning middle class brought people into the cities, and their children into schools. As secondary education became the norm, the teenage demographic began to emerge: a social group with school as their locus of identity. By the middle of the twentieth century, teenagers were a recognised, and coveted, set of consumers, separate from children and from 'youths', notorious for their quickly passing fashions, their obsession with music and records, and their spending power. Although teenage boys have always had their own stereotypes to contend with, it is the girls who've been most conscientiously documented, courted and criticised—for their incorrigible silliness, mostly. Consider how we are encouraged to conceive of teenage girls. Airheaded fangirls, vacuous Valley girls, boy-crazy, trend-obsessed, shallow, gullible, clumsily sexy, easily scorned, easily dismissed. Teen girls are mocked for the way they talk, the way they look, the trends they participate in, the music they love, for their earnestness, for their passion, for their cliqueyness—basically, for everything.

When I was a teenager I was constantly aware of my status as a teen girl, and constantly attempting to distance myself from it. I was not obsessed with my looks; I made it very clear that I didn't care about Justin Timberlake; I was happy to tell people that I was not like those other girls.

It should be clear, however, that 'those other girls' are almost entirely a myth. Image-obsessed mean girls do exist, but no teenage girl is the kind of caricature that appears in high school movies or op-eds about selfie culture. And in the decade and a half that has passed since I entered my teens, there's been an incredible shift in how teen girls are represented and how they represent themselves, thanks mostly to the internet and platforms like *Rookie*, the online magazine started by prodigy Tavi Gevinson, and Tumblr, the democratic blogging site where many teen girls find a thriving community of like-minded compatriots formed around everything from Harry Potter to fashion to Wicca to social justice to Justin Bieber. Teen girls these days are approaching their lives with agency, even the famous ones— international pop star Lorde, who rose to fame at age sixteen, is so tuned in to the intensity and fluctuation of the teen girl experience that she titled her sophomore album *Melodrama*.

But when I was a kid, the internet was just getting started. I didn't have Facebook or a Tumblr, and although I considered myself to be entirely above the mainstream and mundane, I swallowed the vapid teen girl myth completely. It's a shame, because looking back on that time now—that hyper-saturated period at the precipice of adulthood—it seems like a dream. I wish I hadn't resisted the magnetic pull of teenageness into that roiling heart of communal feeling.

When I was a teen I felt a sense of power that I haven't felt since—a vivid magical thinking that meant I was certain, in some unarticulated way, that I could make things happen. I felt powerfully joyous and powerfully angry and powerfully, unrequitedly in love. Of course I felt like the force of my emotions was enough to change things around me, like a shifting magnetic pole knocking things out of place, or a conduit for some huge emotional current. Being an adolescent girl feels like something huge is happening to you; it doesn't surprise me that young women throughout history have often ridden that brink between the mortal and the divine.

•

In the period just after Christ's death, Christians were a per-
secuted minority. Still a fringe cult of fanatics and strange,
street-shouting preachers, they were feared and reviled by the
Romans. Rumours spread that Christians were cannibals who
committed incest at their household church meetings, thanks to
Christians' habits of referring to one another as 'brothers and
sisters' and their secretive ritual of taking the body and blood of
Christ. Their refusal to publicly worship Roman gods offended
and frightened the Roman populace; their emphasis on bodily
and spiritual purity through chastity and self-punishment, their
distaste for worldly pleasures, and their 'superstitions' took them
from offensive to despicable. Members of the sect were tortured,
crucified, fed to lions, stoned to death, driven out of towns and
otherwise hassled by both the general population and by the law.

Many of the passionate disciples of early Christianity were
young women: desert virgins, teens from aristocratic families
breaking their vows to future husbands and taking vows of
chastity instead. *The Acts of Paul and Thecla*, an apocryphal
story written around the same time as the New Testament of
the Bible, describes a young, wealthy woman in the first century
AD, living in the Roman city of Iconium in what would later
become Turkey. Thecla was engaged to a young man named
Thamyris, until she happened to hear the sermons of Paul
from her bedroom window. He was preaching on chastity. She
became so absorbed by what she was hearing that she sat transfixed by her window for three days, neither eating nor sleeping,
and unable to be moved by her increasingly frantic mother and
fiancé.

(I remember being struck dumb in my teen years by something that felt greater than myself—stories, mostly—reading Diana Wynne Jones and Katherine Mansfield, looking up from the page and staring into space—being absolutely, profoundly changed.)

Eventually, Thecla came to enough to tell her mother and Thamyris that she would no longer marry, that she would take a vow of chastity and devote her life to God. Her mother, frightened and enraged with the prophet for poisoning her daughter's mind, rounded up a mob that took Paul to prison. Overcome with longing to see her spiritual leader instead of only hearing him, Thecla crept out at night, bribed the prison guard and sat with Paul in his cell, listening to his sermons and kissing his chains. When she was discovered the next morning, she was brought before the local governor and asked why she would not marry Thamyris. When she refused to answer, her mother called for her to be burned at the stake.

The story goes that she was saved from that fate by a fortuitous hailstorm that put out the fire and drove away the angry mob, and that she survived many other trials as well, including being thrown to wild beasts and tied to the back of an angry bull. (The story also says she slapped a Roman governor in the street after he tried to convince her to marry him—a badass for sure.) Eventually she went out into the desert to live in a cave, and came to be known for working miracles of healing. When the jealous doctors of the city sent a group of men to rape her, the ninety-year-old virgin called on God for help; a rock doorway in the cave opened, she stepped inside, and she was never seen again.

Though Thecla's story is fantastic, it's not uncommon for

the era. The fervour of early Christianity emboldened young women to disobey their parents' orders to marry, and their religious devotion earned them praise from the male figures of the Christian church. Teenage girls played a significant role in legitimising Christianity in the first centuries after Christ, by being vocally, defiantly devout, flouting Roman tradition and law in order to remain unmarried virgins, following the desert mothers and fathers into the wilderness to become spiritual leaders themselves, and leaving behind lush lives of aristocratic comfort for days spent in penance and spartan, spiritual reflection.

It's likely that Thecla stands in place of any number of remarkable teen girls of the period who turned their considerable emotional energy away from marrying and raising families as the Roman law dictated, and towards building what would become a globally influential religion, in the process risking torture, death and condemnation. Unsurprisingly, many of these founding maids have been written out of the accounts of the church in its infancy; stories like Thecla's remain only on the fringes.

•

Unlike Thecla, Joan of Arc is a teenage girl whose legend has endured. You probably know the story: a peasant girl from Domremy who lived during the Hundred Years' War in the fifteenth century, Joan, who had her first vision from God at age thirteen, was the catalyst that changed everything for France in its struggle against the invading English. As only a young woman with a mission can, she devoted herself to fulfilling her calling to protect France and restore the rightful king. She convinced the French Dauphin, Charles VII, to put her in charge of his armies, and then, incredibly, she led them to victory—

an illiterate cattle maid still in her teens with no military experience, who nevertheless was possessed of such blazing-eyed conviction that she turned the war with the English into a religious experience.

You also probably know how the story ends: she was burned at the stake as a heretic at age nineteen, by the pro-English Bishop of Beauvais. But her passion and resilience has seen her remain an enduring figure for more than five hundred years. Now she is the patron saint of France: a teenage girl, driven by some unseen, unstoppable force; a passion that changed European history.

•

Of course, Thecla and Joan are girls acting alone, girls allowed to be special by the exceptionalism of history (Malcolm Gladwell calls it 'moral licensing': letting one member of a marginalised group achieve greatness and then clamping down on all others); they're allowed to exist outside the easily trivialised demographic of teen girls because they really *are* 'not like other girls'. The single girl is an enduring and beloved tool of the patriarchy—Joan, Thecla, Buffy, Juliet, almost any Disney princess . . . even Joan was said by her contemporaries never to suffer another woman riding with the French army.

However, two hundred years later a group of teen girls was at the centre of another nation-altering moment: one that changed America's spiritual landscape irrevocably.

The witch trials of Salem, Massachusetts, lasted from February 1692 to May 1693, and thanks to them the name of the town has become synonymous with dark paranormal doings and religious paranoia. The trials also ushered in the dawn of an era of scepticism and a move away from the strictures of the Puritan

Church. And the whole debacle, which saw nearly one hundred people arrested for witchcraft and twenty-four lose their lives for it, was started by adolescent girls.

Abigail Williams and her cousin Betty Parris, aged eleven and nine, were the first to exhibit symptoms of affliction by witchcraft: fits, twitching, feeling that they were being pricked by pins and poked by phantom fingers, screaming, throwing things, contorting themselves into peculiar shapes—all after, it was rumoured, they had been taught fortune-telling by the Parris family slave, Tituba. Soon, the symptoms began to spread among the teenagers of Salem: Elizabeth Hubbard, seventeen; Elizabeth Booth, eighteen; Mercy Lewis, seventeen; Mary Walcott, eighteen; and Susannah Sheldon, eighteen, all complained of being hexed.

Plenty of historians and medical specialists have had a go at pinning down the cause of the witch hysteria. Theories range from poisoning by the hallucinogenic fungus ergot, which grew on the rye stores, to epilepsy, to sleep paralysis, to encephalitis, to old-fashioned boredom. All we know for sure is what's preserved in the court records: that a group of young girls accused nearly two hundred townsfolk of witchcraft, and the town believed them.

In the end, nineteen people were hanged as witches; one man, 71-year-old Giles Corey, was pressed to death; four others died in prison, including two infants. One of the young women, Ann Putnam Jr, eventually wrote a moving apology for the significant role she played in the witch trials, but even in this she could not resist referring constantly to her fellow accusers: 'I justly fear I have been instrumental, with others, though ignorantly and unwittingly, to bring upon myself and this land the guilt of innocent blood'; 'I desire to lie in the dust, and to be humble for it, in that I was a cause, with others, of so sad a calamity to them and their families'.

•

Teen girls are often at the centre of outbreaks of mass hysteria. Consider the case in 1962 of the Tanganyika laughter epidemic, when three students at a mission-run girls' boarding school in present-day Tanzania began uncontrollably laughing, apparently for no reason at all. The laughter spread so rapidly and so thoroughly that the school had to be closed down. The illness then travelled with the girls back to Nshamba, the village home to many of the students, afflicting their school-aged siblings, young adults and finally older village people. Ninety-five out of 159 students were affected with the laughter epidemic, 217 people in Nshamba suffered attacks, and it did not stop there— the epidemic spread to another girls' school, where it affected forty-eight pupils, and then to two boys' schools nearby.

If this doesn't illustrate the stealthy cultural heft of teen girls, I don't know what does. Did any of the girls at the boarding school know that they were the genesis of a malady that would disable entire villages? Of course not; to be a teen girl is to be part of something bigger than you are without ever realising it.

Here is an embarrassing story: when I was a thirteen-year-old nerd, I was very deeply in love with Legolas, the elf from the Lord of the Rings movies. So obsessed was I with Orlando Bloom in a blond hairpiece that my mother, who is a fundamentally good and giving person, went to six department stores in order to find me one particular screen-accurate Legolas action figure for Christmas. Why six department stores? Because they were sold out *everywhere*. Eventually, my mother, the perseverant, found a single Legolas that had been squirrelled away behind all the other Lord of the Rings dolls, presumably by some other harried mother intending on returning at a later date with the outrageous sum required to buy the damn doll—some other mum also attempting to do the right thing by her suddenly unfamiliar daughter and her wildly oscillating, unpredictable desires.

The Arwen and Aragorn and Frodo dolls did not sell out—only the object of my, and thousands of other pubescent girls', desire. I was part of an impressively disruptive, collective lust for a man in a very nice wig, and I never really had a conscious sense of it until basically right now. My passion for the sexy elf was entirely personal. I had rich fantasies about this long-haired fictional man; I dreamed about him; I harboured passionate desires that I told no one about. But this intensely private obsession was part of a movement far beyond me: thousands of other girls, propelled by the same desires, overwhelming the world with our emotions so fast that they couldn't even keep the shelves stocked.

Teen girls are probably not aware that, right now, they are choosing our pop idols and our classic hits—that while the media may provide them with a draft of the menu, they are the ones choosing what dishes will be served to the rest of us. I didn't know it; the Tanganyikan girls didn't know it; the girls of Salem, of Iconium, even Joan of Arc didn't know it. We're all part of something bigger, so big we can't see it at all.

•

In Japan in the 1920s, girls' schools, usually run by Christian missionaries and embraced by middle- and upper-middle-class

Japanese parents for their implicit promise to preserve girls' purity, were the site of the emergence of 'passionate friendships', an entirely new way of understanding spiritual love that drew on romance novels of the era and translated it into homosocial, but not necessarily homosexual, relationships between school friends. This in turn drove an entire industry of girls' magazines and love stories completely devoid of men and boys, which in turn developed its own lexicon so complete and pervasive that it has altered the way women speak in Japanese to this day. In the United States of the 1950s, teen girls' enthusiastic invention of and devotion to fashion fads, from backwards sweaters and men's pyjama shirts to saddle shoes and bobby socks, saw the clothing manufacturing industry sent into a scramble to keep up with ever-changing, and ever-profitable, teen fashions. Those teen trends regularly went on to become mainstream influences— including the acceptance of blue jeans as everyday clothing.

More than any other demographic, it's teen girls who shape our popular culture. They are the curators of our contemporary cultural artefacts, creating our cultural world by selecting, engaging with, disseminating, critiquing, re-creating and obsessing over certain products—particularly music. If you want one example of how the emotions of teen girls shape everyone's lives, you need to look no further than pop music. For every cigarette-smoking 35-year-old music critic in a denim jacket, there are thousands and thousands of teenage girls doing the same job, but more efficiently and without the eye-rolling resentment. Despite being beaten down by gatekeepers of the club ('Oh, you're wearing a Rolling Stones T-shirt? Bet you can't name five of their songs'), teen girls are the driving force behind almost every superstar musician and pop group, and have been since at least the 1930s.

In 1937, Benny Goodman, the King of Swing, played at the Paramount movie theatre between film sessions and was unexpectedly greeted by a horde of hundreds of teen girls dancing on their seats and in the aisle. Frank Sinatra's career was launched in earnest with what came to be known as the Columbus Day Riot in 1944, when thirty thousand teenage girls swarmed Times Square in New York to see 'their Frankie'—the riot coming just a month after the startlingly successful launch of the first teen magazine, *Seventeen*. The Beatles arrived in the United States in 1964 to full-blown Beatlemania, selling two million records in just nine days.

Could the Beatles ever have gone on to the genre-redefining, indulgent weirdness of Sgt. Pepper or the White Album if they hadn't had the cultural and financial cachet that teen girls' love provided them during the 'I Want to Hold Your Hand' era? Would Frank Sinatra have achieved the kind of success he needed to become the firm favourite of every red-faced, mid-sixties bloke if thirty thousand screaming schoolgirls hadn't drawn the country's attention to him on Columbus Day 1944? Would swing have become the iconic sound of the mid-twentieth century had a bunch of teenage girls not sat by their radios every lunchtime and every evening after school, and gone and bought the records they loved hearing with their allowances?

Teenage girls, as much as it goes against our accepted narrative of seasoned *Rolling Stone* music criticism, are tastemakers. Brodie Lancaster, a critic and author whose work often focuses on fandom and boy bands, has examined the phenomenon intimately, most incisively with a keynote speech at the annual music conference BIGSOUND in 2016 titled 'Music to Watch Boys To'. In the address, she dissects the scorn and infantilisation directed towards 'fangirls': they're considered interlopers on 'real' music whose very involvement devalues their object of obsession. Of course, if they were men—especially older men—we'd use a different word for them: experts.

We can watch the cycle in real time with One Direction, one of Lancaster's topics of expertise. The phenomenally successful boy band has now disintegrated into its separate parts, with each member going on to a solo career of varying success. Harry Styles, (arguable) front man and fan favourite, has received the most critical acclaim, much of it in the same coolly surprised tone any early Elvis fan would remember from his contemporary critics: *Wow*, they say, *this guy who used to sing pop songs for teenage girls can actually make real music.* And the teen girls say, *Tell us something we don't know.*

But the lovely thing about girls engaged in fandom like that around One Direction—or Ariana Grande, whose very young fans rallied bravely around one another after the terrorist attack at her concert in Manchester in May 2017—is that they don't need to engage with older male critics who dismiss their contributions. Like so many other groups of teen girls, they are creating their own culture; the rest of us just happen to feel the impact of that boundless, obsessive joy.

•

At least now, nearly a hundred years after being conjured into existence by a rapidly changing world, after fifty years of being blamed for moral decay and the pollution of true art, spoken of with disdain, dismissed as hysterical, weak, gullible and out of order—at least *now*, teenage girls seem to be recognising and encouraging each other's power.

And it is thrilling to live in a world where teenage girls finally appear to be coming into their own. Teen culture, in the form of magazines, young adult books, films, photography, blogs and websites, makes believers out of hardcore sceptics (like me) in the healing power of communal girlhood, providing a place for young women to learn about and from one another. During the 2016 United States presidential election, it was *Teen Vogue* that ran some of the most incisive political coverage of presidential candidate Donald Trump, and this time, when older journalists acted shocked that a magazine for teenagers could be so engaged with the real world, *Teen Vogue*'s readership executed a mass eye-roll.

The online magazine *Rookie*, which was started in 2011 by then fifteen-year-old fashion blogger Tavi Gevinson, was a hub of twenty-first century girl power that captured the inimitable emotional state of teenage girlhood with gauzy photo series and gritty personal essays alike. In December 2018, Gevinson announced the closure of *Rookie*, prompting an outpouring of affection from those who had grown up with the site. On Tumblr, teen girls make and curate their own aesthetic, much of it aggressively soft, with pink and glitter and flowers, or organised around sprawling and intricate fandoms, often set on a foundation of remarkably engaged feminism and gender theory. Young women like Gevinson and actor Amandla Stenberg led the way for teens to talk, in interviews and social media and in their own, self-made publications, about girl culture, the fluidity of gender, creativity and community with enviable fluency; this is a generation with not just a connection to each other, but confidence, open eyes and a sense of the fleeting force they possess together in those fragile years between being a kid and being in the real world. In January 2016, a Los Angeles high schooler and budding activist named Alexia Sambrano wrote an essay that was published in the *LA Times* called 'Why I am a feminist', in which she neatly encapsulates the growing awareness teen girls have of their unique place in the world: 'I am a feminist because, as a teenage girl, I am constantly told I should watch more news, and get more involved, but the minute I open my mouth and speak, I am told I am just a teenage girl, and do not understand, but I do understand.' I believe her.

The young women who I spoke to in the course of my research are like their predecessors in lots of ways. Their lives still largely revolve around school; grades and end-of-year tests loom large in their minds, and those who had graduated high school already had the slight aura of melancholy that comes with disengaging from the place that's been the hub of your identity for the past ten years. Like teenagers in the 1940s and '50s, these girls go to movies with each other, window-shop, listen to music, share books and secrets. But unlike those teenagers, and unlike me at the same age, they seem to have a much greater sense of the world around them. When I asked them what they thought were the greatest challenges teenage girls face today, their responses were thoughtful and informed: unrealistic beauty standards thanks to celebrity culture and Instagram; pressure from schools and parents to succeed; pressure from peers and society to be 'perfect'; mental health; sexism and discrimination; the ongoing challenge of learning to love oneself. While none of these girls had heard of *Rookie* or Gevinson or Stenberg, they were clearly engaging with the issues those personalities raise on a public level—once again, participating in something broader and more powerful than themselves without knowing, or caring, that much about it. Overwhelmingly, these young women were focused on creating positive change in their environments. Petra, who's thirteen, told me that while she feels like she's only one person in seven billion, she wants to make a difference to the world with whatever she ends up doing. Grace, who's seventeen and from a small town in north Queensland, spoke insightfully about her motivation behind going into nursing and her desire to give back to her small community in order to help people in whatever way she can. Others raised issues of internalised misogyny and systematic discrimination against young women, issues that they hoped to address with their future careers. It was gobsmacking, really; I'd spent most of my teen years thinking very hard about boys, and almost not at all about the world at large.

One of my enduring regrets from that time is that I wasted so much of my teens hanging out and attempting to curry favour with boys. It's remarkable to me the levels of boredom that I tolerated in my pursuit of male approval: hanging out in my best guy friend's bedroom while he played video games, playing in bands with tedious jazz police, listening to daft boyfriends talk about their plans to become personal trainers. A memory that stands out from this blur of Lynx deodorant and bad haircuts is this: one night, at a male friend's house, six girls from school and I ended up drinking Vodka Cruisers on a bed together, and I felt something strong, gentle and warm bloom in me as we ignored that male friend, talked about musicals and created in-jokes, kissed each other for fun, and fell asleep in one another's arms. It didn't last; my fear of losing male approval was too strong for me to overcome until I was much older. But I remember that moment. I don't remember much, but I remember that feeling.

•

On Valentine's Day 2018, while I was writing this chapter (absorbed in digging through the soft focus of my own teenage memories—boys, flared jeans with frayed hems, inventing codes to pass notes with my girlfriends), nineteen-year-old Nikolas Cruz entered Marjory Stoneman Douglas High School in Parkland, Florida, and opened fire on his former classmates. Seventeen people were killed, and a further seventeen injured; it was the deadliest shooting at a high school in United States history.

I was ready for the wave of shock and disgust to sweep the world as the news broke of yet another school shooting, yet more innocent lives lost. I was not ready for what followed next: not, as I had expected, the standard, resigned silence after the cry of rage (how accustomed we've become to children dying en masse in America), but a phalanx of high school students—survivors, friends of the dead—rising impassioned and amplifying that cry like I'd never seen before. One young woman in particular has become, in the months since the shooting, the face of anti-gun activism: Stoneman Douglas senior Emma González.

Shaven-headed, dressed in an army jacket, she first commanded the world's attention at a gun control rally in Fort Lauderdale, where she blazed through a speech with the casual brilliance of someone whose natural talent has been transfigured by tragedy into virtuosity. 'We are going to be the kids that you read about in textbooks,' she told the crowd, incandescent with rage and grief, declaring that Stoneman Douglas would be the last school shooting in US history. Then, at the March for Our Lives protest in Washington, DC, on 24 March 2018, González again stepped ably into the role of figurehead: after listing the names of the people killed during the shooting, she stood in perfect silence, tears streaming down her face that she did not brush away, for six minutes—until a timer rang, and she told the crowd gathered that *that* was how long it took for seventeen of her classmates and teachers to be murdered. The *New Yorker* ran a piece by Rebecca Mead called 'Joan of Arc and the Passion of Emma González', drawing a line of legacy between González's tear-streaked silence and Renee Maria Falconetti's extraordinary performance as Jeanne d'Arc in the 1928 silent film *The Passion of Joan of Arc*. In the film, Falconetti's head is shorn almost to the scalp. The drawn-out extreme close-ups of her face show it alight with vivid emotion; she weeps, she turns her eyes towards God, she scorns her captors. Mead is right to suggest that González is the inheritor of Falconetti's powerful performance. The clear-eyed leader of a teenage movement with the kind of vigour not seen since the Vietnam War protests, she feels like the closest thing to Joan of Arc this generation will see.

To me, González represents everything good and precious about teen girlhood. Not just that she's demonstrated her impressive natural oratorical skills in the wake of unimaginable trauma, but that she is wielding, with wit and care, the enormous emotional power that teen girls have. The contemporary anti-gun movement is led by teenagers, and it's powered by the white-hot core of teen emotion: their anger, despair, betrayal, hope. No one's more passionate than a teenage girl. I am ready to see that passion start to change the world.

2

GIRL BANDS

In concert

I joined my first band when I was thirteen. It was a pop-punk fourpiece, extremely of its time (2003), with my best friend, Lauren, on bass, our friend from music class Maddy on guitar, and a boy called Andy, who I had an enormous crush on, playing drums. I was the lead singer, though I was quickly demoted to 'frontperson', because Lauren and I spent most of our time fighting bitterly over who would get to sing the lead in whatever New Zealand classic hit we were covering that week. (We're still in touch; she's an opera singer now.)

I don't think it occurred to me at the time to consider the gender make-up of our group. We were just four friends having a bash at stuff in Andy's garage, arguing over names and playing too loud in local battle of the bands competitions. But in the fifteen years since then, try as I might, it's been impossible for me to ignore the way issues of gender and discrimination permeate the music industry at large, and almost every band I've played in since that garage.

I have often been the 'girl in a band', a role examined in depth by Sonic Youth's Kim Gordon in her book of the same name: 'When Sonic Youth toured England, journalists took to asking me a single question over and over: What's it like to be a girl in a band?' It's an old question, but one I keep coming back to. I spoke about it with one of my former bandmates, Heather, who recently came out as trans. We were talking about her transition and the nature of identity and knowing yourself, and she asked me when I first recognised my own gender, my girl-ness. I realised that it has most often been reinforced when I played music. I've never been more self-conscious than when setting up to play a show with an all-male band and an all-male tech crew in an all-male-staffed venue. The music industry is still overwhelmingly, depressingly male. What's it like to be a girl in a band? Lonely, and disorienting, and uncomfortable—because in an industry still so driven by male ego, there's vanishingly little room for girls and their ideas.

At least, that is how I used to feel. After talking to so many women who make music, my mind is starting to change, along with—I think—the culture. It feels like a shift is taking place. The industry might still be dominated by men, but women who make music are getting together to change things for the better.

•

I meet Ruby McGregor at a café on a cool, sunny day. Ruby is a guitarist, drummer and singer, an accomplished songwriter and a veteran of the Brisbane music scene. I want to talk to her about her time playing in Go Violets, a disarming all-girl indie-pop group that disbanded in 2014. I'm nervous; Ruby is the first person I'm talking to about the mysterious mechanics of girl bands. I've never played in an all-female band. I'm desperate to know what it's like.

'I think playing with women is delightful,' she says, and I think, *A-ha*.

For a long time I have had suspicions that playing music with other women is something special. Though I've played in mixed-gender acts before, I have watched with envy the apparent cama-raderie of my friends' all-girl bands and admired their technical know-how, and I've always treasured the artistic closeness I have felt with my own female bandmates. So many women told me about the relief they felt when they finally joined a band with only other girls, after spending years trying to squeeze into the spaces between their male bandmates. Not just relief, though: a tentativeness, a sensitivity to one another and, many people told me, a rapid and profound bond.

In *Girl in a Band*, Gordon talks about how she used to covet the electricity she saw flying between male musicians on stage: 'I wanted to push up close to whatever it was men felt when they were together onstage—to try to ink in that invisible thing. It wasn't sexual, but it wasn't unsexual either. . . . In retro-spect, that's why I joined a band, so I could be inside that male dynamic, not staring in through a closed window but looking out.' While I can't say I was ever motivated to make music by those particular longings, I know what she's talking about— that not-sexual-but-not-unsexual dynamic is a hallmark of musical collaboration, and it's as elusive and alluring as being in love. The word I keep coming back to when I try to write about that very specific experience of making music with other people (something that, weirdly, I've never tried to write about before) is *intimacy*. Playing music with someone, crammed together in a sweaty rehearsal room, trying to write songs or learn parts, requires a surrender of the ego and a suspension of existing personal dynamics in ways you'd almost never have to in any other context.

Reaching that point of intimacy is an unsettling process, but that's what we do when we join bands: go into a room with people we might barely know and try to strip down our many thorny layers of creative defensiveness until we get to some Art. At least, that's the plan. In many women's experiences, including my own, the reality is that being a woman who plays music with men often calcifies those layers back on. It doesn't even have to be the men in your band. Others in the industry, in your rehearsal space or at your show will make it clear that they're waiting to pounce on your slightest fumble as yet more evidence that girls can't—and shouldn't—play music. When you're working in conditions like this, how can you possibly access the intimacy needed to make music together? Unsurprisingly, the best music I've made with other people has always been with boyfriends—people with whom I've already had a separate, romantic intimacy to exploit in the name of creating something bigger together.

But all of the women I spoke to told me that there really is an easy vulnerability to be had when making music with other women. As hesitant as many were to pin this on gender differences, the trends stood out: women who make music with other women feel more comfortable, more free, and more creative, and the rewards are richer and purer—because, as Sarah Thompson of Melbourne band Camp Cope told me, they're no longer 'scared of people picking what you're doing apart'.

When we talked, Ruby, who now plays in mixed-gender acts Babaganouj and Lexicon, mentioned something else about making music with other women: it fast-tracks your friendships. 'That's how [former bandmate] Olivia and I became friends, and it happened at the speed of light. We went from zero to one hundred and were, like, super best friends. [That] vulnerability and opening up creatively—it already feels like everything's out on the table.' Plus, when you're necessarily fighting to be taken seriously as a bunch of girls playing music by the male majority, that shared experience sticks you together. 'There's this sisterhood thing. It's like we all kinda get it.'

Olivia is Ruby's Go Violets and Babaganouj bandmate. On the phone, she echoed Ruby's sentiments about playing with women. 'It was definitely this bonding experience that I've never had with any other friends, because you're touring together and doing all these stressful things together and have so many ups and downs together that you become family. I found that that happened a lot more being with girls than being in a band with guys.' Like most of the women I spoke to, she found it hard to put these feelings exactly into words. 'It's just a different level of understanding, and intimacy is a really good word for it. There's just something different about it.'

The three women in Camp Cope have had to put up with a lot in the few years that they've been playing and releasing music. Not only are they three women making punk music that has broken into the mainstream, they're also groundbreakingly vocal about inequality in the industry, setting up safe-space hotlines at their shows and festival gigs and using their slot at Falls Festival in January 2018 to publicly put the pressure on organisers for only booking nine women for the touring line-up.

It's safe to say that they rub a certain kind of bloke the wrong way, and it's clear that their trajectory has not always been an easy one. When we spoke, drummer Sarah 'Thomo' Thompson brought up the frustratingly common experience of having your male peers do a one-eighty once you've reached a point of success that appears threatening. 'Everyone in the punk scene in Melbourne were really nice to us when we first started. Then the minute we got bigger than them they just hated us, and now they don't talk to us anymore.'

This, of course, did not stop Camp Cope from making music. In fact, they point to their ostracism as a creative blessing: if you're already forced outside the mainstream just by dint of being women, then you have the freedom to do things the way you want to. Bass player Kelly-Dawn Hellmrich puts it like this: 'If we had tried really hard to [play by the rules] and do that traditional pop-punk sound and sing about things that weren't controversial, they would still find a way to pull us apart or criticise us. It's like, anything we do is going to annoy you, so we might as well explore and make ourselves happy.'

As for playing and writing music with other women, there's no contest. Kelly-Dawn again: 'There's a lot of freedom and respect when we write. You're not feeling like someone's going to patronise you or pat you on the head for being a musician. I know that I'm going to go into the room and write music with Georgia and Thomo and they're going to respect me for who I am and my music ability, not because of anything other than that. When you're working with men, there's that fear—your experiences with men teach you to be on guard. But you can more freely and comfortably write music when you're not ready to be defensive. You make your best art when you're comfortable.'

•

I think about the first time I felt the beginnings of that rare, precious comfort, in the band I used to play in when I lived in Brisbane.

The boys have stepped out for a cigarette and for the first time it's just me and Kate, our new bass player, in the fluorescent-lit rehearsal room. She's come to us from hyper-cool rock band Martyr Privates, and I love every bass part she's written, and we're already telling each other everything. I like her nail polish. I like her hair. I like her unexpected, encyclopaedic knowledge of hip-hop. We write a tiny joke song together on two synths, squiggling out silly arpeggios and fake funk bass riffs. When the boys come back, we get shy and put the song away. I've got an iPhone recording of it somewhere, still.

Much later, Kate will send me her first solo track, a brooding minimalist croon she's conjured out of a Korg Electribe synthesiser and her bass guitar, and I'll cry with pride and gratitude, and then, when she asks, write her a chorus.

•

All the women I spoke to mentioned the unpleasant dynamic that comes with being a gender minority in a mostly dude band room, and all seemed to have had the same experiences of being talked down to or harshly criticised by men. That phenomenon that Thomo from Camp Cope mentioned, of being constantly picked apart, is a micro version of what happens on a macro scale for most women in the industry: a relentless criticism and scrutiny, from sound engineers who assume you don't know how to turn on your own amp to fledgling music journalists who spend six hundred words describing your sex appeal and fifty talking about your songs.

It's a dynamic that is at last being scrutinised, in large part thanks to musicians like Camp Cope, Vicki Gordon and The Preatures' Isabella Manfredi, as well as a global climate that is, for once, taking women's stories of harassment and discrimination seriously. The #MeToo movement prompted a response from the women of Australian music: an initiative called #meNOmore, itself inspired by a similar response from women in the Swedish music industry. Spearheaded by Manfredi and a number of other industry veterans, #meNOmore launched with a letter co-signed by more than 360 female Australian music industry workers, and included a litany of stories depressingly familiar to any woman or non-binary person who's engaged with the music scene: being groped at shows. Being told to be grateful you've even got a gig. Being talked down to by your male bandmates, or having your achievements downplayed by men in your circle, like Camp Cope, or Go Violets, or any number of other bands who are told that they've somehow got it easy because they're girls. From the huge injustice of sexual assault to the tiny, grating indignity of being ignored by the sound guy who's just greeted all your male bandmates, these shared experiences provided concrete evidence of a casual hostility to women in music that had been taken as a given for far too long.

Vicki Gordon is one of the women responsible for this starting to change. She is a powerhouse: a musician, CEO, founder of several charities and tireless champion of equity in the industry. I met her when she was in the process of setting up the Australian Women in Music Awards (AWMA), the first ever national awards for women in the Australian music industry, the inaugural round of which were awarded in October 2018. I don't know anyone who's as engaged as she is with the issues that women face in the industry, so of course I wanted to get her perspective on the phenomenon of girls making music together. I knew that the work I did with other women in bands had a different quality to it, but I was still finding it hard to pin it down.

'The one thing that I think like-minded women do bring to one another is a sense of connection that can only happen between women who are working in a safe space,' Vicki told me. 'We need to be able to do that in order to be creative.' As for making music with men—well. 'Because we all exist within this crazy patriarchal system, men always assume a position of power. It doesn't matter how liberated they are or how evolved they are or even if they call themselves feminists—most white men will always put themselves into a position of dominance. That dominance doesn't always take the form of aggression, either—that dominance can actually take the form of a passive kind of presence, an arrogance that assumes superiority.' Those small, exhausting moments again: having to repeat yourself four or five times in the studio before the engineer will recognise your contribution. Having your own equipment explained to you by another sound guy at another venue. Your new bandmate pretending not to hear you tell him that he's playing the wrong chords, and being forced to listen to the dissonance over and over again until your other, male bandmate repeats exactly what you'd been saying all along, and the tune finally changes.

·

So it does seem like many female musicians are more comfortable making music with other women—often even more comfortable than making music on their own. In fact, the more people I spoke to, the more research I did, the more it appeared that the salient difference is maybe not making music with girls vs. making music with boys; the important difference might be making music as a single girl vs. making music with your girlfriends.

Grace Stevenson is an electronic musician who plays industrial dance music solo under the moniker Rebel Yell, and with two female friends in electro-punk three-piece 100 %. 'The good thing is,' she told me, 'when I'm performing with 100 %, I know that the other girls have my back when I'm on stage. The crap that I go through with Rebel Yell by myself . . . there's no one there to support me, and I'm just there on my own and I can't say anything, and if I do then of course I'm the bitch.' She's referring to the depressing standard of behaviour towards women playing music in club settings (towards all women in club settings, to be honest)—men climbing on stage with her, touching her equipment, shouting at her during her set. But it's different when she's playing as part of 100 %. 'If we all clap back as a team, other people see that and are like, "Yeah, look at those girls all standing up for themselves, that's awesome." But if it's me, it's like, "Oh, she can't take a joke" or whatever. I think it's easier to be three divas than just one.'

It feels to me like this is a fairly recent development in the discourse of women playing music—that it's actually better, easier and more productive the more divas there are in the room. The term 'diva' itself is still a negative one, implying old caricatures of female musicians who take themselves too seriously, who make insane demands, who can't perform the much-lauded act of being 'one of the guys'. In a widely shared 2014 Noisey article titled 'How to survive being the only girl in a band', Mariel Loveland, the singer of American pop-rock outfit Candy Hearts, dispensed a quantity of suspect advice, including 'stop giving a fuck', let blokes carry your gear, and learn how to put make-up on in a moving van. It's all designed, implicitly or otherwise, to get you to the coveted 'one of the guys' status— the absolute opposite of a diva. You are allowed to be a girl in a band, this discourse tells us, but only if you're cool with getting squashed in the worst seat of the tour van, if you can piss outside like the dudes, if you're willing to put aside those annoying reminders of your femininity, and only if you're the only one.

I was drip-fed the toxic notion of the Only Girl from childhood. When I think about the bands I looked up to as a teenager, not one of them had more than one woman in the liner notes: at first, I was into jazz, and all the great solo singers (Nina Simone, Billie Holiday, Lena Horne). Then, as I started listening to the radio, my heroes were Alanis Morissette, Garbage, the Cranberries—bands or solo artists where the women sang and the men played most of the music. No wonder it never even occurred to me to try to start a band with other girls for so long. After that first band, which I formed with my best friends, all the bands who invited me to sing were composed solely of dudes. I just didn't know any female musos who played anything except classical.

Until very recently, girl bands—at least, girl rock bands— were a novelty, the exception rather than the rule. For women who wanted to be rock musicians, they had a limited set of icons to aspire to be like: Kirn Gordon, Courtney Love, Debbie Harry, Stevie Nicks—all amazing women, but all alone among men. I shouldn't talk in the past tense. According to 'Skipping a beat', a report by the University of Sydney Business School examining the state of gender equality in Australian music, things are still pretty dire. Women account for only a third of all employed musicians, one fifth of songwriters registered with APRA AMCOS (Australia's music rights and licensing organisation), and, according to the 2011 census, zero percent of sound engineers. That's right: zero women reported that they worked as engineers in sound recording and music publishing in 2011. Only thirty-one of the top one hundred songs played on commercial radio in 2016 were by female or female-fronted acts. In a ten-year analysis of popular radio, Triple J's 'By the numbers 2018' report found that, on average, all-female or solo female acts only made up 28 per cent of the most-played songs; mixed-gender acts made up just a tiny sliver of the breakdown. The rest: all-male or solo male acts, or male producers using a female guest vocalist. It seems that when girls look to popular music for inspiration, they still see a sea of men, dotted with isolated and often objectified women. When I was growing up I never questioned it. I want to question it now.

The thing is, questioning it brings us up against decades of degradation, dismissal and division of women who play music together. Consider, for a moment, 1980s icons the Bangles. An all-girl four-piece formed in 1981 by sisters Vicki and Debbi Peterson, their friend Susanna Hoffs, and bass player Michael Steele (formerly of the Runaways), the Bangles fascinate me because they were effectively broken apart by an industry that pitted women against one another—an industry that rankled at four women trying to make music on an even footing. In a revealing episode of the television program *Behind the Music*, the band's former manager, Miles Copeland, complains about their insistence on always having 'four people in the photos, four spotlights', as though it's some kind of outrageous, prima donna request to ask that everyone in the band be present and visible. He goes so far as to call it an 'oppressive rule'. At the time, Copeland, the band's label, Columbia, and the general music media were all trying to push rhythm guitarist Susanna Hoffs into the role of lead singer—the media even took to calling them 'Susanna Hoffs and the Bangles'. As a group who had always split singing and songwriting duties evenly, it was this pressure that caused the most tension between band members. Hoffs was courted by the label, lavished with media attention and promised a solo career; the others were ignored. Unable to bridge the gulf that had been driven open between Hoffs and the other members, they split. Watching Copeland spit out the word 'oppressive' to describe four women sticking to their guns and refusing to compromise their principles of doing shit together made me feel winded. That's what the Bangles were up against, and what many women in music are still up against now. The myth of the Only Girl runs deep.

The most upsetting thing about the Only Girl myth is how thoroughly many women have absorbed it. Both Grace Stevenson and Melbourne-based artist DJ Sezzo mentioned during our conversations that they'd faced conflict and friction from other solo women in their scenes. Electronic music, like most genres, remains male-dominated; it's no surprise that there are female electronic musicians who have accepted without question that there's only room for one person like them in their circle, and taken on the role of gatekeeper. What a huge disappointment, that we've been conned into preserving the boys' club. When I spoke to Vicki Gordon about this, she called it a 'conscious objective' of the system: 'The patriarchy has been most effective in the way that it has set women up to work against each other.' Internalised misogyny is no new concept: if you swim in the anti-woman soup we call Western culture, you're going to swallow some of it. It can be hard to bring it back up.

Once you start looking, you can see it everywhere. Kim Gordon, a formidable artist and musician in one of the most successful and admired rock bands of all time, Sonic Youth, nevertheless cannot mention another female musician in her book without delivering some backhanded remark. (On Madonna: 'She didn't have a perfect body. She was soft, but sexy-soft, not overweight but not as sculpted or as hard as she would become.' On Lydia Lunch: 'I wouldn't describe Lydia Lunch as a friend, since friendship requires trust . . . and she was always trying to seduce Thurston [Moore].' On Lana Del Rey: 'Today we have someone like Lana Del Rey, who doesn't even know what feminism is.')

Being the Only Girl is a rough gig. You might get taken more seriously once you've proven yourself worthy of being 'one of the guys', but what a demoralising uphill slog it is to get there— and what shabby rewards await you once you've reached that lofty plane of male acceptance. But there's no innate reason for women in music to be hostile towards other female musicians. It's an artificial state. When I asked Olivia about whether she felt a sense of competition with other women, she said it was 'the complete opposite', and listed a bunch of female-majority bands who openly supported her projects when she was just starting out. Once you beat through the internalised garbage and the scales fall from your eyes, it becomes impossible to ignore how much bullshit you really put up with when you make music with just men.

So what do we do about it? We make music with other girls.

•

In April 2018, I had the very good fortune of catching Beyoncé's historic Coachella performance during the brief window in which it was available online. For those short, shining moments, I had a glimpse of what music could look like—what it might look like if things keep changing the way they are.

Beyoncé is arguably the greatest star of our generation. A prodigious performer, a virtuoso talent, a business savant, a political icon, a game changer, a fearless champion of Black women's power and value, she is history in the making. And for more than ten years, she's been backed by an all-female band. Not just guitar, bass and drums, but a full ten-piece touring band with keys, horns, percussion and backup singers. The band is known as Suga Mama and was formed in 2007, a result of Beyoncé's deliberate choice to represent women playing music professionally. She sets it out clearly to a young fan in a YouTube video from 2009: 'I had an idea to have a lot of women onstage playing instruments, so hopefully young girls can see that, and it inspires them to play instruments.'

Elle magazine's 2017 deep-dive oral history into the band, featuring interviews with guitarist and musical director Bibi McGill, drummer Nikki Glaspie, saxophonist Kat Rodriguez, bassist Divinity Roxx, trumpet player Crystal Torres and percussionist Marcie Chapa, proves that Suga Mama has delivered on that grand plan. Right at the end of the article, Torres reflects on the impact the band has made on a new generation of musicians: 'I didn't realise this new wave that we created with Bey until recently. We always got messages saying that we were inspiring people, but those people we inspired are now in college and high school, like my student, Arnetta Johnson, who plays trumpet for Bey now. It's come full circle.'

Watching Suga Mama live is exhilarating. At Beyoncé's astounding Super Bowl performance in 2013, McGill joins her in centre stage to bust a screaming solo while pyrotechnics shoot from either end of her guitar; in a YouTube video from the 2009 I Am . . . World Tour, keyboard player Rie Tsuji executes an impeccable classical breakdown, complete with winks and twinkling spirit fingers. The cohesion, the joy, the sheer chops of everyone involved is palpable. Something deep and rare stirs in my cold heart when I see a bunch of chicks killing it live; I can't even imagine what it would have felt like to see that as a teenager.

Thanks to artists like Beyoncé and Suga Mama, I think we're finally seeing the end of girl bands as novelties. Not since the 1990s and riot grrl have we seen so many high-profile all-girl acts, built under their own steam and agency and celebrated for their music, not just their gender: the expansive, indulgent psych/prog/pop jams of Warpaint; the grand, noisy post-punk of Savages; the sunny garage-pop of Hinds; the wry country-folk-pop of All Our Exes Live in Texas; the unapologetically feminine, intimate indie of Girlpool—and that's not to mention the hundreds of solo female acts choosing to collaborate with other women, like the regal, groundbreaking African Australian rapper Sampa The Great, electronic multi-instrumentalist Alice Ivy, or the genre-bending powerhouse Ecca Vandal.

Things are looking good for the next generation. Right now, I might be drawing attention to the fact that all these bands are women, but hopefully—surely—in another ten years, that will be laughably passé. The musically inclined kids of today have all of these talented, independent non-dudes to look up to, along with social enterprises like AWMA and the excellent Girls Rock! program, which provides week-long camps for female, trans and nonbinary teens to learn instruments and form bands—I think we can dare to hope that in ten years they will have seen enough women playing drums, playing lead guitar, playing their own music with their own friends, that they'll be doing exactly the same thing, and we can finally put the novelty of the girl band to bed for good.

•

This week I will go to a show featuring only bands fronted by women. It is, shamefully, the first show of its kind I've ever knowingly been to. It's fundraising for a local rape crisis shelter, and will be held on International Women's Day. I want to see how it feels to be there, in a mostly female audience, watching mostly female bands, as we raise money for a cause that overwhelmingly affects women. Since I started writing this chapter, I've started my own all-girl band. My sister, a gifted singer, moved in with me; my old band broke up, and I wanted to keep working with the new bass player we'd recruited; I wanted to write some cheery pop songs, and I wanted to do it with only other girls. I wanted to know what it was like. My new band hasn't played any shows yet—hasn't even had a rehearsal—instead, we're indulging in purely electronic means of production, emailing bounces back and forth, embroidering beats and synth lines onto our growing collaboration. It does feel different. I feel optimistic. I feel airy, like a white linen dress. I feel like I have nothing to prove.

3

MAKE-UP

The beauty club

I'm watching a woman put on her make-up. She's taking me, viewer number 1,596,359, through a detailed step-by-step routine—foundation and concealer, liquid liner and false lashes—while I lie in bed, the laptop doing double duty as a heat pad on my crampy stomach. I'm exhausted and stressed from missing sleep and deadlines, but instead of sleeping I'm bingeing on beauty tutorials, because there is no better self-care and nothing more soothing than watching someone do their face.

The woman I'm watching is re-creating Audrey Hepburn's make-up from *Breakfast at Tiffany's*, in response to hundreds of requests begging for a tutorial on that exact look. As the video plays, I scroll through the comments below it—thousands of other women lavishing praise on the artist in the video, sharing tips and techniques, asking for and receiving advice. The combination of this unending stream of positivity and the make-up artist's warm monotone has the calming, restorative effect of spending quality time with a very old friend. When I'm feeling lonely and disconnected, or limp and uninspired, I turn to the world of YouTube beauty.

•

Any woman with even a passing interest in make-up will have encountered one particularly unsettling idea, whether it emerges from her own self-doubt or from the well-meaning people around her: isn't the point of wearing make-up just to attract men?

I remember having a conversation with a male acquaintance about make-up. He had been browsing Reddit and had stumbled onto a make-up discussion forum, which he read for some time. He was shocked.

'These girls,' he said, 'were talking about make-up the way I talk about basketball.' He meant that they were being technical, trading stats, arguing for or against certain products and brands like experts in their field.

'Well, yeah,' I said peevishly. 'Women have hobbies.'

Make-up seems to be one of the few hobbies that women can have, in fact, that isn't dominated by men. Even if the whole premise of cosmetics really *was* solely to attract a man (and it's not), the places women go to learn about it, to exchange ideas and skills, to bond, gripe and commiserate—they are women-only spaces. The few men in those communities are gay and femme-presenting; the straight ones who wander in, like my basketball-fan friend, are soundly ignored.

I love make-up, not just for what it does to my face, but for the space it makes for women to be together in culture. It's easy to think of make-up as being inconsequential; for a long time, I did. But once I began to think of make-up not as a commodity but as a community—a clubhouse, a church, a coven millions strong—I began to understand how important it really was.

•

In her 1990 book *The Beauty Myth*, Naomi Wolf spends three hundred pages taking apart the vast, oppressive mechanism of modern beauty standards and showing us its grimy insides. She explains how, as women's civil rights have broadened, social expectations of physical attractiveness have constricted, compressing us in novel, insidious ways. During and after feminism's second wave in the 1970s, fashion models were elevated to positions of higher and higher prestige, commanding more money, fame and attention than almost any other women in any industry besides actresses. As equal rights bills passed, the cosmetics, diet and retail industries doubled and tripled in size, eating disorders in girls and young women skyrocketed, and advertisers stopped trying to sell women fulfilment in the form of kitchen appliances and started telling us that we'd only be happy and successful in this new, gender-equal world if we looked like *this*. The 1980s ushered in an era that has not yet come to an end: an era in which women *must* be beautiful.

Wolf makes a compelling argument for the pervasiveness and tyranny of the beauty standard. It costs women billions of dollars a year, thousands of hours and immeasurable distraction to fall in line with compulsory standards of physical presentation that would never be expected of men. Interestingly, Wolf argues that these non-negotiable rules of beauty are in part designed to isolate women from one another. If you've grown up surrounded by images of impossibly gorgeous women, usually on their own, always as emblems of desirability and personal fulfilment, how else can you conceptualise your own success? The ideal woman is physically beautiful, thin, young, rich and solitary.

This was my understanding of beauty as I grew up. I was a cute kid, but an acne-riddled, flat-chested, clumsy teen. I understood beauty to be capital, and capitalism to be a zero-sum game. I recognised my beautiful peers' physical wealth and understood with painful clarity my own poverty. It made me feel resentful, and jealous, and lonely. The media I consumed did not help. No matter how often *Girlfriend* and *Cosmo* told me to love and accept myself, I knew I'd never look like any of the models in their pages, and I knew that that was what I *should* be.

But things changed for me—and the rest of the world— when Web 2.0 came of age in the mid-2000s, bringing with it social media, rapidly developing, niche online communities, and every lonely, ugly girl's best friend: YouTube.

•

Beauty culture is maybe the second-biggest secret girls' club there is (menstruation still takes the number one spot). Most women in the modern world participate in beauty rituals—from digging out a years-old lipstick to swipe on before a major life event, to getting up early enough to apply a full face of warpaint for the day. You might not remember signing up for the club, but you're probably in it.

And the club dates back millennia. Some evolutionary anthropologists argue that cosmetic use predates language, theorising that early human women formed groups called female cosmetic coalitions, which were designed to disguise menstruation through carefully applied red pigment. The Egyptians lined their eyes with kohl and coloured their upper and lower lids with ground malachite, smoothed their skin with castor and sesame oil, and coloured lips and cheeks with red ochre and henna— regardless of gender, class or caste. Make-up was for everyone, ensuring not only beauty but holiness, and improving your chances of passage into the afterlife by looking good for Osiris. Greek women whitened their skin with lead and chalk, coloured their hair golden by bleaching it with vinegar, and drew on uni-brows with soot. (It was considered the most fetching form of eyebrow.) The Bible references make-up regularly, and is not kind to the women who use it. The painted women of the Old Testament are whores, harlots, murderers and witches, including the most famous witch of all, Jezebel. The story goes that Jezebel was a Phoenician princess who married Ahab, a king of Israel. She coerced him into abandoning his worship of Yahweh in favour of worshipping Baal and Asherah instead. She had the prophets of Yahweh put to death and fabricated evidence against innocent landowners in order to take their property, and she was a devotee of make-up. Her comeuppance inevitably arrived in the form of a vengeful prophet of Yahweh, Jehu. When she heard he was coming to kill her, she painted her face, adorned her head with jewels, and was summarily flung from a window by her own servants (on Jehu's orders) to be eaten by dogs. Only her hands, feet and face remained—the parts of her body she coloured with make-up.

During the late Middle Ages, to be a beautiful woman meant to be lily-fair, with a high, noble forehead and sparse or non-existent eyebrows. This meant that noblewomen of the age plucked their hairlines back, removed their eyebrows and painted their faces, necks and breasts with something called ceruse—

a mixture of white lead and vinegar that was powerfully toxic, but resulted in alabaster skin the texture of fine porcelain. They were soundly chastised for it. 'How base is her shape,' wrote the poet Richard Brathwait in 1631, 'which must borrow complexion from the shop? How can she weepe for her sinnes . . . when her teares will make furrowes in her face?'

Women then, as now, were under intense pressure to be beautiful without a hint of artifice—incredibly difficult when the standards of beauty required unearthly paleness and unnatural hairlines, during a time when ugliness was considered to be a punishment from God. Then, as now, the threat of men's disapproval did not stop women from wearing make-up. In fact, Queen Elizabeth I turned her use of cosmetics into a political force.

Elizabeth understood the need for her public to see her as virtuous and chaste, a beautiful virgin bride for England. She also understood that she needed to distance herself from her mother, Anne Boleyn, who had been accused of witchcraft. As Sarah Jane Downing explains in the book *Beauty and Cosmetics 1550–1950*, 'Common Tudor belief held that witches had some kind of ugliness or deformity, so it was particularly important for Elizabeth to be beautiful'. She appeared at her coronation made-up with what would become known as her Mask of Youth: white ceruse, vermillion cheeks, and her red-gold hair, daringly, worn loose and long. She understood her country's need for her to be an icon, and she wore her make-up to her death.

•

The beauty club is bigger, broader, more secretive and more ancient than any Freemason or Illuminati collective. Beauty rituals haven't always been as harshly enforced as they are now, but they've always been something that women shared.

I knew this all along, even in the depths of my lonely plain-girl doldrums. My mother never wore much make-up, but I vividly remember going through her modest make-up bag with her and listening as she explained what each arcane item was for: a jade pencil for lining your eyes, a concealer stick in Barbie-tan orange, dried mascara that clung to your lashes in clumps. When I was fourteen, she took me shopping at a huge mall pharmacy for make-up that I could wear on stage in my school rock band. By then, my little sister was four years old, and it had been a long time since Mum and I had spent time together outside the house. I remember everything about the trip: the sales assistant selecting slim glass bottles of foundation, cakes of powder, pencils and pots of eyeliner and smoky eyeshadow, and applying these unusual substances to my face with soft brushes and cool fingers. I remember feeling absorbed in the ritual, re-creating it myself in the bathroom at home. I also remember my sister finding my make-up bag and spilling green-gold eyeshadow all over the floor—she was as fascinated with it as I was. Later, she'd ask me to do her make-up for her, and obviously I would say yes.

For women who choose to participate in them, rituals around beauty and make-up are a prime source of female bonding experiences, moments that bring us closer to other women: being taken to get your hair or nails done for the first time, doing each other's faces at sleepovers, borrowing your friend's GHD straightener before graduation, sharing lip gloss in pub bathrooms. Membership in this club might be forced upon you, but the upside is admission to a worldwide VIP room full of secrets, esoteric knowledge and your best friends.

I recognised this when I started watching YouTube make-up tutorials. I can't remember the first time I watched one; there's no way I could have known that it would be a turning point in my life. It must have been before any real feminist awakening—before I'd read any Judith Butler, before I understood just how much of my gender was performative, before I'd started to unpack my many concessions to a patriarchal beauty standard—because I can't remember ever questioning the politics of learning how to make myself look conventionally attractive from women on the internet. I only remember feeling a frictionless calm, a feeling I still get when I sit down in front of a twenty-minute Lisa Eldridge skin-perfecting tutorial.

Beauty vloggers are some of YouTube's biggest stars. Michelle Phan, one of the first vloggers to achieve cult-idol status, has over eight million subscribers, more than a billion cumulative views, and makes three million dollars a year. She's been using the platform since at least 2007. Phan's videos follow a soothing formula: she greets her viewers with her famously soft, American-accented voiceover ('Hello cuties'; 'Hi, gorgeous'). She appears with a full face of themed make-up—the Spanish Rose, maybe, or a red-lipped Chinese New Year look—explains what she's about to do ('I have here a beautiful look for you to try out to ring in the Lunar New Year'), and then the video snap-cuts to Phan bare-faced and staring down the barrel of the camera, starting with skincare and going through a routine, step-by-step, until her transformation is complete. Phan has been around long enough to become an often-referenced source of inspiration for the thousands like her, who collectively embody every possible variation on the same theme: women doing their make-up for an audience.

It's a beautiful world, the one these women on YouTube inhabit. Their faces are lit like they're sitting in front of their own small, friendly star. The music in the background is sweet: Creative Commons guitar loops or massage-therapy pan flutes, or the kind of uplifting techno that could also be the soundtrack for montages of snowboarding stunts. The demeanours of the women lie somewhere on a continuum from big sister to fairy godmother, from the ASMR-inducing almost-whisper of Phan, to the calming British authority of Eldridge, to the charming goofiness of Katerina Williams. They pluck apparently limitless products seemingly from the air, accompanied by wisps of text telling us their incantation-like names (Guerlain Terracotta 4 Seasons Bronzing Powder 00 Nude, D.J.V. Beautenizer Fiberwig LX Mascara). They have a wealth of secrets to share, a never-ending series of beauty memes and tags (put your make-up on without a mirror! Kylie Jenner lips!), and they don't demand anything from their viewers except that they like and subscribe. Beauty vloggers tend not to talk politics. But they are still, without even trying, political.

The more beauty tutorials I watched, the more I came to believe that I was witnessing something extraordinary: the creation of a realm that could not exist in such an unfettered form anywhere but digitally—a space *just* for women. Somewhere for us to nut out the often difficult business of being women, to discuss the trappings of performed femininity that would be uncomfortable to raise in the company of men—covering acne blemishes, contouring one's face to appear slimmer, enjoying the art of disguise. It's a space in which to divorce the pressures of the Beauty Myth from its products. Like many activities historically pushed to the fringes because of men's contempt for anything coded feminine, the online beauty club makes a place for women to spend time together, share knowledge, bond, and do the practical work of surviving in a patriarchy that is trying to pit us against one another. The women on Reddit's r/Makeup-Addiction forum aren't in competition, and they're not trying to snag a man. They're enthusiasts swapping stats on fibre count and polymer quality.

Collectively, beauty vloggers construct a narrative completely devoid of the male gaze. I have never heard any YouTube beauty celebrity mention a man's opinion. I've never even heard any of them address a potential male viewer. Which might seem weird, on the surface of it, because a broad cultural understanding (read: a male understanding) of make-up is that it's supposed to appease and attract men.

Despite literally thousands of years of cosmetic use by all human civilisations, despite many hundreds of thousands of women making a living from doing make-up for themselves and others for fashion, TV, movies, magazines and more, and despite every woman in the public eye wearing it at nearly all times, make-up is still coded as deceit. I know I grew up buying into the idea almost entirely. For a very long time I felt that make-up was supposed to be something secret, even shameful—probably because I fiercely wanted to be the most virtuous kind of beautiful: 'naturally' beautiful. Make-up defeated the point, which was to be gorgeous without even trying. This attitude is a popular one. Just look at the scorn many young men reserve for women who are obviously made-up, and their approval for women who pass as 'naturally' pretty. You can find their comments on any YouTube beauty tutorial if you scroll down far enough: among the hundreds of women commenting 'You look great!', there are the ugly boils of 'This is why men have trust issues', 'Take her swimming on the first date', 'False advertising' and, my personal favourite, 'You're hotter without make-up'. All of these attitudes are evidence of a tired and prevalent male understanding of cosmetics, which is as a tool of seduction and nothing else. The joke's on chicks, these guys are thinking, because they've put all this shit on their faces and men don't even *like it*.

Maybe the joke is on us. It is expensive and time-consuming to wear make-up; why would we do it, if not to attract the opposite sex? This is something I have grappled with long and hard. Men definitely pay more attention to me when I'm wearing make-up, and I've definitely worn make-up to attract male attention. But I'm not looking for male attention at all these days, and I still feel compelled to wear make-up. I'm well-enough entrenched in modern feminist subculture to happily let my leg and armpit hair grow out; why can't I leave the house without putting on my face? And if it's just for me, why don't I put it on when I'm home alone?

Maybe it's because cultural norms allow men to pass through the world unchallenged as long as they are washed and fully dressed, but to access the same privileges women need to spend money and time painting on a better-looking face. It's not just men who are nicer to me when I wear make-up, it's everyone. No amount of recognising this for what it is—utter gendered bullshit—will change the fact that me with a bare face and me with BB cream and filled-in eyebrows experience the world very differently. The beauty standard might be artificial, but its effects are profoundly real, and much further reaching than sexual attraction. Numerous studies have shown that women wearing make-up are more confident, receive better treatment from the people around them, and earn more than their make-up-free sisters. Make-up makes a difference.

But we know this. We know that beauty is not as simple as trying to outcompete our peers for male attention or praise. We know that an understanding of beauty, and membership to the club, is really about gaining and sharing the means to move through the world easily, skilfully, without detection—a means of smoothing the system from the inside.

What I've come to believe is that part of the reason make-up is still scorned and coded as deceitful is *because* we do it with other women. Pleasures and activities that exclude men automatically become the object of suspicion and fear (What are they talking about when we're not around?), which is defanged by turning fear into derision and contempt (Those silly women, they don't even know how ridiculous they look).

But the beauty club, when it's gathered in force, is a subversive collective. Unlike the women's magazines of my teens, with their implicit confirmation of make-up as Secret Mate Attractor ('Date night make-up', 'Ten beauty trends he hates!'), YouTube make-up tutorials are a feminine space totally abstracted from the churn of heteronormativity. If they say anything to straight men, it's that *this isn't for you*.

The politics of modern cosmetic use is a tangle, and women much smarter than I am have tackled this topic with vigour. (I'm thinking particularly of Rian Phin, a former *Rookie* contributor and prolific blogger and vlogger; her incisive work on why she, as a Black woman, wears make-up provides a framework in which to understand a whole raft of other opposing pressures.) But one of the things I love about YouTube beauty tutorials and the rest of the online beauty community, including websites like xoVain and subreddits like r/SkincareAddiction, is how easily they smooth out that tangle. They don't engage with uninvited male opinions. They don't ask me to interrogate *why* I love make-up. They just teach me how to do it better, and make me feel good while they do it.

·

Beauty vloggers strip away the layers of artifice shellacked onto any mainstream image of beauty. By that I mean: I have had bad skin since I was ten years old. Acne, oil slicks, giant pores, scars, hyperpigmentation, the lot. I spent a long time feeling ashamed of the way I looked without make-up because I never saw anyone who looked like I did in any of the culture I consumed. Nothing has made me feel better about my skin than watching beauty vloggers.

They appear bare-faced and unashamed of their acne, dark circles, pigmentation and blotchiness, disentangling the cultural myths that imply that beauty and virtue are synonymous, and they show, step by step, how the illusion is created. 'Beauty' as understood by the broader culture is largely trend-based and deeply connected to the cosmetic industry—almost no one looks beautiful to the standards demanded by advertisements and popular culture without cosmetic help. As Dolly Parton says in *Steel Magnolias*: 'Ain't no such thing as natural beauty.' Online make-up communities embody this philosophy entirely— beauty is by nature artificial, and by recognising that truth we can disconnect beauty from inherent goodness or correctness, and connect it instead to skill, effort and ingenuity. Being beautiful is like carving castles out of eggshells: it's impressive, difficult, time-consuming, and not everyone wants to do it—but if you do want to, you can learn how. Now, sometimes, I leave the house without putting foundation on—not because my skin is different, but because I'm no longer ashamed of it. I never would have made this progress had I not seen the effort that goes into making those effortlessly beautiful women in magazines look the way they do.

More importantly, beauty vloggers transcend physical boundaries like geography, which is pivotally important for many young women of colour in majority-white countries. As multicultural as the Western world has become, it's still rare to see non-white faces in women's media, particularly in the context of make-up. When I asked my friends what they loved about YouTube beauty tutorials, this was the strongest response: the videos gave them a chance to see themselves. There are beauty vloggers of every race and creed, just as there are beauty vloggers of every skin quirk and eyebrow idiosyncrasy. There really is someone for everyone, and for women and girls who don't have representations of themselves elsewhere in their lives, those YouTube videos can be life-changing.

'Do you know how hard it is for an off-white/brown girl to learn to do make-up here? YouTube taught me everything.'

Ebony is in her mid-twenties, an engaging, energetic graphic designer and sometime model.

'If we're talking community, there is no greater solidarity— to me, regarding beauty—than learning how to make myself pretty from other light brown girls. YouTube tutorials taught me all the things I never knew about being a "girl", especially 'cos my mum doesn't wear make-up or have long hair.'

The broader digital beauty community helps to create concrete changes as well. A couple of years ago, a friend put me onto an online community of women who are DIY experts in skincare. This community encompasses sites as diverse as subreddits like r/SkincareAddiction, personal blogs and the websites of amateur scientists in a sprawling, unaffiliated and self-taught network of women taking control of their appearance in a fascinating way. Here were women who have turned their participation in the exhausting rigmarole of being a woman in the world into an engaging, stimulating hobby—and some of them are as informed about the mechanics of human skin as some dermatologists.

As soon as I began trawling through this enormous body of crowdsourced material, I was hooked. For one thing, I was struck by the generosity of the community. Participants spend hours sifting through published research papers, sharing their findings in easily digestible blog posts; they post pictures of themselves without make-up, and praise the vulnerable selfies of others for the progress they have made towards reducing acne, hyperpigmentation or fine lines. They candidly discuss their goals, and their concessions to the reality that they will never be 'perfect'. Some women go even further into grassroots skincare and create their own formulations. Many active ingredients found in skincare products, such as vitamin C and glycolic acid, are available to purchase in stable states on Amazon and eBay; thus, the internet has given birth to a generation of at-home chemists, happy to be taking the state of their body into their own hands to the fullest degree. The community is so strong and so vocal that some skincare brands (the Korean company COSRX in particular) are starting to create new products that address specific issues raised by the community. Most importantly, these women's work and curiosity, and their willingness to share their knowledge, allows women without access to expensive specialists and high-end brands to begin to understand and address their own issues; demystifying the science of skincare allows us greater control of our bodies without an intermediary.

And I was astonished at how much I could learn. From message boards, blogs and online communities I learned about the skin's moisture barrier or 'acid mantle', the layers of epidermis and dermis, the methods by which vitamin A strengthens the skin, the importance of pH levels to skin health. From YouTube beauty tutorials I learned how to cover my acne, use a lipstick everywhere except my lips, put highlighter on without looking like a disco ball, and a never-fail cat's eye. And I learned to shed the shame I'd felt for a long time: shame about being plain, wanting to be beautiful, feeling afraid to pursue prettiness, resenting other women and then being guilty about resenting them—a whole morass of weird, bad vibes washed down the drain, bit by bit, along with my oil cleanser.

In order to function, the Beauty Myth requires a disconnect between our selves and our bodies. We are separated by shame and ignorance, taught that our physical selves are our enemies. Knowing your body closes the gap; knowing the skills and how to use them puts power back into women's hands. So many beauty vloggers are careful to tell their viewers that they don't need make-up. Beauty is not about *need*; it's about choice.

Society's beauty apparatus has a way of making you feel desperately alone. As Naomi Wolf's book highlighted, a woman isolated and worn down by the pressure to be beautiful, robbed of her financial freedom by the requirement that she purchase products, clothing and diet plans to maintain her beauty quotient, and suspicious of other women whom she considers obstacles to her success—this woman does not agitate for change, argue with the status quo or walk away from a discriminatory workplace. The isolated woman feels incurably ugly, struggling alone in uncomfortable shoes up an unscalable mountain, putting on lipstick in a locked toilet stall and worrying about doing it wrong, always feeling like the only one failing at correct womanhood. But we're lucky to be around in a time that gives us access to the best antidote to this debilitating solitude: an internet connection and the right search terms.

Look through any comments section on a beauty vlog and you'll see outpourings of admiration from woman to woman. The openness of this admiration is part of the appeal of these online spaces: here is a place in which women publicly demonstrate their care, affection and admiration for one another. There has been a recent cultural boom in the 'girl gang', a phenomenon of famous women working with and championing each other that's best encapsulated by Taylor Swift's notorious 'squad'. But in terms of spaces that allow ordinary women to access a form of femininity that encourages collaboration rather than competition, digital beauty communities are unique. Once I started to talk to other women about make-up online, it opened up channels in my real life as well. Now I talk to all my female friends about it. Make-up talk is coded as shallow, but it makes for deep connections. We talk about the tricky aspects of beauty; we tease apart the political mess of wanting to be pretty but maybe not *wanting* to want to be pretty; we get theoretical. I couldn't do the work that I do on this topic without those women to work through things with me.

In digital spaces women find community, even in the very aspects of culture that seek to separate and oppress us. Many of my friends tell me they feel something unusual after they watch beauty videos or engage with online beauty communities: they feel calm. I don't think it's just because beauty vloggers tend to have soothing voices. I think something about harnessing the Beauty Myth, saying its name aloud, and sharing it, in all its joy and confusion, with people you love and admire, makes the weight of performing beauty turn powder-light.

4

SPORTSWOMEN

The body is a verb

I can hear the weightlifters long before I see them. As I step out of the car at the sports complex in Brisbane's outer suburbs, secreted away in a pocket of peaceful eucalypt forest, I catch the muffled racket of hundreds of kilograms thundering against a rubber floor. Tessa, a former student of mine and a competitive weightlifter, has invited me here to meet the women she lifts with. The gym itself is a small warehouse paved in rubber tiles, with big industrial fans blowing the March humidity around. On a mounted TV, Olympic heavyweights lift hundreds of kilos high into the air, but no one in the gym looks like them: cartoon strongmen, thick and massive. On the floor, watched by their coaches and peers, men and women of all ages and all shapes snatch and jerk, sweat and roar.

In a few weeks I'll be back here for the club competition, and I'll witness a moment that will seem to sum up the whole experience of being a weightlifting woman: from the hard metal spectators' benches I'll watch another club member, having just failed to lift 95 kilos in the clean and jerk, raise herself from the corner where she's slumped in disappointment to scream her support for Tessa, who's about to lift the same weight—and scream louder when she makes it.

Tessa is a graceful, preternaturally helpful 24-year-old who seems gifted with a limitless enthusiasm. She can also lift a hundred kilos over her head and barely flush from the effort. We got to talking one afternoon last year, after a class on Virginia Woolf; I don't remember how we ended up talking about sports. But when she mentioned she did Olympic weightlifting, I asked if she'd be interested in speaking to me for this book, thinking how fascinating it would be to talk to someone embedded in a physical discipline that seemed so thoroughly masculine. Instead, she invited me to see the sport for myself, and meet the other women who love it as much as she does.

Women have only been competing in weightlifting at an Olympic level since 2000, after receiving their own world championship in the sport in 1987. The sport itself traces its origins to European competitions of strength in the nineteenth century, and has been around in its recognisable form (with some variations) since at least the first Olympic Games in 1896. Weightlifting is different from powerlifting and these days includes only two lifts: the snatch, in which an athlete places her hands in a wide grip on the barbell and hoists it over her head in one smooth movement, and the clean and jerk, which is a two-movement lift: the first, from the floor to the shoulders; the second, an almighty push into the air. During competitions, weight is added to the barbell incrementally, and each athlete has the opportunity to make three attempts; the athlete attempting the lightest weight goes first. Each will attempt to lift more than they have ever lifted before. To watch a weightlifting competition is to see athletes at the very brink of their abilities. It's absolutely thrilling.

At the weightlifting club I meet Paige, Tandia, Alyce and Mia—just a few of Tessa's clubmates. They've come from wildly different sporting backgrounds, and Mia's only thirteen years old, but they all tell me the same thing, straightaway: they *love* their sport. They love how hard it is, how supportive their teammates are, how good it makes them feel about their bodies. When I was fourteen, I played soccer at school. I was on the team below the Second XI, and I played defence. It is a dreary, damp, cold portion of my memory. I don't know if we ever won a game; my most vivid recollection is of jostling with another player during a free throw and sarcastically calling her 'sweetheart'. I don't know any of my teammates anymore.

The women at the club, though, seem like best mates. Tessa says there's an immediate bond between women who train together. I think this has something to do with the nature of the sport. The whole time I'm there, everyone keeps telling me it's so much more than just lifting heavy weights: it's a test of character. Mia, the thirteen-year-old, came to the sport from CrossFit, where they wouldn't let her advance as fast as she wanted to. She tells me the endeavour is as much psychological as it is physical. 'You need more mental strength than anything else.'

Tandia is a sports science graduate who started as an intern at the club and fell in love with it. She was a ballet dancer for fifteen years before she realised, in Year 12, that she'd never have the body to succeed professionally. She referred to leaving dance as a divorce—a real heartbreak, after so many years of devoting her life to it. But when we talk about weightlifting, she lights up. She emphasises the enormous, positive difference it's made for her to move from what she calls a looks-based discipline to an achievement-based one. 'You've got set numbers to achieve,' she says, rather than an elusive body goal that means that you feel 'never good enough'. She's also full of praise for the sport itself.

'The culture, particularly around women, is so great,' she says, mentioning as well that although weightlifting is a sport where gender differences are obvious, they're refreshingly immaterial. Everyone is stoked on their results, whatever their gender. Over and over again, these women tell me that this is what they love about the sport: that it's a battle against yourself.

Alyce is one woman who will, technically, be competing against others: when we spoke she was preparing to compete in the 2018 Commonwealth Games on the Gold Coast, in the 48 kilogram division. She's a diminutive, impish young woman with brown hair in a ponytail on top of her head, whose coach films her while she trains so that she can correct her form. She came to weightlifting via circus performing, hoping to lift her circus game as she lifted the weights. She did, but ended up finding weightlifting so personally satisfying—that sense of challenging oneself again—that she's made the switch for good. When I ask why she was attracted to the sport, she says: 'I was always the weak kid in the gym. I didn't want to be the weak kid.'

Like many of the women I spoke to at the club, Alyce likes how technical the sport is—one wrong movement at the start of a lift will ruin the rest of it. It's a sport for perfectionists, she says. And a sport for those who are chasing a rush: there's nothing like clearing the bar you've set for yourself, after months or years of hard work. Later, at the club comp, I'll think about this as I watch the competing athletes transform before my eyes.

As they drop their weight, they change, their closely furled focus, intense and internal, blossoming into open-faced smiles of pride and release. Pink-cheeked, relieved, their gaze not turned inward but seeking out their friends and coaches, they seem a different person to the one who picked up the barbell. They make me think of buds bursting open. As always, when faced with the profundity of the human body, I will have to hold back tears.

As I sit with Tessa and Paige, a former cyclist, on a bench to the side of the training area, they begin to talk about their bodies. They're both rosy and glowing, taking turns training under the eye of their coach, Miles. They swap stories of injuries—Tessa's kept her out of the running for the Commonwealth Games, Paige's is so recent it will cost her the upcoming club comp—but they talk about their bodies in an overwhelmingly, unusually positive way. Just like Tandia, they're not focused on what their bodies look like, but what they can *do*. I feel a warm rush of envy and admiration. Of course, they are both happy with how they look, and Tessa says she's much happier now than when she was a runner, when she would compare herself unfavourably to other runners. Now, she says, she never feels like that; instead, she sees that her body reflects the love she has for her sport and the hard work she's put into it. Paige agrees: when you lift weights, she says, 'You get a different perception of what beauty is.'

She's luminous while she says this, still slightly out of breath from lifting 40 kilograms moments before our conversation. She looks strong—everyone around me looks strong—but there is no consistency of form or shape here. Everybody here looks remarkably different, because how you look doesn't have a whole lot to do with how much weight you can hoist into the atmosphere with just your muscles and a little powdered chalk.

Miles, Paige and Tessa's coach, is a soft-spoken British man, gently encouraging to his athletes, talkative with me, eager to ensure the club makes a good impression. He tells me that the club is probably an even 50/50 gender split, with a number of young girls, like Mia, around the age of thirteen or fourteen, who've recently joined. He pairs them up with older women like Tessa and Tandia in a kind of mentor relationship, an open encouragement to be inspired to challenge themselves. He's wry when he talks about the differences between the boys and girls who train there. Sometimes, he says, boys on their first visit to the club are surprised and intimidated by the girls because they can lift more than many of the men. Sometimes this causes a surprising level of recidivism among the boys. Meanwhile, the girls, he reckons, often train harder than the boys and improve more because of it. And the culture within the sport seems to be reflecting this: fifteen to twenty years ago, when he started coaching, the few women who were interested in weightlifting would disguise their bodies in baggy clothes, attempting to fit in with the men. Now they wear what they want—fitness gear, T-shirts, clothes that are easy to work out in. No one seems to be hiding who they are. I remember something Mia said to me as soon as we started talking. I asked her what she liked about training here, and she said immediately, 'Everyone is treated really equally.'

Later, I meet up with Tessa again over coffee, and I ask if lifting weights has improved her self-esteem. 'Yeah,' she says. 'One hundred per cent. I think it comes back to what we were saying before—my sport isn't focused on how I look. I'm just working hard, enjoying what I'm doing, and it's reflecting on myself. I like what I do so I like how I look. It took me a while, because coming to weightlifting I was really scared about putting on weight and getting bigger. But now I don't mind that I'm ten kilos heavier than I was when I first started. I only [realised] a couple of weeks ago when I was like, I actually haven't looked in the mirror and wanted to change anything. I haven't been like, "Oh, I wish my legs were a little bit thinner," or this or that. I just haven't done that in a really long time. She pauses, then shrugs. 'I got to a point where I was like, you know, I'm just going to do what I love. I'm finally starting to feel that love back for myself.'

•

I remember being uncomfortably aware of my body at an early age. I remember, in fact, standing in front of my bedroom mirror with my childhood best frenemy while we openly compared each other's figures, looking for hourglass curves on our prepubescent bodies. As I got older, my hips stretched out but my chest stayed flat; I grew long-limbed and awkward, not tall or thin enough to be remarkable but enough to feel scrawny and half-formed. These days, when I flirt with depression, it's my body that catches the brunt of it. I stand naked at the mirror willing my thighs not to touch, trying to conjure a ballet dancer's posture out of my decades of slouching, pressing my stomach down—*flatter, flatter*. When it gets really bad, I start to work out. In secret, in my room, usually in the nude, I do squats and sit-ups and planks and Jane Fonda–style leg raises. It's boring and inexplicably shameful and I hate it, and as soon as I perceive a change in the legs I've deemed too fat or the stomach that's started to protrude, I stop. I am aware that this is not a healthy relationship with my body, with exercise, with what I am physically capable of.

It's not always that bad. In the cloying heat of Brisbane summers, I seek out my old friend, the public pool. I used to ride my bike everywhere, and would love the feeling of my legs pumping and the blood pumping in them, loved showing up to places wind-whipped and pink in the face. But I don't love cycling the way I love the pool. In the mid-morning, after the unsmiling, Speedo-clad office workers have been and gone, I snap on my silicone bathing cap, wriggle into a long-sleeved rash shirt, press the goggles onto my eyes. I have not shaved my bikini line and the cap's plastic grip gives me an unnerving facelift, but I'm not here to look good. I'm here to swim, slowly and steadily, with no sound but the water and my own breath, no thought but the numbers as I count the laps.

Walking home, my skin tight from chlorine, I can sometimes feel myself settle back into my body. It's easy to spend most of my time hovering in an anxious knot of consciousness above my corporeal form; after the pool, my legs a little unsteady beneath me, my heart rate unnaturally slow, I relax once more into this muscular vehicle. I feel myself become one thing again, at least for a moment. Psychologists call this mindfulness; it's a large part of a lot of modern meditative techniques, this sense of awareness of your bodily sensations. I suck at meditating, but, on those walks back from the pool, I get it. I get why you'd do sport.

·

Traditionally, for young, athletic, team-oriented Australian women, the acceptable sporting pursuit was one sport only: netball. A rule-heavy, technical and ferociously competitive game, netball was developed in the United Kingdom in the late 1800s as a sport specifically for women—it was known in the early days as 'women's basketball' for its hardwood court, forward passing, and objective of scoring baskets. In a fascinating 2001 article titled 'Gendering sport: The development of netball in Australia', Professor Tracy Taylor, an expert in sporting dynamics, suggests that netball in Australia has always been posited as an 'acceptable' physical activity for women and girls, in part because it 'could be played in a manner that retained femininity and decorum'.

The restricted physical movement and lack of body contact distinguished netball from more robust men's sports and meant that the game never directly competes with coded-male sports like basketball. Taylor argues that throughout its history the sport encapsulated 'a particular form of "compliant femininity"'—in other words, netball has always been a girly-girl's game.

Netball is an interesting paradox: it was conceived and popularised as a sport for delicate, dainty women, and as such can be perceived as something that upholds restrictive ideas about femininity (the rules, the skirts, the emphasis on decorousness). But it's also the only sport in Australia that is predominantly run by women. In fact, up until the 1970s, the All-Australia Women's Basketball Association (AAWBBA), netball's governing body, enforced a women-only policy at all levels of the game, from players to coaches to executives and administrators. So, as Taylor says, it 'was able to offer girls and women the rare opportunity to control and shape the direction of a sport'. And it pro-vided a space in which women could access all those benefits of team sports that have been available to men without question for centuries: comradeship, leadership, tradition, social bonds and, for some, the option to make a career from the sport they loved.

Team sports are overwhelmingly a positive influence on girls and young women. According to the Women's Sports Foun-dation, a non-profit organisation founded by Billie Jean King, high school girls who play sports are more likely to do well in school, graduate and avoid unintended pregnancy than those who don't. Research also suggests that girls and women who play sports have better body image, higher levels of confidence, well-being and self-esteem, and lower levels of depression. The foundation argues that playing team sports sets up young people for success in the world of business and life in general, by providing a unique sociocultural learning environment. Team sports prioritise people's strengths and competencies over their popularity, as well as teaching players how to project the illusion of confidence—you can't let your opponents or your teammates know you're nervous or doubting yourself. People who play team sports learn to be calm under pressure, to deal with mistakes, to practise loyalty and to believe that they can achieve whatever they commit to achieving. They learn to take direction from coaches and captains, to disengage self-worth from winning or losing, to enjoy challenge and competition, and to persevere. These are all qualities encouraged and expected of young men, who are also encouraged and expected to play sports, especially in a sports-obsessed nation like Australia. For Australian women and girls, there are few avenues where they can find similarly genuine encouragement other than netball.

But the paradox of the girls' game doesn't seem to be going anywhere.

Speaking to my friend Lizzie, a lawyer who grew up in a country town that had sports at its core, in a family with a sporting dynasty several generations long, it becomes clear that netball is a fairly fraught issue for many young women. Lizzie played the game all through school until her academic studies took precedence in her senior years, and she now plays in a social league in Brisbane, in a team with eight or nine other women who have full-time professional jobs. Over coffee on the ground floor of her inner-city workplace, she tells me that part of the reason she enjoys playing as an adult is that she finds it difficult—intimidating is the word she uses, actually—to open up to other women in her everyday life.

'Netball's good in that I can be around females that I don't have any preconceived knowledge about, because I just join teams with people I don't know very well. I don't have to talk about my life, I can just talk about what we're focusing on, which is the game. I find it really nice and comforting to have that kind of female support. It's being around women but not being scared of women. It doesn't matter how much you despise your opponent, if someone falls over on the court or hurts themselves, there'll always be someone standing behind them to help them up.'

I can see the appeal, and the important social function of sports like netball—sports that exist, implicitly at least, to be an outlet for female competitiveness, but also an opportunity to help each other out on an egalitarian level, one without agenda or prejudice about one another. Except, Lizzie tells me, 'There is that weakest link that everyone kinda gangs up on.' If you are that weakest link—which Lizzie was, back in her home town, when she was a teenager—netball seems like it could be outstandingly uncomfortable.

'It always felt like if you were a girl you had to play netball, in that town. If you didn't, you were just on the outskirts of everything.' She describes the dynamic courtside as 'like *Toddlers & Tiaras*'—the reality TV series about child beauty pageants— and I laugh, but I can see her point. The sport is handed down matrilineally over generations and, in certain parts of Australia, constitutes the majority of women's recreational engagement outside of work and the home. Curiously, Lizzie uses the word 'fury' in her description of the sport, and I wonder if there's something to that as well: to the precariousness of the one outlet for focus, passion, physicality and anger that women might have in their lives. Netball does, after all, cross socio-economic and geographic boundaries: everyone from wealthy inner-city private school girls to girls at tiny country state schools put their bibs on and learn to yell 'Here if you need'. And how many of those girls have mothers who played netball, who grew up to find their whole lives revolved around child-rearing and household-running, who felt stifled by social obligations to be accommodating and courteous and kind, whose one opportunity to feel and act on the physical expression of emotion was on their childhood netball court? It's depressing to imagine that for generations of women, netball was the only sport open to those who wanted to socialise, exercise, realise ambition—to be in their bodies for themselves, and not for the service of others.

•

Of course, there's another sporting discipline emerging as a place for women, with great fanfare and wholehearted support from legions of fans: the brand-new women's league of Australian Rules Football, known as AFLW.

Even I, a soft, sports-illiterate poindexter, have been swept up in the phenomenon that is AFLW. Australian rules football, that ludicrous, spectacular sport around which much of the country, regardless of gender, organises their lives, only officially opened channels for women to become professional players in 2017. After nearly two hundred years of campaigning (according to AFL/AFLW podcast *Play On*, women have been asking for a league of their own since 1880), the AFL ran a series of women's exhibition matches between 2013 and 2015—the last of which was televised and attracted phenomenal ratings. Since the start of the women's league in February 2017, the game has broken records all over the place, including attracting the biggest crowd ever to attend a standalone women's sporting match (Fremantle vs. Collingwood, 10 February 2018, with 41,975 people in the stands). With eight teams currently in the league, AFLW will expand by another six teams by 2020, with at least one team in every state.

Basically, women's AFL has shattered even the highest expectations. Although there is the standard-issue chorus of naysayers (old-school sexists and garden-variety trolls), the refrain from players and organisers is exuberant: they're setting up a league that will inspire many female sports fans for generations to come. In a quote on the official AFLW site, Carlton player Brianna Davey says, 'I'm inspired by all the women and girls who used to be spectators but now want to play. It's not just about the sport. AFLW is a movement.'

A leader of the movement is Breeanna Brock. CEO of the Brisbane Lions AFLW team—the first female CEO to be appointed in the AFL, in fact—and a seasoned sportswoman herself, she led the Lions through a magnificent debut season, and is an influential advocate of the sport's importance to women both on and off the field. She also received the Football Woman of the Year Award in 2018 in recognition of her contribution to the sport—which includes doubling the Lions AFLW team's revenue in their first year, acting as development manager for AFLW Queensland and successfully revitalising the club after the men's team's dismal losing streak.

She tells me that AFLW has democratised the sport again. Because the league is still in its infancy, the venues are small enough that fans can meet and interact with the players at every match.

'You get kids who are just coming because they can stick their hands out and touch you,' she tells me. 'It's the third-highest reason for people to attend our games—they know that they will genuinely get an opportunity to meet a player.'

And the players they meet seem like real people—something that sounds obvious to me, but which is a total novelty to fans raised on men's AFL.

'In the boys' system, they come out as an eighteen-year-old kid never having done anything except train for football. The most interesting thing they might do is play golf. Whereas all our girls work or study.' There's been a flurry of media attention around these women's lives outside football, as audiences realise that their players' day jobs actually make them interesting.

Brock says it's having a positive effect on the men's team as well, as the two teams train in the same facilities.

'Often the girls and boys are in the gym together and they'll talk, and the boys will finish their session and be like, "What are you guys gonna do?"' Most of the women are heading off to work an eight-hour shift at wherever they earn most of their money. The boys' plans to go home and play video games tend to look a little pathetic in comparison.

'And because we're winning, and the boys are not winning,' Breeanna says, 'they're like, "Hmm . . . so you guys work, and train, and win, and we're . . . "' She trails off, laughing. 'It's been great, really fantastic for both groups to interact with each other.' Brock has seen the football landscape change so much as to become almost unrecognisable in the past five years. At her previous job, she spent her time going to community clubs and encouraging them to bring on girls' teams; a significant portion of them told her, in her words, 'Over my dead body.' Now, several years later, there's eighty new women's teams across Queensland, and the gender shift is having effects beyond just the women playing.

Girls' teams mean new opportunities for daughters to bond with the parent who takes them to football—usually their father.

'Dads are now bringing their daughters, so they're having a different kind of relationship around the sport than they previously would have, because the daughters would have gone off to netball with Mum. There's some great research that says if you've got a boy in the household, it'll be his sport prioritised first, because Dad will take him to that sport on Saturday. Mum's still got to do the shopping, so daughter goes with her, she's not playing a sport. But now that daughter can go off with Dad and brother, and play the same sport. They're not getting left behind as much.'

And there are visible benefits for getting girls and women into team sports. As Brock says, if you join an AFL team, you automatically have twenty-two new friends. The team forces you to build trust, to learn to protect one another, to be aggressive and demanding and to go after what you want—and to use your body, and get muddy, and not have to apologise for it.

'Imagine a little ten-year-old girl being told, "You can do all these things that you're never allowed to do anywhere else." Their eyes light up. What they all say, particularly around that ten- to twelve-year-old mark, when you ask them, "What do you love about footy?": "I love tackling. I love the physicality of it."' Even to Brock, a dyed-in-the-wool AFL supporter, the code doesn't matter when it comes to women in sports. The stakes are so much higher than league loyalty. 'The more we can get girls out doing something—who cares if it's AFL, rugby, soccer, tennis,' she says, 'as long as they're out, active and doing some-thing, that breeds self-confidence, physical confidence, physical health. It's all that intangible stuff that you couldn't put a dollar figure on—the influence of what seeing more women playing sport can do for girls.'

For a long time, the options for women to play sports pro-fessionally have been thin on the ground, and tucked out of sight. Which is frankly insane given that in many disciplines Australia's national women's teams far outperform the men. The Matildas, Australia's women's soccer team, were ranked sixth in the world at the end of 2018; the Socceroos, their male counterparts, were ranked 43rd. The pay gap, as widely com-mented on by the media, is appalling: in 2015 it was reported that world-renowned player and Matildas co-captain Lisa De Vanna made about $27,397 for the whole year, while Socceroos star

Tim Cahill made about that figure per *day*, even before bonuses or endorsements. And although there has been progress—including a complete overhaul of Cricket Australia salaries in 2017 that saw female players' payments jump from $7.5 million to $55.2 million—implicit value placed on women's sports continues to lag. AFLW games are still free to attend; women's State of Origin NRL matches cost $10 to attend, as opposed to $300 for the men's. Nonetheless, the response to AFLW has been ecstatic. The closeness of the players, their devotion to their fans and their ease with becoming legitimate—and admirable—role models means that there's a whole generation of new players about five years away from hitting the field. It's a wild moment to witness, the stirrings before the storm. Brock says egos are already starting to blossom among the Lions' women's ranks, and it fills me with a fierce kind of triumph: let them be arrogant, let them be rich, let them play the game in front of the millions of eyes they deserve.

•

While walking to the dentist, I turn onto the Kurilpa Bridge and am confronted with four women in fluorescent pink, ponytails swinging, jogging in step. I immediately prickle. I want to walk in the shade, and they are running on the shady side. I think: I'm not moving for these jogging bimbos. But then I stop. I am taken aback that after months and months of writing about women collaborating and caring for one another, I'm still reflexively anti-woman—particularly anti–women in groups. I move to the side and let the joggers pass; I think they might be training for a charity run, from what I glimpse on the pockets of their running shirts. But would it matter if they weren't? They all look very young, and being young and long-haired and wanting to stay fit and doing it with your friends is not a crime, or even something to scoff at. How long is it going to take to unpick this knot that misogyny has tied me in?

I remember a friend, several years ago, telling me conspiratorially that when she was at school, she'd had such bad anger issues that she'd been sent to see a psychologist. What helped, in the end, was contact rugby, which she played with vigour until the end of high school. When we spoke, during our undergraduate degree, she said she was starting to feel mad again.

The other night, at a dinner party with some girlfriends, someone asked me if I exercised to keep my figure, and my face got hot and I changed the subject.

I still think about jostling with girls on the soccer field, and how differently things might have worked out for me if I'd kept playing team sports, kept negotiating those relationships with other women in the context of codified competition, if I'd always appreciated my body for what it can do instead of what it looked like. But there's still time. I've booked tickets to the next Brisbane Lions match, and Miles has promised to take me through a weightlifting training session. In the end, I'm only competing against myself.

5

DANCERS

Moving together in time

I remember attending tap class as a four-year-old. It is one of my earliest memories: the plastic clickers on elastic bands that my mother slipped around my shoes before class, and marching around a school hall, *heel, toe, heel, toe, click click, click click, click click*. Vividly, I remember when my parents bought me real tap shoes, black patent leather with the bright, cruel silver taps on toe and heel, and how I skittered noisily around the house in them. I remember showing off in class, bossing my classmates around. Then I remember the dance concert at the end of the term, how the teachers told our mums that our stage make-up needed to be blue eyeshadow and red lipstick, and how my mother didn't have either of those cosmetics, so I appeared in green eyeshadow with a fetching coral lip. (Sometimes I wonder how I would have felt if I'd gone on stage looking just like all the other girls. My pride tells me I would have been disgusted. But I don't know. Maybe I would have loved it. Maybe it would have felt just right.)

In high school I flirted with Rock Eisteddfod (I recall some kind of unitard with flowers and leaves on it, and the horror of getting my first period the day before the show) and learned the foxtrot and cha-cha before graduation, but those days tapping around a school hall were the closest I came to being a dancer. Sometimes I think childhood dance classes are a defining experience of girlhood—that everyone has some memory like this, whether real or simply absorbed by osmosis from a culture that aligns dance with everything Girl.

These days, though, I have a stoop and a sheepish relationship with my remedial masseuse, the products of too many hours at a screen and too few thinking about my posture. I never feel confident on a dance floor; I am always joking, trying not to fall over, only feeling credibly at ease with the music when I'm alone or drunk or high (or, once or twice, on stage with a band, in a particularly ecstatic moment). Dance—and dancers—seem like even more of an alien world than that of sportswomen. But I am so curious. The last time I danced in public, to disco at a tiny bar close to my house, after a long day and without changing out of my work clothes, just by chance I felt the flickering of something transcendent. Imagine what it would be like to be a pro at this, I thought.

•

Dance is one of the oldest forms of art. Because it's done with the body, prehistoric evidence of it is hard to find, but the earliest confirmed records of dance come from 9,000 years ago, in cave paintings in India, and we can assume with some confidence that we've been dancing for a lot longer than that. Anthropologist Andree Grau even proposed that it was dance, specifically 'moving together in time', that precipitated collaboration between individuals, and therefore language, culture and the seeds of human civilisation. She also spoke about dance creating a 'heightened state of consciousness' by combining intellect and affect, the mind and emotions, in the movements of the physical body.

All of the dancers I spoke to referenced that heightened state in one way or another; they talked about being able to cease conscious thought and embody pure feeling, or coming to sudden revelations while performing their steps. The concept pops up regularly throughout literature about dance as well, from investigations of the social dynamics of affluent Californian ballet schools to documentaries on hula dancing champions. An article by Anna Aalten examining embodiment in ballet, in which she talks to several professional ballet dancers, is titled after their most commonly used phrase: 'The moment when it all comes together'.

I think about Charles Tansley in *To the Lighthouse* telling Lily Briscoe, 'Women can't write, women can't paint.' Women have been excluded from capital-A Art, as a tradition, pretty thoroughly. Maybe it's more common now to talk about an artist or writer or musician who happens to be a woman without first mentioning her gender—but it's nowhere near universal. Women are too embodied, too caught up in childbearing and childrearing, or too silly with thoughts of attracting and keeping a mate, to make Real Art.

Except for the Real Art that is dance. No one has a problem with women dancing. It is one of our culture's most valuable loopholes.

Dance offers its practitioners a unique opportunity to combine the pursuit of physical prowess with an absorption into the near-spiritual realm of emotion and artistry. The bodily aspect alone is a big deal, considering how often women are discouraged from fully inhabiting their physicality. It's like an escape clause for women who long to move their bodies in a society that still prefers women to be still and passive: the same parents who might frown at their daughter playing touch rugby have no problem at all with taking her to jazz or ballet classes. Indeed, many girls start formal dance classes because their frazzled mothers enroll them in dance schools hoping to provide an outlet for their troublesome excess energy.

But dance, like any art form, is more than just fulfilling for the individual. The women I spoke to use dance to preserve culture, tackle body dysmorphia in refugee girls and facilitate discussions about race and intersectionality. Ask the vast fan base of superstar choreographer Parris Goebel what dance means for them, and you'll learn it's so much more than a solitary pursuit. It's a community, a social movement, a history—and, when it comes to forms like ballet, a puzzle that I just cannot figure out.

•

But ballet can wait. First I'm meeting Esita Maen at a café in the outer Brisbane suburb of Underwood. She's a short, animated 23-year-old with hip-length black hair and impeccable eyebrows, and she speaks powerfully and eloquently about the role dance plays in her life.

For Esita, her dance group is not just an opportunity to teach and to dance; it's a method of passing down culture to the girls in her community. She calls it a 'front': dance is just a way she can get a bunch of girls from Kiribati—a tiny atoll nation in Micronesia—together so that they can share their traditions, preserving a vital part of themselves that she feels is at risk of disappearing completely in the Pacific diaspora. It's not enough to just have the blood, she says—you have to have the culture as well.

I had known, in a cursory sort of way, that dance could be a route into one's culture, but I'd never properly thought about it before. Hearing Esita talk about the work she does with the women and girls in her dance group suddenly threw it all into focus. For those who participate in Esita's classes, the time they spend together is as much about learning how to be an i-Kiribati woman as it is about learning the dance steps. It can be difficult to preserve cultural traditions when you're part of a tiny minority in a mostly white Australian city, but the classes provide an opportunity to talk about, for example, the traditional celebrations that take place when a girl gets her first period.

'Because these girls are coming to practice and they're getting asked, you know, "Oh, did you have your period party?", it really helps them to understand what exactly they come from. And it helps us teach them life lessons, in terms of how they carry themselves, not just as a girl from the islands growing up overseas, but as a culturally aware Gilbert Island girl.'

Kiribati dance is beautiful and intricate. Esita tells me that the moves are based on the movements of birds. I watch YouTube videos. I see it. The dancers wear flower-shaped ornaments, on their biceps, forearms and sometimes fingers, that look at a glance like tiny finches flitting around as the dancer repositions her arms. But the most striking thing is the movement of the dancer's head—just like a bird, quick and sure, little flickers from side to side. It's surprising and a little eerie, but absolutely magnetic. Some dancers wear voluminous pale-brown skirts made of shredded pandanus leaves, which Esita tells me can highlight the hip movements of a skilled dancer with devastating effect. Some, she says, can make the outer edges of the skirt flick so high that they reach above the dancer's head.

I ask about the impact doing dance like this can have on body image, and she laughs. It's hard sometimes, she says, convincing girls that they do have the confidence to perform in just a bra and a skirt. But: 'It really comes down to pushing them to remember that this is your culture, you have a right. Not even that—it's almost like an obligation. And your body image is almost irrelevant. The only thing you have to worry about is if you're healthy, and everything else will fall into place. If you have a few extra curves, like, so did our ancestors. It's going to be fine. Chillax.'

•

After my conversation with Esita, I decide I am going to participate in a Groove Therapy dance class. Designed specifically for people who aren't confident or experienced dancers, Groove Therapy is supposed to be a little oasis of support and community in a world of dance that can be very intimidating to non-dancers like me. The dance class I'm going to will be held in Byron Bay, a two-hour drive from where I live in Brisbane, at ten in the morning on a Saturday. I'm going with a friend—more an acquaintance, really—the only person on my Facebook friends list who was also attending. I messaged her immediately to ask if we could go as a duo. The thought of going it alone was horrifying.

When I asked her, Esita compared the feeling of dancing in sync with others to how it feels when you're 'in the pocket' playing music, and I finally, almost, I think, got it: when you're doing something right with a bunch of other people, the sense of connectedness to one another and the satisfaction of performing to the fullest extent of your abilities combine to create something bigger than all of you. In Helen Garner's essay 'In the Wings', as she watches the Melbourne Ballet Company at the barre, she relaxes 'into the peculiar bliss provoked by the sight of bodies moving in unison'. I think about how pop psychology tells us to mirror our conversation partners' body language to put them at ease. I think about how few opportunities there are for urban-dwelling, Western women to do collaborative physical work together. I think about the time I spent fifteen minutes chatting with a new friend while we both absentmindedly picked bits of dog hair off a scarf, how good it felt to do that together, and how surprised I was. I almost never put my body into step with another's.

At the dance class in Byron Bay, a move requires us to partner up. One dancer must execute a 360-degree spin, right arm extended, while the other drops dramatically into a squat so that the arm sails over their head. It is by far the best part of the routine, not just because of the incipient danger of copping a forearm to the face, but because we are deliberately partnered with total strangers. I enjoy communicating in this elegant, unfamiliar way; together, we make our bodies legible, we create something, however ungainly.

Beyond the satisfaction of not blackening anyone's eye, though, I don't take as much as I'd hoped from the class. We are gathered on the brick-tile floor of a beachfront pub, and bemused

Saturday morning punters are watching us over the rims of their mid-strength beers. I am sweaty and self-conscious. I feel fat.

At home that evening, I try to perform some of the routine we learned in front of the mirror. I look ridiculous. Groove Therapy always operates without mirrors, which is a smart move, as I'd immediately have gathered my things and left had I seen how stupid I looked during class. It felt good to move my body, and to learn and remember the steps (and to swing my arm wildly without concussing anyone), but trying to re-create those moves in the mirror feels dreadful, like a cruel prank. I wanted to have a revelation in that pub, surrounded by fifty other women lifting their feet and sweating through their activewear. But it will take more than one class to dislodge my gaze from the outside of this weird, awkward body, and put it back where it belongs: in here, looking out.

Vanessa Marian, the director of Groove Therapy, is invested in making positive changes to the way girls and young women relate to their bodies. When we spoke, she'd just run the first class in her program Groove Rising, a street dance class for new immigrant and refugee girls. After an unsuccessful first go at it with an organisation in Western Sydney, Vanessa sat down with one of the girls from the original program and co-designed Groove Rising, a project that prioritises tackling body dys-morphia. She says that teenage girls coming to Australia from conservative cultures end up thrown against the juggernaut of beach culture, often with disastrous consequences.

'It affects the best of us who have grown up here our whole lives, and it affects almost every woman of colour that I know, and I can't even imagine the culture shock of not even having grown up with that.'

Dance, she says, is the right way to counter the sense of distortion many young women have about their bodies, not only because of the basic processes of exercise releasing endorphins but because of the ease with which this particular physical activity fosters a mind–body connection.

'And also the idea of reinforcing appreciation for your body in a way that isn't aesthetic. That's a really big one. A lot of it is subtle. It's the idea of not saying a single word about how people look, and just having a good time. Also, all of our teachers, by default, are all women of colour. All of our bodies range in size. And I think, just by being in the room, that is powerful enough for a lot of [the students].

'For us,' she says, 'it's about just giving our students one safe space a week where they can come and explore their own identity and what it even means, because as women of colour ourselves we all understand what it means to not really fit in one world or the other.'

•

An artist, choreographer, dancer and teacher, Amrita Hepi has been called a 'dance activist' for her work centring the body in questions of culture, authenticity and decolonial imagination. She's also well known for her Beyoncé and Rihanna workshops, which she runs in nightclubs, teaching women how to work it like the superstars and engage with big cultural ideas at the same time. 'I realised that when I'm teaching it's a really great way to talk to people about things, especially about subjects that concern the body and shame. I can run a dance class and do an acknowledgement of country and I can talk about all the things that I feel like don't get talked about in other forums. And obviously because we were dancing to a lot of Black music, we talked about black- and brownness. Sometimes it feels like the conversation could be one-sided, but the thing I was getting in return was that, what I would teach the class, I would be able to see coming back at me. It became a conversation.'

Amrita has worked all around Australia, crossing cultural and socio-economic divides, and says that dance is a universally positive thing—that people are changed by it. Even after just one class.

'I've watched people walk out straighter and more full of energy and life force, and I've watched people who have changed in that they've kept coming to classes, and I keep updated on their story, and they're like, "Because I did this dance class by myself I felt like I could do [something else] by myself." It's being able to focus on something, it's being able to remember something, it's being able to conquer a small thing with the body, but it can leave a pretty lasting impact.'

I ask if she thinks dance helps women because we feel disconnected from our bodies. She says it's not that simple.

'I think that inherently our bodies are scrutinised so much that we are actually quite in touch with our bodies a lot of the time. So we kind of know what's going on at a bigger level because we know the pressure we're under.' The pressure to have children, to look a certain way, to take contraception, not to mention the need for constant vigilance in order to preserve our own safety, means that women are actually hyper-aware of their bodies. Dance does something, though, to change that awareness.

'Maybe this is a way that we can acknowledge that our bodies exist for more than the purpose of reshaping them, or making them quieter or making them louder. Maybe the best analogy is that when we are dancing we are in control of the volume.'

•

Amateur dance is a means of empowerment for many of the women around me. There's the enduringly popular dance night No Lights No Lycra, which, as its name suggests, is a party held completely in the dark so that you can dance secure in the knowledge that no one is watching. There are initiatives like Amrita's and Vanessa's, dance classes marketed to people 'too scared to dance'. A number of my friends have taken adult ballet classes; nearly every Brisbane neighbourhood has community-run classes for Bollywood dance, belly dance, hip-hop, not to mention the fitness/dance crossovers like Zumba and barre. But my favourite part of dance culture happens on Instagram.

For several years now I've been following the career of Parris Goebel, a New Zealand woman whose prowess as a choreographer has seen her, and her dance crews ReQuest and The Royal Family, collaborate with Justin Bieber, Nicki Minaj, Jennifer Lopez, Rihanna and a phalanx of other pop ultra-stars. Goebel is a self-taught visionary who dropped out of high school to start her Palace dance studio at age fifteen, and whose dance style is a vigorous blend of hip-hop, Jamaican dancehall, Pasifika, and some ineffable expression of that concept we call 'squad'. In the video that catapulted her into the public consciousness, Justin Bieber's 'Sorry', Goebel's dance troupe, all women, whine and gyrate, gurn and posture, playing with femininity and sexiness with a total lack of propriety. It's full of unapologetic stunting, clownish exaggeration, mean faces, the kind of schoolgirl joie de vivre only the coolest kids have. She calls the style 'polyswagg'. It still gives me goosebumps.

Goebel is a trailblazer in dance. She has an uncanny knack for choreographing on a massive scale, as evidenced by the many exhilarating videos of The Royal Family competing, thirty strong or more, at events like the World of Dance Championships (drawing the biggest cheers with the smallest, most precise movements, like when the entire ensemble freezes except for a minuscule and devastating 'whassup' nod). But spend a moment on her social media feeds and you'll see she's a genius at putting together moves for duos and trios as well, a virtuoso at freestyling, a true scholar of her chosen form. The first time I saw one of her videos, even I knew I was witnessing history in the making.

Recently Goebel made her directorial debut with a music video for a track by Ciara called 'Level Up'. In it, the pop star and the entirety of Goebel's female dance crew pump out the frenetic, high-energy moves I've come to expect from them, in the red-lit surrounds of the Auckland War Memorial Museum. Their opening sequence in particular is the visual equivalent of an earworm: legs akimbo, dropped into a half-squat, heads tilted to one side, the whole group swipes circles with their hands forming blades, forearms cutting shreds out of the air. It does what it's supposed to do—it makes everyone, even me, want to try to do it.

I follow Goebel on Instagram, and in the week after the video dropped all of her Insta stories were videos sent to her of fans copying the moves. It is an instantly iconic dance, nailing the sweet spot between visually impressive and technically achievable, and I tapped through hundreds of clips of Goebel's followers interpreting the moves. People put all kinds of twists on it, from all kinds of modern dance traditions: they twerked, they vogued, they turned it into cheerleading routines, and Parris put heart emojis all over every one of them. It felt kind of voyeuristic, but I couldn't help but be transfixed by all that joy bouncing between smartphones around the world.

Most of the people Parris posts doing the #LevelUpChallenge are women of colour, and I think about how dance forms like hip-hop, dancehall, polyswagg, pantsula and vogue, forms like Groove Therapy and Amrita's Beyoncé-inspired classes, and cultural forms like Esita's Kiribati dance troupe, are art forms where non-white women are not only welcomed, but are in control of their bodies, their cultural narratives and their physicalities.

•

Here are the topics of some research papers on dance I've read: the effects of dance classes on older women in retirement homes; the impact of community dance programs in rural and remote Western Australia; belly dance as a method of recovering from gendered violence; ballet as a source of pleasure; what happens to ballet dancers if you instruct them without a mirror. They appear to have higher self-esteem, is the answer to that last one. It's an interesting paper, written in 2002 by Sally A. Radell, Daniel D. Adame and Steven P. Cole in a journal called *Perceptual and Motor Skills*. I found it after searching 'ballet women psychology' in my university library database; it was on a list after an article titled 'In defence of ballet'. I know what assumptions these articles are writing back against: that ballet is harmful to women's psyches and self-esteem; that ballet is unhealthy; that ballet does, in fact, need defending.

My first date with my partner was to the ballet. I had never been. We went to a Sunday matinee session of the New York Ballet Company to see them perform three contemporary works. We had cheap seats, up the back in a mostly empty auditorium at the Queensland Performing Arts Centre, and I was shocked to find that, even from such a distance, I loved it. Most of all, I loved the stark, disorienting disconnection between the visual and the auditory experience of it: I watched these dancers float across the stage as though made of smoke, but even from the back of the half-empty auditorium I could hear their feet, the hard toes of their pointe shoes knocking against the boards. I could hear the effort, but I could see no trace of it. It was a beautiful way to spend time with someone I was already falling in love with—to be awed in each other's presence by something that seemed totally alien, totally untouchable.

·

The beauty of ballet, says Dutch dance academic Anna Aalten, 'is created by the straight lines of the extended human body going outward and upward and by the artificiality of the movements'. It is an art form constructed entirely in opposition to the body's natural form; it asks a soft, curved, earthbound thing to become straight, stiff, and weightless. This is where the tension and the wonder of the dance come from, why it's so breathtaking to see a ballet dancer float across a stage en pointe—she's making her body do things it was never meant to do. It's one of the greatest examples of mastery of the flesh I can think of.

It's also deeply problematic. Ballet does need defending, because it has a history of hurting women. Not just their famous feet but their bodies, their self-image, and their position in society. In an article titled 'Five things I hate about ballet', *LA Times* writer Lewis Segal references the art form's notoriously restrictive approach to the bodies of its female devotees, 'who starve themselves to match a skeletal ideal and then stop menstruating for the length of their careers'. This extremely narrow body ideal can lead to eating disorders, mental health issues and slow cognitive development in young dancers. Female ballet dancers learn from a young age that in order to be employable, they must be obedient and willing to conform; they learn that they are replaceable. And that's to say nothing of the numerous dancers seriously injured in the course of their career.

Feminist criticism of the dance form is plentiful. Dance scholar Ann Daly calls it 'one of our culture's most powerful models of patriarchal ceremony', and says it's 'rooted in an ideology which denies women their own agency'. There's certainly no denying that ballet is an art form in the long and storied tradition of the patriarchy and all the gender roles that accompany it: a ballerina is supposed to represent the patriarchal ideal of Woman, beautiful, delicate and passive, lifted and moved around by her male partner, an aesthetic object to be put on display.

Do you think any of this deters, in the slightest, the girls who want to dance?

What I love and fear about ballet is how it can, simultaneously, rigorously adhere to heteronormativity, beauty standards, old rubrics of what it means to be a good woman, and still function—however unintentionally, however unconsciously—as a subversion of a system that continues to deny most women access to both real physical strength and true artistic expression. Aalten writes, 'In western culture, physical strength and femininity are believed to be incompatible.' Ballet dancers get to have both in spades.

•

I spent a long day watching YouTube videos of ballerinas preparing themselves for their work. There are so many ballet videos on YouTube; I must have watched hours upon hours of them by now. In one, a very young woman—possibly a girl, it is impossible to tell—demonstrates, for nearly nine minutes, how to scrape her fine blonde hair up into a perfect ballet bun. Her movements are so practised, I can tell that she has to think about slowing them down in order for them to appear legibly on camera. In another, a woman talks us through the preparation of her pointe shoes. This is a common theme for ballet videos, one that borders on the fetishistic: beautiful, lithe women, and the salacious contrast provided by their gnarled and hurt feet. In one video the ballerina uses the word 'pain' a lot. She does not make a secret of her suffering. She unevenly slices off the bottom of her new shoes, creating a rougher surface that will give her more traction. She cuts a thin sliver out of the shank to allow her to bend her foot into an unnatural arch more easily. She uses gel pads around her toes to cushion them from the shoe, but she says some girls will use tooth-numbing gel on them instead. Looking at this woman's feet, and her taut, smiling face as she describes the pain of being en pointe for eight hours a day, I have a rising sense of horror. The dance is starting to seem old and savage, like fox-hunting, or a public execution.

But maybe not. I wrote an essay for the Australian literary

journal *Kill Your Darlings* that linked what I called 'new fitness'—the current trend towards performative exercise as disseminated by young, activewear-clad women through Instagram—and mortification of the flesh. I was trying to connect new fitness with early Christian asceticism, which required adherents to mortify or punish the sinful body in order to purify the spirit—my point being that followers of new fitness, with all their no-pain-no-gain mantras, muscle-isolating gym exercises and time-lapse evidence of gruelling workouts, were also attempting to punish the body in order to gain purity. The difference is that the purity gained from broadcasting your virtue on Instagram with the hashtag #cleaneating isn't spiritual at all, but a purity of conformity to newly developing standards of femininity and the desirable body.

I am starting to see the same compulsion to punish the body in ballet, too, and here at least I can understand the motivation a little better. It is a long tradition to be continuing, wounding yourself in the name of art. It troubles me that it's overwhelmingly women who bear the cruellest and most extreme physical punishment: the torturous shoes, the diets so restrictive that their periods stop. But maybe in doing all that, they begin to approach something sublime—to literally sublimate their own most fundamental needs (comfort, food, rest) into a higher project than themselves. Are all ballet dancers of the same ilk as those people who leap off cliffs in sail-suits, hoping to dance ever closer to the edge of death, and thus to the divine, thrilling in the pain and balance it takes to not tip over entirely? It hurts to force your body to be something it does not want to be; it hurts to pursue perfection.

•

I think the shock of seeing ballet dancers' feet has more to do with gender than anything else. They are gnarled and raw, sure, but any sportsperson alters their body in pursuit of their goal, and we don't linger indecently on the cauliflower ears of rugby players—or, indeed, on the calloused fingers of professional string musicians, or on farmers' sock-tans. I think there's something magnetic about the juxtaposition of a realm that seems superficially to be entirely feminine with something as genuinely hardcore as wilful self-mutilation in the pursuit of artistic excellence.

I think about the perceived femininity of ballet as well. Maybe there's something attractive about that to girls: a space entirely (or apparently entirely) dominated by women, where everyone wears pink and make-up is mandatory, a full-bodied surrender to girliness without apology. From the outside, ballet seems like a semi-secret girls' club, with its own language and rituals and social mores, and its own terrible secrets.

Maybe this is why popular culture is so fixated on ballet, particularly as (body) horror. It's a potent form of the monstrous feminine, something sinister and unknowable and possibly unnatural—the uncanny psychological transformation of Natalie Portman's Nina in *Black Swan* speaks to the sense of faint disgust we feel at a woman so thoroughly consumed by her work, her passion, her ambition. She can't just be good at her job or her art; she's going to lose her mind and stab herself with a piece of broken mirror during a psychotic hallucination where she tries to murder a spectral doppelganger. We strap those pretty shoes on to the ballerina; we don't like it when she uses them to run, to fly.

•

I walk to the Queensland Ballet studio on a sunny winter afternoon to sit down with a couple of the dancers in the corps. Sophie and Vanessa are best friends as well as colleagues. I don't know what I'm expecting. In the past week or so I've watched *Centre Stage* and *Black Swan* and counted the ballet clichés: eating disorders, arrogant, egotistical maestros, visionary young men, gifted and boring young women, body issues, bitter rivalry, bitchiness, interminable scenes focused on their poor, battered feet. But at the Thomas Dixon Centre, a circa-1900 chocolate-brick building in West End, I'm shown into a bright room lined with desks where a number of dancers are eating lunch, chatting with each other and the company's marketers and choreographers.

Sophie and Vanessa are both in their mid-twenties, both, like all ballet dancers, willowy and strong (they hug me when they leave to prepare for rehearsal, and I feel their fine muscles as we embrace). Vanessa is aristocratic, Gallic; Sophie, blonde with high, wide cheekbones. They are relaxed and open with me, and I don't feel like I am transgressing, here at this table in this light-filled room. I ask, Why ballet?

Like everyone I've spoken to, they both started dancing almost as soon as they could walk. They were both drawn to physical movement, but did not love the sports they played as kids—Sophie says she was so stressed by the competitive aspect of athletics that she'd cry.

'It's funny, because dance is competitive as well, but it's different. I think it's because you don't get first, second, third, like in a race. You go out there and dance, and there's no medal at the end; you're just doing it for others to enjoy, and for yourself.'

This almost makes me laugh, because I remember talking to Tandia at the weightlifting club, who started lifting after quitting ballet, and who said the exact opposite: that the intangibility of success in ballet was what made her lose her love for it, and the concrete numbers of weightlifting was what made it so appealing. For Vanessa and Sophie, though, the athleticism is necessary, but not the goal itself.

'I think movement is just something that comes naturally to a person,' says Vanessa. 'You just feel the need to do it, and it's very expressive. You can portray emotions that you might not be able to say in words. It's really special.'

Then she says something I will think about for the next three months: 'And there's also this element of trying to be perfect. But you'll never reach the perfection that classical ballet is, because it's so technically hard.'

'That's what drives you,' says Sophie, and I imagine, briefly, what it would be like to have that pure a goal.

Later, I watch a video by Vice that follows Theresa Farrell, a dancer with the American Contemporary Ballet in Los Angeles, as she drops one and a half pounds before her next performance. She says it's about striking the balance between strength and lightness of limb—if the leg is a pound heavier, it's harder to lift over your head. And she says this: 'The athleticism is a means to an end for the ultimate artistic goal.' She's talking about being perfect. They all are.

•

When I first started thinking about ballet, I wanted to talk about competition between female ballet dancers. It surprised me a little how completely fascinated I was by the idea of a dynamic of rivalry in the dance. ('Girl dancers!' snorted one friend, himself a former ballet dancer, when I told him what I was working on. 'They all hate each other. Spend all their time hoping their enemies get injured or pregnant.') Maybe there's something satisfying about seeing those old myths played out for real, for our entertainment, for the guilty tingle of seeing that puzzle piece slot in. Maybe there's something exhilarating about seeing women who are experts in their field jostle for position, just as there is something exhilarating about seeing anyone at the absolute pinnacle of their physical prowess.

But that's not what I care about now. Vanessa and Sophie are so calm about that aspect of their lives. When I suggest that there's a strong sense of competition in ballet, they gently correct me: when auditioning for contracts, yes, it is competitive; but so much of what gets you a role, it seems, is out of your control. It makes no sense to hold on to rivalries when your success often depends on something completely beyond the realm of your mastery. Maybe you are the most talented, but the company needs to replace a tall dancer who's just left, and you're too short. Maybe the director of this production likes the look of you; maybe the director of the next won't. You can be a beautiful dancer and still miss out, for reasons you might never know. It sounds nightmarish to me, but Sophie and Vanessa seem completely at ease with it.

What I care about now is perfection. I have always had an uneasy relationship with the idea of perfection, because I've always connected it to appearance and nothing more. But though

Ann Daly (and many others) criticise ballet for perpetuating women's status as objects to be looked at, the dancers I speak to locate their pursuit of perfection not on the body, but in the ephemeral art created by it. The pursuit of perfection in dance is not limited to ballet. Modern hula competitions prize the same combination of athleticism and effortlessness. But, once again, the core of the art form is about what the body *does* more than what it looks like—and, as one of Aalten's participants puts it, the opportunity to maybe, even just three times in a season, finally achieve a moment of physical, mental and emotional unity.

•

At the Thomas Dixon Centre, I'm shown into an airy, high-ceilinged room on the second storey and seated in a folding chair next to the piano. Huge windows line three of the walls, and the place feels like an eyrie. The company is preparing for a regional tour of *Swan Lake*, and they've agreed to let me sit in on a run-through of the first act. I realise, too late, that I have been seated in front of the mirror, which has the disconcerting effect of putting me directly in the eye line of the dancers as they watch themselves stretch out in fluffy cardigans and leg warmers. I try to become as small as possible, but no one really looks at me, except for Sophie and Vanessa, who wave enthusiastically.

In the part they're rehearsing today, Vanessa plays the Prince's mother, the Queen—she's well suited to it, stalking gracefully and haughtily about the floor in enormous UGG boots—and Sophie plays a swan. The company seem so young I have to remind myself that I'm about to watch a rehearsal, not an afterschool class. Once they start dancing, I don't have to remind myself anymore.

Act 1, Scene 2, commonly known as the White Act, is my favourite part of the ballet. Even without costumes, with the dancers garbed in a haphazard collection of rehearsal tutus and trackpants, the many swans gliding across the lake in unison are breathtaking. They look like liquid, or like underwater reeds, waving fluidly in the current. I can't help it: I imagine myself as one of them. I imagine what it would be like to have that strength of command over my corporeal form. I imagine being reassured by the clarity, the tangible nature of the positions, augmented by the ethereal, unnameable beauty of the human body in exquisite movement.

Every one of these dancers, I think, is trying to be perfect. Sometimes it is hard to watch. During the Dance of the Little Swans, where four dancers with interlinked arms perform a difficult routine in near-exact unison, one of the little swans stumbles and swears aloud. She does not make it back into formation—her sisters continue without her—and I watch her approach the directors, apologising, near tears, and then stagger to the side, where she massages her leg. When she swore, I smiled; it was such a candid moment, and I was immediately reminded of the many times I've made some silly, public error and blurted out 'Shit!' before I could stop myself. But the little swan does not smile at all, and I feel terrible.

Sitting this close to the line that marks the front of the stage is quite a different sensation to watching a ballet in a concert hall from the cheap seats. As the dancers go past, smiling, leaping, I hear their breath rushing heavy and hard through their bared teeth. If I shut my eyes I'd think they were sprinting, brows furrowed, but I watch their faces as they waft past and they are absolutely serene. I see the sweat on them. I can smell some of them. It's thrilling. I watch all of the swans, wings elegantly raised, expressions uniformly and delicately distressed as they float across the boards, and I want to burst into tears. They are individually extraordinary, but as a group they approach something divine. The very gesture towards perfection feels rapturous. Maybe I'm just easily impressed. I have wept freely many times during the Olympics, almost always during the women's events. But maybe I'm not wrong to be moved by seeing women at the peak of their bodily mastery, considering how often I am reminded of how little mastery I have over my own. Women's bodies are not often the sovereign realm of women. I am still no good at placing myself right here, in my physical self. Watching ballet dancers, even when they're performing steps decided for them, even when the steps are decided by men, I get to see something shining at the centre of that patriarchal murk: I get to see them own their flesh.

•

Alexandra Kolb and Sophia Kalogeropoulou are the authors of 'In defence of ballet'. Their work, they say, responds to 'feminist critique . . . which seemed to us to deny women's own agency and the pleasure they take from dancing'. In the course of their study, they spoke to several adult amateur women's ballet classes about why they danced. Pleasure was the universal response. Their respondents loved the discipline and rigidity of the steps, the opportunity to challenge themselves physically, the pursuit of the elusive connection between emotion and body. Anna Aalten's research subjects, all professional dancers, said much the same. Regardless of its feminist credentials, the people who do ballet are in love with it.

Girls don't grow up longing to be ballet dancers, attending classes in every spare moment and eschewing social lives in order to spend more time at the studio just because they're thoroughly taken in by the patriarchy. Ballet is strung up in the corsetry of gender, yes; it's also overtly white, thin, able-bodied and wealthy. But it remains one of the few opportunities available to girls and young women to be unapologetically physical, to strive for athletic excellence, and to be rewarded with unadulterated praise. Ballet books and movies and TV shows, more than just being examples of unhealthy body ideals, provide young girls with active, energetic, ambitious role models; ballet itself encourages a drive to achieve and excel physically. Ballerinas, for reasons good or bad, occupy an exalted position in Western society, above female athletes, above female musicians, far above female visual artists.

But ballet dancers are an unusual choice for a paragon of femininity. They do not use their bodies to care for others, in the way so many women in coded-feminine professions do (nurses, midwives, aged carers, sex workers). They use their bodies for art. They spend a lifetime whittling their bodies into ethereal objects, mangling their feet permanently, in order to spend a comparatively brief moment making something beautiful. That they work within a structure so rigid it dictates every aspect of themselves only makes their art purer. I can't help it: I am more amazed by ballet dancers than by astronauts. Ballet is grotesque and gorgeous, sublime and strange. I can't look away.

6

TRANS WOMEN

Transitioning to girl power

With Liz Duck-Chong

Every time I make a new female friend I feel like I've hit the jackpot. As an adult woman, making new friends can be difficult, particularly as my anxieties about approaching people I don't know have deepened and developed in novel, unexpected ways as I've aged. Without the sweaty press of school, with all its accompanying hormones and shared English classes, or the giddiness of undergraduate university classes, it can be hard to find people—particularly women with whom you share a bond.

Forgive me for getting mushy, but Liz is one of those people for me. We met on that other platform where people bond in the twenty-first century: the internet. Liz is a fearless and deeply thoughtful writer, photographer, musician and self-confessed sexual health nerd. She writes about, among other things, sexuality, transness and queerness, for places like *Archer*, the *Guardian* and *Meanjin*, and has a regular column on the teen sex education website Scarleteen. We only met in person for the first time in

September 2018, but we'd been talking on Facebook, on Twitter and over the phone for months before then, sharing and critiquing our writing, working through wildly complicated ideological issues as a team. Our friendship embodies all the things I love about the idea of women collaborating: together, our ideas get better, bigger, more refined. We challenge each other. We share what we know and we address our moments of ignorance. It's the very best of the girls' club. It's so *cool*.

I bring this up because right now there's a small but vocal group of self-identified feminists who want to bust that girls' club apart. Debates about gender—its fluidity, its legal recognition, its restriction to one bathroom or another—are heating up around the world, and conservative opinions are finding unlikely allies in trans-exclusionary radical feminists, or TERFs. Those conservative opinions—that there are only two genders, that whichever one you're assigned at birth is it, and that those who move from one to the other or who occupy the space in between are aberrations—are not backed up by science or by lived experience. But they are influencing the law, the social treatment of transgender individuals, and the precious and hard-fought sense of unity among women.

•

When Heather, one of my old and dear friends, came out as trans last year, I was surprised at the immediate and uncomfortable resistance I felt to her transition. She was the first person I'd known before and after a transition, and the change spooked me—but only for a moment. Now, it's as if I get to learn this person I love all over again from another angle. When we spend time together, we're closer and more curious about one another. And she's happy—so happy. It didn't take long for me to put aside the childish petulance I felt at my friend changing in a way I didn't really understand. I understood pretty quickly, I think.

I'm a cis woman—a straight, white cis woman at that—and while I know several trans people and am lucky enough to call some my friends, I am by no means an expert on the intricacies and complications of gender identity. When I spoke with Heather about this, and my hesitance to get into the trickiness of gender and trans identity, she asked me a question I've been thinking about ever since: When did I first know that I was a girl? I said in the chapter on girl bands that I was most aware of my girlness when I played in bands as the only woman, but it's hard for me to pin down exactly when I first started thinking of myself in gendered terms. My parents tried hard to raise me, their first child, in a girl-positive way; I remember my mother telling me, 'Girls can do anything.' She was a landscape designer who worked on every one of her sites, lifting and digging and building beautiful bamboo fences, and ordering a herd of male labourers around while brandishing secateurs. I was not a tomboy, but I did not love pink (though I adored my Polly Pockets and lusted after the Barbies my parents would never buy). I think I scorned girly stuff not by nature but by encouragement; I was a girl, *but*.

I remember reassuring myself as a child that although I was a girl, I wasn't stupid, I wasn't vapid, as I had been told other girls were—I was smart and independent and bossy. This was the nature of my girlness. A shape picked out by negative space.

What makes a woman? Right now I'm menstruating; is that it? But will I cease to be a woman after I reach menopause? I have breasts, what they call secondary sex characteristics; but if I underwent a mastectomy I would still be a woman. I have a womb, but women who've had hysterectomies are still women. I have a vulva and vagina, but women are born with these parts missing or partly formed, and they are still women.

These are not profound insights. Scholars and activists and many other people thinking carefully about the nature of gender have come to the same conclusions. Gender doesn't live in the body. Judith Butler, the original authority on the ephemeral nature of gender, says that gender is a phenomenon that is being produced all the time; that nobody really is a gender from the start, but performs a gender through a series of actions, gestures and so on. Gender is formed out of cultural expectations of what a 'man' and a 'woman' look, act and dress like. It's not really *real*. And neither, really, is biological sex, or at least our understanding of sexual dimorphism into the male/female binary. Anne Fausto-Sterling, a professor of biology and women's studies, wrote in a 1993 paper that the monumental resistance to letting intersex individuals live as they were born, unchanged by surgical intervention, 'seem[s] to lie in a cultural need to maintain clear distinctions between the sexes'. We get the heebie-jeebies when something as fundamental as sex, with all its baggage about who cares for the kids and who brings home the bread, gets shaken up a bit.

Fausto-Sterling also astutely notes that 'one can find levels of masculinity and femininity in almost every possible permutation', from the chromosomal to the anatomical; sex and gender, she says, are not on a spectrum from male to female, but are instead points in a multidimensional space. Isn't that beautiful?

Considering all this, in a lot of ways, gender seems to be

about trust: do you trust someone when they tell you that they feel like a woman? Do you trust that that feeling means that they are a woman?

I do. Trans-exclusionary radical feminists do not. TERFs position trans women as the ultimate enemy of all other women.

They use language extremely and uncomfortably evocative of that of white nationalists: trans women are a threat to womanhood, they say, as though womanhood is a territory upon which a hostile force can encroach, as though there isn't enough womanhood to go around. Like many religious conservatives, they cling, bafflingly, to biology—a phrase I saw recently was 'two men and two biological men identifying as women is not a balanced panel'—as though Butler had never printed a word, staunch in their refusal to acknowledge that the issues women face are multifaceted and nuanced and changing. It's unsettling to see this rhetoric espoused by women who claim to be members of the very broad church of feminism. It leads to moments where I sit at my computer staring glumly into the electronic abyss between the community that I thought feminism was and the rapidly receding shorelines of the many islands it's fractured into.

But I'm getting ahead of myself. The truth is that all of the things I might immediately grab on to in order to assert my womanhood are fleeting. When you think about gender, it dissolves. As I went through my checklist of what makes a woman, striking each one off, I saw, before my eyes, the illusion disintegrate. Just as I menstruate and have breasts, I also sprout thick hair on my legs and offensive odours from my pits. The line between male and female is as unreal as national borders, and we're all in a state of suspended disbelief in order to keep it like that. So it seems absurd that anyone would take someone else to task for emigrating across those borders and asking politely to have their new citizenship recognised. Especially when that emigration is such a treacherous one.

Gender is like money, or manners: imagined, held together by shared belief. Professor of English and comparative literature, gender theorist and author Jack Halberstam encourages an understanding of the concept of transness as an undoing, an indeterminacy. I like the idea of breaking down this centuries-old crust of brittle binary bullshit. I like the idea of detaching myself from gendered pronouns, mine and others'. What might it look like, a world in which we could shrug off the scratchy shawl of gender? And who better to ask about it than Liz?

•

This is a world I often imagine, one devoid of gender and its trappings, but it clashes with the gendered saturation of how we live today. The attire with which I cover my body and shoe my feet, the state in which I keep the hair on my head and the rest of me, the products I use to clean my house, wash my skin and brush my teeth, hold my money, store my possessions and transport myself from place to place are all given a gendered nod, if not an outright pink or blue label. As a woman who was not always seen as such, I spent many years navigating the ways that gender is not able to simply exist, but rather is thrust upon us, living on the receiving end of it with all the enthusiasm one would have about a late-night copped feel.

By contrast, I cannot for the life of me remember the first time I was asked when I knew that I was a girl, having been asked it for so long now. The white lie is that I always knew, but it's a universal one—whether transgender or cisgender, we all had to figure it out at some point. My teenage years were full of doctors, psychologists and psychiatrists asking what girlhood meant to me, and how I felt that I fit within its bounds; writing down the answers I gave them and cross-checking them to what I'd said weeks and months before, being afforded a level of gender scrutiny for which my cisgender peer group would be found wanting, so narrow was their definition.

Many trans women say they first noticed their gender as a difference; that is, that my clothing is not like their clothing, my chores are not like their chores, my body is not like their body, but I think all of us notice like this. We grow up in a society, if not always a household, that is full of masculine men and feminine women, and the associations we have with our own bodies are often made in reference to that blueprint, whether we decide to follow it or let it burn.

For trans women, the gendered ideals that all women confront or conform to are heightened even further, with the validity of our very identities being held hostage to whether or not we perform an acceptable version of womanhood. My trans lesbian and androgynous sisters, my butch and nonbinary sisters, they all continue to take up space even against the pushback they receive for not fitting a model of girlness that others designate as appropriate for them. With their shaved hair, short shorts, button-ups, ballerina flats, combat boots, sensible heels, piercings, bangs, block colours, all-black ensembles, polka dots or whatever they're feeling themselves in, they sketch the outline of a new feminine, or something beyond the feminine entirely.

Even as I live and breathe today, a femme queer woman who fits a lot of expectations and archetypes, the narratives my body rubs against the wrong way are all around me, managing to get into the gaps between my stockings and my skin. That I don't have a vagina is enough to disqualify me, until I have one, and then it's that it doesn't menstruate, ignoring the cis women who do not or never did. That I don't have breasts is pointed out, until I grow them or have them augmented, at which point it's that I can't feed a child with them, until I do and it's something else, throwing cis women of so many diverse body experiences under the bus yet again. They run roughshod over what we are and are not, ignoring the beautiful space between, where we could be—and this is where we find the magic of being girls.

When reference is made to my body as not being woman-like, or woman-enough, I wonder what hand-drawn plans people are referring to, navigating gender with the colonial land survey while we're all out here using Google Maps. Besides, it's all just the same topography. As an adult, I take medication that reverts the flow of the river, and my body carries on as it sees fit, adjusting many of my secondary sex characteristics like it was created to do so (and indeed it was). Not forgetting that, before we're born, we spend around two months bathing in amniotic fluid without any definable genitals at all. Instead there are a set of various outcrops and culverts that, with a gentle hormonal touch, will go on to form something we can label with far more decorum.

And yet, for all the brain scans and blood tests in the world, we already know that gender is far more than our bodies. Chromosomes, the gotcha card often slipped into conversation by those critical of me, are as diversely created as the bodies they attempt to erase by naming them. I remember a paper that described a woman who went through puberty, menstruated, and had two children before finding out she had XY chromosomes, oblivious to the apparent impossibility of her reality. As these critics whittle away the wood to create a likeness of gender as they see fit, they lose the picture of the vast tree that the image stems from in the first place, and just how many branches and roots it took to get to where we are now.

And that tree is almost unimaginably complex. Even without

bringing in the further complication of gender, as we socially construct it, the realm of biological sex is far from binary. Just like the mother who gave birth to children despite having XY chromosomes, there are myriad ways the human species combines its genetics to create new bodies. Mosaicism is the lyrical name for the genetic condition in which individuals have genes that differ in chromosomes from cell to cell, with a whole spectrum of phenotypical expression. Around one in every thousand female infants is born with triple X, an extra X chromosome that manifests in those women (often) being taller than average, but little else. Some apparently male infants are born with XX chromosomes. Many, many infants—as many as are born with red hair—are born intersex, with the physical features that we associate with assigned sex in a wide array of variation. The existence of, in the words of the United Nations, a significant percentage of the human population who have bodies that 'do not fit typical binary notions of male or female' should be quite enough for us to recognise that our feeble reduction of this many-limbed gender tree to just two awkward branches is a foolhardy one.

And that's just the physical aspect of it. Gender itself is a construct, a shorthand created by humanity to simplify the complex task of interacting with thousands of other humans—but the shorthand we use in the West was hastily adopted and is badly in need of revision. This should be obvious, too, considering the many iterations of gender adopted by cultures other than the globally dominant Anglocentric, heteronormative, patriarchal one: many Native American nations recognise a third gender, two-spirits, with some nations recognising four or more genders; in Samoa, the Fa'afafine occupy a similar cultural space, as do brotherboys and sistergirls in some Australian Indigenous communities. Gender can be freely accepted as ambiguous and mutable in the cultures where it is allowed to be so. The external performance/presentation of something as complex as gender— how it links you to others, how it defines you in a cultural space, what doors it opens to you, what doors it shuts . . . once you start thinking about it even a little bit, the idea of mashing that into one of two boxes seems laughable.

So it's even more disconcerting that, in the past few years, certain factions of the feminist movement have made that segregation their central goal. TERFs are a vocal minority in feminism, who base their activism on excluding what they term 'male-bodied transgenders'—that is, trans women who were assigned male at birth—from women's spaces, women's discussions and the women's movement in general. Thanks to the recent debate on marriage equality in Australia, along with that surrounding the Safe Schools program, trans issues have been prominent in the public conversation. Much of the anti-trans rhetoric that appeared in the media and in the No campaign's PR material during the course of the marriage equality vote is directly descended from TERF ideas.

While the term TERF was coined in 2008 by writer Viv Smythe in order to differentiate anti-trans radical feminists from other, trans-inclusive or trans-neutral radfems, the ideology itself dates back to at least the late 1970s. In 1978, trans woman Sandy Stone, the audio engineer at American lesbian record label Olivia Records, resigned after controversy spiked over her gender, and the fact that she was working for a self-identified lesbian business—a business that, it's worth noting, had welcomed and supported her. That same year, the Lesbian Organisation of Toronto (LOOT) voted explicitly to exclude trans women from its ranks. The 'womynborn womyn' rhetoric precipitated by this cultural climate has had ongoing effects. In the early 1990s, lesbian music event the Michigan Womyn's Music Festival ejected an attendee, Nancy Burkholder, after discovering that she was transgender; in 1995, the Vancouver Rape Relief & Women's Shelter did the same to volunteer worker Kimberly Nixon, saying that her gender meant it would be impossible for her to understand the experiences of the women she was assisting (despite Nixon's own experiences of intimate partner abuse). Australian scholar and writer Germaine Greer resigned from Newnham College, a women's college at the University of Cambridge, after her transgender colleague Rachael Padman was elected to a fellowship in 1996.

In recent years, TERF rhetoric has made the leap from certain lesbian feminist communities to the mainstream. In 2018, the Pride in London parade was disrupted by a protest from a group calling themselves Get the L Out—an organisation of lesbians agitating for the expulsion of trans women from lesbian spaces and movements. Former University of Melbourne professor Sheila Jeffreys has argued, both in interviews and in print, that 'transsexualism [sic] should be seen as a violation of human rights'; her 2014 book, *Gender Hurts*, was criticised by many trans people and allies for its poorly researched attack on transgender individuals. The frustrating thing about TERF ideology is that some of its foundations seem to make sense. Many TERFs feel that they are rejecting the idea of gender as a whole, pointing out the fallacy of suggesting there is such a thing as a 'woman's brain'. As British writer Julie Bindel has put it, 'Feminists want to rid the world of gender rules and regulations, so how is it possible to support a theory which has at its centre the notion that there is something essential and biological about the way boys and girls behave?' She's referring to the oversimplified explanation of trans identity, which is that a trans woman is simply a woman's brain in a man's body—an idea that's both reductive and inaccurate. You *can* want to get rid of gender rules and regulations, and still recognise that someone who is deeply unhappy presenting in one way should be allowed—encouraged, supported—to present in another way that alleviates their despair.

If there's one thing we should all be able to agree on, in a post–third wave, post–Safe Schools, post–marriage equality era, it's that gender is profoundly complicated. Superficially it may seem paradoxical to want to get rid of gender and to recognise gender transition at the same time—but humans and our absurd brains are paradoxical in all sorts of ways. TERF rhetoric focuses fetishistically on the operative status of the woman in question (is she pre- or post-op?). There seems to be the perception that trans women are interlopers amid a group of 'real' victims of oppression, who are deeply invested in jealously guarding their in-group status. The most upsetting aspect of TERF ideology is not its rigid adherence to what they consider to be fundamental feminist truths; it's the appalling lack of empathy, and the effect it has of further dividing women from one another. Our community, our togetherness, is already so hard-won when we manage to make it happen. Why do we have to invent new ways to keep us apart? What perverse psychology is at work that suggests we're furthering the feminist cause by falling into line with the great patriarchal conspiracy to isolate and distract women from what really matters: unity?

Every time I talk with a TERF, or read something they've written, there is always a moment when I realise that they think they've backed me into an ideological corner: that they've come up with some angle or question or doubt about my gender and body and life that I've not already gone over a million times myself. They think if they just weasel-word me into admitting some potential privilege I hold on to, or some doubt I have about my existence and my appearance (negative self-image being an exclusively trans experience, apparently), or some fear I have about my future, that my world will come crumbling down around me—totally ignorant to the fact that I have already catastrophised so far beyond their reach that I have not just made peace with where I am, but laid solid foundations there for self love. Julia Serano, a trans biologist and theorist, writes of seeing in trans women the 'wisdom that can only come from having to fight for your right to be recognized as female, a raw strength that only comes from unabashedly asserting your right to be feminine in an inhospitable world'.

There is a perception in the way we talk about trans people, especially trans kids, that they're doing this off the cuff; a willy-nilly administering of 'life-altering' medication because it's suddenly cool to do so ('No, Mum, if all of my friends started taking oestrogen, I wouldn't just start doing it too'). They assume we're all snowflakes, when a better analogy would be that we're icebergs, with so much of our history and background and process hidden beneath the choppy blue surface, so much of our power waiting beneath the waves. The assumption, too, goes deeper, taking for granted that there is some objectionable difference between the way we create our identities and selves, simply because mine started a little later, or looked a little different. TERF logic relies on an impenetrably narrow concept of lesbianism, maleness, and even womanhood to function, ignoring the broad church that each of these labels welcomes under their roofs, and the ways that all of us create and continue to cultivate our femaleness to our own image, or the images of those we love and admire.

Serano writes with so much love of transgender women, a love I share and see in the communities we forge and the bonds we share, writing of how 'many of us reject all of the inferior meanings and connotations that others project onto femininity—that it is weak, artificial, frivolous, demure, and passive—because for us, there has been no act more bold and daring than embracing our own femininity'.

In the very nature of their logic, transphobes lay traps for themselves in how they reduce womanhood to a series of haves and havenots that defy their supposedly loftier idea of what gender could be. In reality, it is people of gendered minorities who do this queering the most; we are proficient in our boundary-clashing, true professionals in how we break down who can and can't be a girl, a boy, or something else altogether different and delightful. We live in this liminal zone that they lay claim to but don't even begin to understand, and our boldness and joy wins out.

And yet, despite this total lack of understanding, TERFs are taken as authorities on these topics—that in an effort to find 'balance', the weight is always falling on the side of those who wield these categories like weapons. This false credibility isn't just a neutral thing, however; it leaks and speaks so many forms of harm into being, doing lasting damage in the process.

For all their talk of words, of conversation, and of meeting in the middle, that's easy to say when the conversation you're having is theoretical. For transgender people, that theory is our reality. It results in concrete harm, in discrimination, and sometimes even in our deaths (especially for those trans women who do not share my socio-economic good luck or my skin colour). I need to fight back not because I'm *trying to take up too much space, but because these so-called radical feminists have deemed literally any space women like me take up to be an affront, which is hardly a feminist idea.*

They will only accept a version of me that is paper-thin, a necessary facsimile of the womanhood we feminists have spent decades rallying against. The real trick here is that this is the very same sexism that men have always levelled against us, against women: this squashing of our variety into something quantifiable and questionable, of controlling the existence we are allowed to forge by dousing the coals.

Trans culture is one of consistency—we have never not been and never will not be, and this makes me hopeful for the futures we can create and know will be ongoing; stretching out beyond the imagination into a better place than we are in today.

Transgender women have always carved out space from the people and places that have sought to do this to us, but we are so much more than our heirloom chisels and hammers, existing back throughout history and continuing on for as long as there are people being born. There is a power in trans sisterhood, in the ways we understand and care for each other, but there's an even greater power in our shared womanhood—transgender and cisgender alike—and all its many facets and forms.

·

It's a maelstrom, this gender business. Just as I watched it dissolve under a focused gaze, after these conversations with Liz, I also watch my gendered identity fracture into glittering pieces—no longer a whole, dull thing, but a million brilliant bits. When I spoke to my friend who had transitioned, she said that while she knows—she *knows*—that gender is a construct, and that we only consider certain things and actions feminine because we have coded them that way, it doesn't change the fact that once she started doing those things as a woman, it felt right. Here it feels as though we're veering into gender essentialism again: this is inherently a woman thing, this is inherently a man thing—but that's not right at all. Our ideas of masculinity and femininity have become calcified onto physical sexual expressions: men are masculine, women are feminine, and that's it. But just because we have begun to chisel the two ideas apart doesn't mean that ways of performing gender become meaningless. Recognising that money is a construct doesn't relieve my poverty; knowing that gender isn't real doesn't make my lipstick and ten-step skincare routine any less appealing to me. Wanting to be feminine and wanting to dissolve gender as we know it can exist side by side. Like Liz said, we all contain multitudes, in our minds as well as within our physical forms, all lying latent until they are conjured to the surface.

We don't really talk about this, as a culture that's unhealthily enamoured with a binary in almost any context. Because of this, TERFs and other anti-trans activists would have you believe that it's wrong. But just because we don't talk about it doesn't mean that it's not true—and it doesn't mean that we don't know it, either. A recent survey conducted in cities across five continents found that most women believe that trans women should enjoy the same rights as cis women. A full eight out of ten respondents agreed. This flies in the face of the very loud and public tantrum-throwing of groups like Get the L Out, and in the face of anyone invested in convincing others that the majority of people are scared and angered by trans women. The truth is, they're not. Most people are reasonable and compassionate, and, whether they spend a lot of time thinking about it or not, seem to recognise that at a fundamental level gender is just another story we tell about ourselves. Most people don't want to be the door bitch at the girls' clubhouse. We want to put everyone's name on the guest list. Things work better when we're in them together.

7

MIDWIVES

Maga gravida

Somewhere in my parents' garage there is a photo album documenting my birth. My parents live in Tropical North Queensland, where the humidity pervades everything; some years ago, after a cyclone, my mother unearthed the original album to find the prints turned into gory psychedelia by the damp. Some images still remain: she has cut away the illegible parts, so that the album is full of roughly described circles and oblongs depicting a bloodied infant, held high by white-gloved hands, against a drapery of hospital sheets; and my mother, hair netted under a paper shower cap, her oval, olive face pale but tremulously hopeful, looking at the camera over me, a wrinkled gremlin bundled in a blanket.

I was born by caesarean section after several days of labour. The way my mother tells it, I might have been delivered vaginally had the nurses listened to her. When she was labouring with me, her first child, she was put on an oxytocin drip that induced powerful contractions. I was in the transverse position, facing away from my mother's spine rather than towards it, and

I did not turn. The induced contractions forced my head against my mother's cervix, causing it to swell shut. I got stuck, so the doctors had to cut me free. Only one other person was allowed into the operating theatre with my mother; she chose my dad, who brought his camera, and, in a wanton display of disregard for the sacredness of the moment, snapped the instant I was dredged up from the wound in my mother's belly.

Some of my earliest memories are of my mother showing me, aged four, how she could still produce milk in swelling patterns from her nipples, and, at about the same age, of tracing her silvery caesarean scar in the bath. Those sorts of memories form part of the background hum of a life, easily taken for granted, easily ignored, so it was only recently that I started to pick out that frequency and listen to it—I started to recognise what made my mother a mother.

I had not known how alone she was during her pregnancy and labour. A New Zealander living in Sydney, only recently divorced from her unfaithful husband, in a tumultuous relationship with my father, willingly and stubbornly cut off from her own parents, she did not have many female friends, fewer still who were mothers. During the labour, she says, my paternal grandmother appeared in the hospital room's doorway, took one look at her, blanched, and left, not to return until after I was born. It reminded her too much of her own traumatic labours, she said. But this left my mother without women around her, in the care of an indifferent male doctor she barely knew. She told me that she knew at the time if she could just 'hold on' a little longer, he'd eventually go off shift and she could hope someone better would come along. (They did, and she says the doctor who delivered me was 'lovely'.) It was 1990, before midwives became a common part of the public health system. My mother had no one to advocate for her. She was exactly the kind of person who needs a midwife.

Midwives are fond of saying that their job title literally means 'with women'. When I spoke to Rebecca, a student midwife in her third year of study, about her chosen profession, she told me that midwives need to straddle the line of medical professional and emotional support person—they need to be simultaneously checking vitals and making medical decisions, and liaising with the mother, her family and the others around her to put everyone at ease. A mother must be able to trust that the midwife has her best interests at heart, along with the experience and compassion to support her through birth, and a doctor must trust that the midwife knows what she's talking about when she advocates for the mother, thanks to her medical expertise and training. It seems a huge responsibility, and a unique role, and I am fascinated by it.

My interest in midwives emerged from an obsession with witchcraft in the Middle Ages. Female physicians faced a campaign of misinformation from a Western medical institution that was still very much in its infancy, but self-aware enough to recognise an economic threat. Eventually the smear campaign took the form of accusations of witchcraft, and countless midwives died at the hands of the Church, by hanging or at the stake. In a gruesome way, it makes sense: childbirth was dangerous for mother and infant; many died. People feared it, and anyone associated with it. A midwife's proximity to death, pain and the mystery of birth and reproduction made her—makes her—a magical figure.

When I began writing about witchcraft I spent a lot of time

wondering about what constituted magic. Most anthropologists do not ask the question of whether magic is real, because for the societies that use and believe in it, there is no question about it. *If* is not a useful question; *where* is, maybe, a useful question. We do not tend to understand aspects of our lives as magical in the modern West. Even in the past, as demonstrated by the witch trials, magic was not a positive thing with which one would want to be associated. But I think there is so much magic in women, together. This is my overarching theory, this is why I'm writing this book: that there's something powerful about women working together, not against one another but in service and celebration of each other.

Now, as I enter what will be the most childbirth-adjacent period of my life, as my friends and co-workers start to have children, my fascination with midwifery and all it symbolises remains. I do think it's magic: to choose a vocation that places you alongside women, in support and solidarity, in a millennia-old tradition of ordinary miracles.

•

I have never wanted to have children. Even now, as I approach my thirtieth birthday, I am sometimes stopped in my tracks by the fear that I will one day be overthrown by a wave of hormones and wake up baby-crazy. It hasn't happened yet. I'm still struck with a bone-deep dread at the thought of falling pregnant. I sometimes have dreams—nightmares—where I watch in horror as my belly expands, and I wake myself up by clawing at my abdomen. Even my friends' babies—I love them, I recognise their goodness and their cuteness and the miracle that they contain, how they are growing every day into real people with motivations and interior worlds . . . But every time I hand a child back to its parent, I feel a little bubble of joy. Procreation is not on the agenda for me.

And yet, I am fascinated, morbidly intrigued, by childbirth, and the rituals around it. There's something unnerving and magnetic about this extraordinary, ordinary thing, about bringing life into the world—about being the vessel through which something miraculous travels. It might happen in hospitals and be accompanied by pastel balloons and giddy Facebook posts, but birth is still blood magic—and death, vague but familiar, ripples on the other side of it.

Birth is a curious thing. It seems fundamentally female, but of course it isn't; it seems both inherently natural and profoundly unknowable, fraught with trauma and judgement and historical wrongdoing, and with the purest joy. And the people who guide those who give birth through these troubled waters have almost as long and complicated a history as birth itself.

Pregnancy often changes bodies irrevocably. Hormones make ligaments loosen and the pelvic cradle change shape. The growth of the foetus pushes organs around, making it hard to breathe and putting unreasonable pressure on the bladder. Although plenty of women are lucky enough to experience the classic pregnancy 'glow', many more have to deal with acne for the first time since adolescence. Lots of women say their hair changes—it suddenly goes from straight to frizzy or vice versa, or it sheds like mad or starts growing in thick and bushy. Pregnant women risk pre-eclampsia and gestational diabetes, amniotic fluid embolism and internal haemorrhage. Ankles and fingers swell, stomachs rebel, ligaments loosen, teeth break; standing is a chore, sleeping a tribulation.

The birth itself is also a phenomenal feat. The cervix, usually the body's best defensive barricade against the outside world, softens, thins and stretches. The uterus contracts rhythmically and excruciatingly. Inside, the baby has its head down, facing the mother's tailbone, and, as contractions peak, is pressed through the birth canal headfirst (ideally—though some babies are born feet first, with their hands pressed to their head, or, like me, facing the sky). Most mothers describe the process of their baby crowning as an intense burning, stinging, stretching feeling—this on top of the internal cramps racking them. And most births are not fast. The median time for a first labour is about eight hours. Many women labour for days.

Yet, in spite of all this, giving birth is also the most normal thing in the world. A miniature crisis for each individual woman, but a process as natural as breathing, when you take a broader view of it—which is what midwives do. In all the literature, and among all the midwives I speak to, the term 'normal' comes up again and again. Women have always given birth. It is a natural thing for the body to do—a perfect thing, even. Hormones released during and after birth mitigate pain and ensure a mother is awake, alert and overjoyed to receive her baby, even after the ordeal of labour. A midwife's job is half done if she can just convince an expectant mother that she is more than capable of handling childbirth; that every woman in her ancestry has done it, that her body knows what to do, that she is strong and sensible and safe.

No mean feat in the face of raw statistics. Around the world, about eight hundred women and eight thousand infants die every day from complications with pregnancy and labour. Every year, seven million women suffer serious long-term problems

related to giving birth. Most of these deaths and injuries are pre-
ventable, and are caused by a lack of hygiene and access to clean
water, outmoded medical knowledge and disregard for women's
autonomy. Alarmingly, the mortality rate for mothers and
infants in the United States is actually rising, with between seven
hundred and nine hundred women dying each year—double the
rate of thirty years ago. Dr Felicia Lester, the medical director
of gynaecologic services at the University of California, San
Francisco, told *Berkeley Wellness* that she suspected this rise was
due to increasing rates of caesarean births (particularly repeated
caesareans, which can cause fatal bleeding), systemic racism (the
risks attached to pregnancy and labour are far higher for Black
women in the US, regardless of socio-economic status), and,
tellingly, 'a lack of emphasis on maternal health as compared to
fetal health'. Obstetric specialists now learn to focus mainly on
monitoring the health and status of the foetus rather than the
mother, which means doctors can be underprepared for complications arising from childbirth, and women can be left feeling
like little more than incubators.

The World Health Organization is a big advocate for midwifery; in the late 1980s, they established a midwife training
program, Action for Safe Motherhood, to train midwives around
the world to support women giving birth safely and naturally,
with a focus on providing information and care that supports
new mothers' decision-making and feelings of competence and
control. Their studies have proven that emotional support, education and involvement of mothers-to-be in the birth process
is as important as pain management in creating a positive birth
outcome for the women. Midwives are there to provide exactly
that.

•

There is still something esoteric about midwives. Although their duties and training are similar to that of nurses, and although they work within the bounds of scientifically tested medical knowledge, they remain slightly apart from the medical establishment.

We must remember, after all, that this is the establishment that tried, with varying levels of success and with inexhaustible persistence, to completely discredit midwives throughout the ages. In Ancient Greece and Rome they were dismissed as drunks and prostitutes; in the Middle Ages they were called witches; in the late nineteenth and early twentieth centuries they were caricatured as gin-soaked charlatans and backstreet abortionists (cf. Sarah Gamp, courtesy of Dickens). Perhaps because no other vocation so devotedly tends to the mysterious realm of 'women's business', midwifery has been associated with witchcraft since before the birth of Christ. The Catholic Church in particular has always considered these stewards of women's knowledge with a deep suspicion.

This is despite the fact that for much of early Western history, all doctors were female. In ancient Sumer, Assyria and Egypt, those responsible for healing were almost exclusively priestesses. In these civilisations, the deities responsible for death and illness were also responsible for life and health, and they were all women. In Assyria, Gula, the goddess of death, was also called 'the great physician'. In Egypt, the fertility goddess Isis also carried with her the symbols of death. Many Egyptian queens, including Cleopatra, were famous healers. Life, death and healing were the realm of women for a very long time.

Things were different with the Greeks, though. Like most interesting Greek innovations, the Hippocratic school of medicine was a boys-only situation, and women were no longer allowed to practise healing—except, obviously, for midwifery. The absolute refusal on behalf of the Greek medical establishment to dirty their hands with gynaecology is coded as disdain. Greek doctors looked down on childbirth as something necessary but incorrigibly vulgar, but, like most reluctances to deal with women's bodies and business, it may well have actually been fear of women and their mysterious, unknowable bodies.

I think it's for this reason that, for much of history, the most damning thing that could be said about midwives was that they worked exclusively with women, a specialisation distasteful to male physicians until uncomfortably recently. Even now, there are stories like my mother's, stories in their thousands, of women giving birth surrounded by indifferent men ignoring her instincts and cutting her open without blinking an eye, or of adding another stitch to a perineal tear while winking at an attendant husband, or of otherwise treating a woman in labour like a difficult and tiresome patient with a treatable but annoying illness.

•

The medical system does not have a fantastic record when it comes to women's health. The spectre of hysteria—that old wandering womb—still hangs over many interactions between women (and nonbinary people) and their doctors. Studies have shown that medical professionals dismiss women's reports of pain more readily than men's. The millions of women who live with endometriosis provide chilling statistics on how women's pain—particularly pain occurring in the reproductive organs—

is ignored or otherwise minimised. Endometriosis is a disorder affecting one in ten people of reproductive age with uteruses, in which the uterine lining, or endometrium, grows outside of the uterus. This causes excruciating pain before and during a menstrual period. My mother has the condition, and some of my most vivid memories from childhood are of being in the car with her and watching her turn pale and pull over in case she was going to pass out from the pain; once, she had to curl up on the footpath on a street behind my school until the pain had passed. At the time she was a landscape gardener, and the toughest woman I knew. But like many women, it took a long time before a doctor recognised that she was not just suffering from period pain. The average length of time before a woman receives an endometriosis diagnosis is ten years. For other female-specific conditions, like polycystic ovarian syndrome, the situation is similar.

Health care's indifference towards women is not limited to reproductive disorders. In 2018, Canadian cartoonist and author Kate Beaton published an essay in The Cut about her sister's death from cancer. The piece was titled 'Our Sister Becky: What if the doctors had listened to her?' Rebecca Beaton had visited the doctor several times for unexplained bleeding, and was dismissed each time, until another doctor finally identified a large lesion on her cervix, and a biopsy confirmed a diagnosis of stage IIB cervical cancer. After chemotherapy and radiation treatment, while in remission, she had pain and swelling in her leg. When she went back to her doctors, they said it was 'nothing suspicious', and one put a note on her file: 'Rebecca continues to be paranoid.' The swelling was due to metastatic cancer. She died in May 2018.

It is against this backdrop that I'm writing about midwives. I know that not all health-care professionals are dismissive of their patients' needs, and I know that even if they are, it's usually because they are caught in a huge, inefficient machine of a medical system that places enormous demands on its employees as it creaks on, understaffed and underfunded, trying to save people's lives. I know that doctors and nurses, gynaecologists and obstetricians included, can be compassionate, sensitive, holistic carers who listen to their patients and trust them to know their own bodies.

But I also know that this has not been the tradition for many hundreds of years. The medical system is still shaking off its last suspicions about women's own bodily knowledge, still coming to terms with the idea that a woman in pain might actually be experiencing something out of the ordinary (that pain is not women's natural inheritance); still learning to trust women's bodies when it comes to the everyday calamity of giving birth. This is where midwives come in.

Not all midwives are compassionate or sensitive. Like people in any industry, they may have their prejudices, their biases, their blind spots and their hang-ups. But they are trained in a tradition of trusting the body and of normalising birth. This does not necessarily mean privileging natural birth over all other kinds (though most midwives would prefer their patients not to have to undergo surgery). It *does* mean treating birth like the normal, everyday occurrence that it is, and, in doing so, trusting the person giving birth to be able to do it.

•

Midwives exist to listen to mothers' instincts. They act as mediators between medical knowledge and holistic care, and they champion the rights of the mother and, above all, the normalcy of birth. They are also the inheritors of ancient feminine customs, sacred rituals, the power of women supporting other women— all concepts high on the 'woo' spectrum, and amusingly at odds with the practical, no-nonsense nature of modern midwifery.

I don't think these two aspects are contradictory, though. One of my friends, a very recent new mother, told me that the moment when she appreciated her midwife the most was not even during labour, but afterwards. Her baby son had a weepy eye, and, like any new parent, she was starting to get a bit panicky.

The midwife took the baby, examined him, and calmly said, 'Look: it could be lots of things. Put some breastmilk in his eye and it'll probably get better. If it doesn't, we'll sort it out.'

The breastmilk worked, as did the attitude of cheerful nonchalance borne of decades of experience on soothing my friend's nerves: more relaxing and reassuring than any number of doctors whisking the baby away for tests and antibiotics.

Another friend tells the story of labouring with her first child, assisted by a midwife whom she had instructed, with the ferocity that comes with intense pain, *not* to touch her. The midwife did not touch her, but talked her through each stage of the labour, based only on what Tash reported happening to her body. I was amazed at this story of total trust between the two women: Tash, trusting completely in her midwife's expertise, and her midwife, trusting Tash's knowledge of her own body. When the baby was born, Tash was on her knees, and the midwife said, 'Reach down and catch her now!' She caught her daughter in her own hands.

Criticism of the over-medicalisation of birth has led to many mothers choosing to seek the services of midwives through their pregnancy and delivery, and a proliferation of other purveyors of birth-related customs and care, including doulas, birthing assistants and independent pregnancy and lactation consultants. There is an element of the mystical about all of them. They deal with the biggest rite of passage in a person's life—birth— and they dole out the healing magic of the laying on of hands. They're also perhaps the last remaining vestiges of women's business here in the West: times and places where women do secret women's stuff, like help each other give birth.

Midwifery privileges women's embodied knowledge and instincts on how their bodies and birth works. Midwifery also recognises that women are stronger and safer when they work together with one another, rather than going through one of the most complicated and difficult moments of their lives in isolation. In this way, despite the tradition's sometimes conservative appearance, we can still understand midwifery as something radical. Despite being faced with unsympathetic lactation consultants and a medical institution that immediately ignored her after her delivery, Tash still considered herself something of a superhero after the birth of her first child. I don't think she would have felt like this if she didn't have a midwife by her side. There are so few times when we encourage women to recognise and take ownership of their own power; considering that new mothers are about to embark on a stage of their life that will involve more challenges and more obstacles and less sleep than any other they've ever faced, it seems sensible to send them into that new stage feeling like they can do anything.

Maybe one of the reasons I like midwives so much is that they elevate that women's business, simultaneously consecrating and normalising the stuff that traditionally remains behind closed doors, relegated to secrecy and whispers among mixed company. (I should note, of course, that it's not as though all midwives are women—there are male midwives, and nonbinary midwives. But men make up just 1 percent of midwives in the United States. Europe and Oceania report similar statistics. In almost every part of the world, midwifery is the one of the most female-dominated of all professions.) A midwife is a visible and proud branch of women's knowledge, a woman in sensible shoes bustling to the front of a crowd and giving people orders, someone whose job it is to take control of a scary situation and make it seem normal, even mundane.

•

I have been watching a lot of *Call the Midwife*. A BBC drama that started in 2012, the show is based on the memoir of the same name by nurse and midwife Jennifer Worth, who cut her teeth working in London's impoverished East End during the baby boom of the 1950s. When I tell people that I've been watching the show, a lot of them scoff. I have started asking them why they are so dismissive (none of the scoffers have watched an episode, of course). They tend to have trouble articulating it. I have started articulating it for them: is it because it's a show about women's stuff? This tends to finish the conversation.

It is a show about women's stuff, almost purely: the challenges faced by women living in slum conditions in abject poverty without birth control or access to abortion, when home births were de rigueur and the doctor only called in the direst emergencies. I cry in every single episode. For this, I will allow a small amount of criticism. The show does list sentimental at times. But it is so hard to separate the miracle of birth—and the joy of being cared for throughout your labour by women who believe in you and your strength and power—from sentimentality. Watching these moments with only women on-screen—nurse, midwife, Sister, mother, grandmother—feels so good. Even when the scenes are tragic, I take some sustenance from them. I think it's because we so rarely get to see this kind of gentle intimacy between women depicted in popular culture, particularly as something to be celebrated rather than something to be mocked or problematised. It's not as anxiety-inducing as *The Handmaid's Tale*, or as vulgarly capitalist as *Sex and the City*; it's just women doing women's stuff, the way women always have. It's enough to make mushy weepers of us all.

I talk to my friend Ruby about *Call the Midwife* and we chortle over the places where we watch it: while doing the dishes, while cleaning the house, while folding the laundry. These chores, this women's work, seem more beautiful somehow when put up against that other women's work, of creating new life and bringing it into the world. It does not seem shameful or oppressive to continue the traditions of women who have come before us, or to take pleasure in the domestic sphere. It seems powerful and ancient.

Fortunately for me, my love of the show is supported by the thousands of midwives who soundly approve of it. There's even been a marked uptick in young women choosing to study midwifery since the series' premiere. Midwives who watch *Call the Midwife*, particularly midwives of a certain vintage, recognise themselves. This is as good a mark of a show nailing its brief as any.

Fortunately for me also is the fact that, despite weeping copiously at the joy and magic of birth depicted in every single episode, *Call the Midwife* has not done a lick to change my own attitude towards childbearing. It's funny, isn't it? I can write thousands of words on the history and social psychology of midwifery and collaborative birth, but the thought of doing it myself still gives me a frisson of dread.

Maybe it's not so strange, though. Midwifery, Rebecca tells me, is not really about babies. It's about women: the purest expression of care for women, by women, with women.

•

As well as being a student midwife, Rebecca is also a vocal and tireless campaigner for abortion rights, much to the chagrin of her Catholic university. The university does not see her two passions as at all compatible, which is baffling, because the people who care about women's health—call them midwives, old wives, folk healers or witches—have always helped women choose when, and if, they want to have children.

Part of the reason Rebecca chose to study midwifery was her desire to bridge the gap between pregnant women and the medical profession. In a conference paper, she calls midwives 'stewards of knowledge that affect a woman and her family, society, and culture well beyond the birth of a child'. Medicine has not always been a particularly safe place for a pregnant woman. Sometimes, you still need someone on your side.

'Advocating for women is the basis of the profession,' she tells me. 'Advocating for women-centred care. You're there making sure that the right decisions are being made. You are an autonomous professional, so you're the one calling the shots unless something needs to be referred to a doctor. You're there to make these choices with the woman. It can be hard sometimes because you're dealing with someone in a foreign environment, and they're in pain, and they might not speak English as their first language or any English at all, and there might be situations when the other people in the room are negatively impacting the environment, so you have to navigate social situations as well as doing medical care, while also caring for the woman as an entire person.'

She describes the same kind of camaraderie and community between staff members as that depicted in *Call the Midwife*. One of the things that she loves the most about working in maternity wards is being side by side with people of all religious faiths and all ethnicities, all attitudes towards feminism and gender equality and what families should look like, who are all there to care for women who are giving birth, and united in that sense of care.

But we also spend a long time talking about when women shouldn't have children. Rebecca sees this aspect as part of her holistic practice: taking the pressure off women to become mothers simply because they can.

'There's such an emphasis on it being the thing that you have to do. I do wonder what it would be like if people fully thought it through—because not everybody stops and thinks before they get pregnant. It's pretty easy to get pregnant. A lot of people don't even consider that there's any alternative at all. You can see sometimes that some people so desperately don't want to be pregnant. You're looking after them and it's a bad situation, or it's a situation of violence or incest or rape, and you're just thinking, What would be better for this woman, if there was an alternative, you know? The thing is, if abortion was normalised, safe and legal, you'd have more people having children as a strong, conscious decision. But because women having children is such an expectation, people just do it without really thinking about it.'

It's not like we as a culture treat mothers particularly well. Having the support of a midwife during labour and birth appears to open up a tiny moment of utopia, of how we ought to see motherhood always: inspiring, emotional, magical. But after that brief moment, when the love and trust flows between everyone present, and women ride the high of giving birth and realising how resilient and strong they really are, the compression of society snaps shut again. In *The Argonauts*, her gorgeous and intimate memoir about motherhood, queerness and gender, Maggie Nelson describes a crystallising moment at a seminar in graduate school, watching the art historian Rosalind Krauss tear to shreds a presentation by literary theorist and new mother Jane Gallop. 'The tacit undercurrent of her argument,' she writes, 'was that Gallop's maternity had rotted her mind.'

Even if you're among the intellectual elite, once the baby's out, you're just a mum, vulnerable to all the criticism and condescension that go along with fresh maternity, following the same narrative that sees so many women distressed and depressed as their identities dissolve into motherhood and the world begins to ignore them.

Tash—the woman who caught her newborn baby in her own hands—is a casualty of the medical establishment's fondness for these old narratives. She describes a moment of emotional whiplash, as she transitioned from maternal goddess genius to incompetent new mother. As she lay recovering, still riding a high from giving birth to her first child, she says a hospital lactation consultant appeared at the foot of her bed, barking at her about colostrum.

Colostrum is the deep-golden fluid that precedes recognisable breastmilk. It contains hyper-concentrated nutrition, antibodies and immunoglobulins. Many people call it 'superfood' for your baby; considering the high nutritional payload and the brief window in which your body produces it (usually only about five days), there is some sense of urgency among certain lactation specialists in getting the stuff into your newborn. In Tash's case, this urgency took the form of belittling hectoring about her inability to get her child to latch. This is not an uncommon experience. Though the days of blanket-prescribed formula feeding are behind us, the Breast Is Best campaign has become just as totalitarian, and just as disapproving of those who would deviate from the party line. What many new mothers will tell you is that breastfeeding can be *hard*. In Tash's case, the difficulty with lactation and breastfeeding among the women of her family was such a big part of her consciousness that she spent her entire undergraduate career writing about it. And despite alerting her postnatal nurses to the likelihood of her own difficulty with breastfeeding, she was not treated kindly.

'I couldn't get her to latch properly, and the nurses were insisting, you know, "She needs it! It's liquid gold! She needs that!"' Exhausted and upset, Tash did everything she was told, but couldn't get her newborn to feed. The nurses told her they'd have to hand-express the colostrum.

'So three or four times, every two hours, this nurse would come back and just mangle my boobs for a while, and use a syringe to suck up this colostrum and then feed it to my daughter, who would then throw up because she was still throwing up mucus. This nurse is coming in, manhandling me, to feed it to my baby only for my baby to throw it up, constantly. For hours.

'It got to the point where every time a nurse would come in I'd just start crying. It was a really shitty twenty-four hours. It's not the worst that could happen in a hospital, but just because it's not the worst thing that they could possibly do doesn't mean that they don't need to change.'

We've come a long way since the strapped-to-the-bed humiliation of birth in the 1940s and '50s (can you blame my grandmother for rushing out of the room, too traumatised to look the memories of her own deliveries in the face?), but when I speak to my friends who are new mothers, this is where they tell me we still have a way to go. As Tash describes it, you go through all these antenatal classes, you begin to believe you really *can* do anything, that you're capable and strong, and then—

'Every lactation consultant and postnatal ward nurse just made me feel like I didn't know what I was doing—which I didn't!—but that I *should*, and that I was stupid for not knowing. I just felt so low. I got home and was totally disempowered. I felt so bad, and I thought, How can anyone come out of the hospital after their first baby feeling like they can do this? I couldn't understand it.'

Tash had a beautiful birth experience—so why was her time in the postnatal ward so different? She says: because the birth is about you, but the postnatal ward is about the baby.

Women in the West have long been denied sovereignty over their bodies. Religion, the medical establishment and the law have all encouraged us to hand over control of our corporeal vessels to the church, to doctors, or to lawmakers with our 'best interests' at heart. As I write, in 2018, the state of Queensland has just decriminalised abortion. We are well into the twenty-first century, and my home state has only just removed the requirement that a pregnancy must pose a serious risk to a woman's physical or mental health in order for a legal termination to take place. In the United States, access to safe and legal abortion remains nebulous as lawmakers bicker over what humiliations to inflict upon women seeking to terminate, and whether female bodies have 'ways of shutting the whole thing down' if a pregnancy occurs as the result of a rape. As a culture we're obsessed with the childbearing potential of women's bodies, but that obsession fails to extend to, for example, post-natal maternity care. Once the baby is out, it's the baby we care about, not the woman who bore it.

While midwifery might have regained its legitimacy along-side a patriarchal medical establishment, we still haven't gone all the way. If we really want to care for women, we've got to extend that care beyond the moment of birth. Midwifery allows for women to control and inhabit their bodies to an extent unheard of in the rest of their lives—which explains why many of my friends speak in such glowing terms about their birth experiences in the company of their midwives. But it is a terrible paucity of joy, to be so supported and loved only in the moment when you're creating a new life and bringing it into the world. In Rebecca Solnit's book *The Mother of All Questions*, she addresses the injustices dealt to mothers: 'Mothers are consistently found wanting. A mother may be treated like a criminal for leaving her child alone for five minutes, even if that child's father has left it alone for several years. Some mothers have told me that having children caused them to be treated as bovine non-intellects who should be disregarded.'

A culture that sneers at *Call the Midwife* sneers at all mothers; maybe because we're scared of them, maybe because we don't understand them. I wish I could know for sure that my pregnant friends will be cared for by their communities, will be stewarded into the tradition of women's business, not just when they're at their most vulnerable but for the rest of their lives.

•

Five years ago, when I first started learning about midwives, I was in a witchcraft rabbit hole; via hoodoo, voodoo, Wicca, Gerald Gardner, Salem, the *Malleus Maleficarum*, the burnings and hangings, the charms and hexes, I finally arrived at the old, weird magic of birth and death. It didn't matter that I was not pregnant, nor planning on becoming so; I was fascinated by the mythos of this independent woman who existed solely to help other women, whose healing powers were so strong and frightening that the Catholic Church considered her to be operating under the guidance of Satan himself. I loved the idea of the raw blood magic of childbirth, the trust and faith a pregnant woman would place in her midwife, the community that would rally around her in the name of bringing new life into the world. Maybe the relationships between the women in Jennifer Worth's memoirs constitute magic. They are rare and precious, unusual and powerful; they glue these people together in strange ways that would not happen otherwise. Sometimes I read articles about childbirth, and their authors talk about the unendurable loneliness of it. They are missing out on the magic a good midwife can weave.

I have been using the words 'women' and 'female' with reckless abandon so far, which is unfair and inaccurate. Women are, of course, not the only people who get pregnant and give birth. There have been several highly publicised cases of men becoming pregnant and giving birth to their children naturally, and many more have flown quietly under the radar—according to Medicare statistics, more than fifty men gave birth in Australia in 2017 alone. Gender is not as rigidly divided down reproductive lines as it once was; we are beginning to wriggle out from under that yoke. Nelson writes in *The Argonauts* about the inherent queerness of pregnancy, 'insofar as it profoundly alters one's "normal" state, and occasions a radical intimacy with— and radical alienation from—one's body'.

But the fact remains that for most of history, childbirth and childrearing was a woman's domain—often her only domain, or the only one in which she might be able to excel. And for much of the medical profession, pregnancy and childbirth remain inextricably female. While talking with *Mel* magazine about her research on trans male pregnancy, University of Leeds professor of sociology and gender identities Sally Hines explained the difficulty many trans men face when discussing their planned pregnancy with their doctors. 'Medical discourse cannot separate pregnancy from the female body,' she said, 'and medical practitioners are unable to offer adequate advice.' The borders of birth are being renegotiated, and we are struggling to keep up. But I can see a moment, maybe on the distant horizon, maybe closer, when a midwife's insistence that giving birth is normal becomes a known fact, regardless of the gender of the person who is doing so.

Until then, maybe it's on us to keep adjusting the borders of this so-called women's space, letting in whoever needs the protection it might provide.

•

I wish that my mother had women surrounding her when she gave birth to me. It upsets me to imagine her, brave as always but alone and in pain, under the care of someone she barely knew.

At least I know that her second birth was different. Ten years later, in a hospital in New Zealand, she gave birth to my sister: again via caesarean, but this time cared for by our family doctor, Eva. I remember Eva as a smooth-faced German woman with the elusive and desirable blend of qualities that makes a perfect GP: authoritative, attentive, willing to listen to whatever hunch you might have about your own malfunctioning body. She was funny, too, and most importantly, had a specialisation in obstetrics. She was not a midwife, but the way my mother tells it, she fulfilled that role, so that Mum, forty-one and giving birth to her second unplanned child, felt safe, capable, cared for. She knew she was not alone.

•

A couple of years ago, after a decade on the pill, I decided that it was time to do something at least slightly more permanent about my mortal fear of getting pregnant. I decided to get a copper IUD implanted. This device—a T-shaped piece of plastic wrapped in copper wire, about three centimetres long—is one of the best forms of contraception available, with a 99.8 per cent efficacy rate. Once inserted, it creates a hostile environment for sperm (although the medical profession is still not completely sure why copper is so toxic to sperm in particular without hurting any other parts of the reproductive system). And it lasts for ten years. I did a lot of research before I chose the copper IUD as my contraceptive of choice. The set-and-forget aspect of it appealed to me; the total lack of artificial hormones and their accompanying mood-fuckery was even more appealing. As was the cost per wear: if I went to a public sexual health clinic, the whole thing would cost me about $80. I made the appointment for a day when I knew I'd have my period (it's supposed to make the procedure easier); I took a Valium and an ibuprofen, and I caught the bus to the clinic, nervous but excited.

The IUD is inserted with a long plastic instrument that is forced through the cervix and into the uterus, depositing the little T inside. For most people who undergo this procedure, it's uncomfortable, and sometimes followed by some cramping, but it's usually bearable. For a few, things go a little awry.

At the clinic, I sat in the waiting room with some other young women. Everyone I'd met so far, from the receptionist on the phone to the greeter at the door to the young doctor who saw me for my initial consultation, was a woman, and all possessed of the sort of no-nonsense kindness that always makes me tear up a bit in gratitude. I was feeling very warm towards the people around me. I smiled encouragingly over the top of my *Marie Claire* at the teenager opposite me, imagining she was taking the first steps towards seizing control of her own reproductive health. Then a young nurse came to collect me and I left the teen behind.

In a pale-green procedural room, the young nurse and her older colleague ran me through what would happen. I am pretty sure this happened, anyway; my memory has been fogged with diazepam and pain. I do remember the older nurse telling me that she'd done the procedure about a million times. She had a very nice face, and I trusted her immediately. I lay back on the special chair with my dress around my waist and my feet in the stirrups, and the older nurse inserted a marked plastic stick to measure my uterus. It hurt. The younger nurse held my hand, and let me squeeze hers hard. Then, the same pain when the IUD went in— quick, no-nonsense, as kind as it could be—I squeezed the young nurse's hand again—I had to get up to use the bathroom—I was dizzy—I was being sat back down and an oxygen mask was put on my face—I was having what they called 'a bad reaction'. What I do remember, through the haze of time and sedatives, is the monumental pain, and the enormous gentleness of the two medical professionals who were with me. They each took one of my hands to stroke with their cool fingers. The older nurse talked me through what was happening: my body had recognised the IUD as something foreign, and it was trying to push it out. I was having contractions. She told me that what I was feeling was very similar to what people giving birth feel, except I didn't have any of the pain-mitigating hormones to go with it.

I don't know if she told me that to make me feel better. (It did—I felt brave.) I do know that it was the worst pain I have ever felt, that I tried my very hardest not to burst into tears and burst into tears anyway; that it made me feel dizzy and sick, that it took over my body in a way I've never felt before, so that without my knowledge or permission I was curling into myself on my side and issuing a high, thin moan as I pressed my hands into my belly; it sucked, it sucked, it sucked.

And that's only pushing out a three-centimetre plastic T. It's not like I didn't have respect for those who go through childbirth before those fifteen shocking minutes of pain on a pale-green examination chair, but afterwards I felt a little like I'd brushed up against my mortality. I can't help but wonder what it feels like to go the whole way through—to not just brush up against it but to make full-body contact with your inevitable demise, in the shape of excoriating pain, in the name of life.

A few days later, I went to another doctor to get the thing removed (it had been forced down into my cervix, where it had lodged, uselessly, until a yank on the strings and another burst of pain brought it out—I remember it dangling bloodily from my doctor's gloved hand, and my impotent surge of hatred for the tiny object). Afterwards, I asked if there wasn't anything *actually* permanent I could do. I wanted to get my tubes tied. My doctor did not try to talk me out of it. She didn't suggest that I wait and see, that I might change my mind. She just looked at me, shook her head very slightly, and said she understood, but that no doctor in Queensland would do it for me. I said that it sucked, and she said she knew.

All of those women—the nurses who held my hand, the doctor who talked over my options with me before the appointment, the last doctor who tugged that plastic bit of shit out of me, the ultrasound technician who commiserated with me because even *she* couldn't get her tubes tied and she'd already had three kids— even now I feel overwhelmed by what they did for me. And I was just a bratty kid who didn't want to get pregnant.

Those women care for people seeking abortions, suffering from STDs caused by assault and incest, pregnant in their teens without a support network, and they do it kindly and without judgement and discreetly, and with very little government funding. When I think about them I see a line of women healers standing behind them, stretching all the way back to the beginning of time, and I feel lucky that I got to experience that unobtrusive expertise in the face of something awful and terrifying. I know they've got my back.

8

SEX WORKERS

Laws of Babylon

When I was about twenty, I worked at a strip club. I was a hostess: my job was to wear a short skirt and high heels and a corset, and take patrons their drinks on a tray. I wrote about this job, which I had for about three months before I went overseas on a trip that the work funded almost entirely, several years after the fact. The published piece gained some traction online, and there was a not insignificant response from sex workers who read it and were very angry about it.

I think they were right to be angry. While I wanted to write about my experiences, which were bizarre and funny and completely shifted my understanding of gender relations in general, I did not recognise the position from which I was doing that— namely, the position of an outsider to the industry. The criticisms levelled at me were accurate: I was a sex-work tourist, dipping my toe in for a few months, gathering some scintillating stories, and hopping out again to parade my street cred around. Basically, I did not know what I was talking about. My time working in the strip club was fascinating to me, but I can't pretend to know what it was like for the people who actually performed the work that drew patrons to the club: the work of stripping, giving lap dances, pretending to be interested in whatever the increasingly drunk bloke in the chair was saying to you.

That labour is hard, often physically punishing, and increasingly poorly paid. Legislation surrounding sex work in Australia is a quagmire of contradictions, grey areas and misinformation, which, combined with social stigma, means that sex workers are often prevented from enjoying the labour rights that Australia's robust union movement has worked so hard to win for all workers. Fortunately, Australia is also home to some of the most innovative and effective sex worker collectives in the world. Sex worker advocacy groups are almost always predominantly female, and they are the inheritors of a long tradition of women unionists. Vixen Collective, Respect, the Scarlet Alliance, SIN, SWAGGER, SWOP, SWEAR, Magenta, Salome's Circle— although they might not be unions by name, their philosophy is the same as their foremothers': that women's industries deserve fair pay, fair work conditions and protection under the law, just like any other. Sex workers have been collectively agitating for change in Australia for more than forty years, and they are a magnificent example of women working together.

•

Sex work is popularly called the oldest profession. While this is a difficult claim to validate, mentions of sex work certainly date all the way back to the eighteenth century BC, when the Babylonian legal document the Code of Hammurabi enshrined as sacred prostitutes' rights to inherit property and collect income from land worked by their brothers. Since then, forms of sex work have existed continuously and around the world. 'Sex work' itself is an umbrella term that encompasses all people involved in the commercial sale of sexual services, including escorts, street-based workers, cam girls and boys, sensual massage parlour employees, pornography performers, exotic dancers, sexual surrogates who work in the context of psychological therapy, and many others; it's used as an alternative to the derogatory term 'prostitute' and in order to encompass all people providing sexual services, not just those who do full-service work.

Whatever you call it, the sex industry has been around for almost as long as human memory, and is responsible for supporting some of history's most interesting female figures. For significant portions of history, female sex workers were afforded more rights and political influence than their non–sex worker counterparts. European courtesans famously rose to positions of real power during the Renaissance; Japan's oiran similarly occupied celebrity niches, influencing fashion and culture among wealthy women while enjoying unparalleled personal and political freedom. In Ancient Greece, educated sex workers and entertainers called hetaerae were the freest of all Greek women, with even more influence and ease of movement than their wealthier contemporaries. The fact that women continued to enter these professions appears to demonstrate that they found the occupation appealing; social attitudes meant that there was not nearly as much sacrifice of cultural capital as that which accompanies modern sex work. Ancient Greek brothels were even funded by the government in the same way as theatres and other entertainment venues. This is not to say that all the sex workers of history enjoyed social, political and sexual freedom; stigma towards sex workers has a long and storied history. But it certainly seems that attitudes were much more flexible than they are today.

According to some estimates, in the late twentieth century approximately 46 million women worldwide were involved in commercial sex work in one way or another. For many of those women, the work is economically empowering, physically invigorating, exciting, challenging and both personally and professionally satisfying. Compared to other female-dominated industries like nursing, early childhood education and aged care, sex work can be lucrative, and sex workers often cite the comparatively high pay rates, independence and flexible hours as reasons they enter and stay in the industry. Some sex workers say the sexual freedom available to them through their work is why they do it; some enjoy the satisfaction of providing a service that is warmly appreciated; and some are in it just for the cash. In other words, sex workers feel exactly how workers in every other industry feel about their jobs.

But the dominant narratives about female sex workers are profoundly one-dimensional. Watch any of the documentaries on women in the sex industry—*Hot Girls Wanted*, *Escorts*, *Life After Porn*—and you're greeted with mournful soundtracks, wistful close-up interviews with mascara-smeared women, and a veritable flip book of childhood photographs illustrating the tragic loss of innocence the job brings with it. Despite the nature of the work being neither inherently dangerous nor degrading, sex workers face unparalleled discrimination because of their chosen industry. Mainstream media often reports on issues related to the sex industry without consulting any actual sex workers, allowing representation to skew heavily towards 'pity porn'. Christians fearing moral imperilment and radical feminists decrying all commercial sex as slavery collaborate in forcing the burden of victimhood onto a population of women who generally just want to do their jobs in peace. Sex workers remain the subject of cruel jokes, and those jokes form the basis of a pyramid of whorephobia with violence, rape and murder at its peak—crimes that often receive lighter punishments when committed against women in the sex industry. And it can be a socially precarious industry in which to work: sex workers participating in hundreds of studies, documentaries and interviews have shared stories of losing friends, partners, the support of their families, their homes and their jobs after being outed for their line of work.

When it comes to sex work, social stigma and the law form a feedback loop: stigma allows lawmakers to ignore or downplay sex workers' rights, and the criminalised nature of the work allows the public to stigmatise it. But, as anyone in sex work will tell you, the reality is that, regardless of persecution, people are willing to pay money for sexual services, and other people are able to provide those services in exchange for money. Data released in 2015 by Havocscope, an organization that collates information about the black market, suggests that globally the sex industry is worth $186 billion per year, and that's without taking into account the $97 billion per year turned over by consumers of pornography. If nothing else, the numbers tell the truth: sex work is work. Like any workers, those in the sex industry deserve protection under the law, not further discrimination. It seems clear to me that the issue of sex worker rights is not a moral, religious, philanthropic or even feminist one; it's about *labour*.

·

The legal status of sex work differs dramatically from country to country. Although there are only a few places in the world where sex work is completely illegal, almost everywhere places restrictions on those who do the work, whether it be on who a sex worker can work with, the areas in which they may do so, the services they provide, or the way they find clients.

In the United States, a dizzying array of laws attempt to control or make illegal some or all aspects of sex work, including buying, selling and organizing sexual services. Only one state, Nevada, allows for legal, regulated brothels, in which employees are required to meet STD testing schedules and curfews; street work still remains illegal. The fact that sex work is against the law in every other state does not, of course, mean sex work does not go on. Many American sex workers operate as escorts, either independently or part of an agency, and often using the internet to advertise and find clients. Some still do mostly street work. Some work in illegal erotic massage parlors or unlicensed brothels. But without the protection of the law, these workers, like those in many countries, are vulnerable to violence, sexual assault, theft and coercion, and unable to seek the help of the police or retribution via the legal system.

Australia is home to some deeply problematic policy on sex work and sex worker rights. For one thing, the laws vary wildly between the different states and territories. Victoria, Queensland and the Australian Capital Territory have legalised sex work in brothels, but with varying restrictions and registration requirements. In the Northern Territory, where brothels are illegal, escort agency workers, but not private workers, must register with the government; Victoria, meanwhile, requires private workers (those who work neither in brothels nor on the street) to register, but with different government bodies. Tasmania allows up to two private workers to work from the same premises, but only if they are not managing or employing each other. All forms of sex work are effectively criminalised in South Australia, which of course does not mean that there are no sex workers there—only that they are breaking the law by doing their job. The justification for all of these laws is that they 'protect' the workers, but their arbitrary application to different workers in different circumstances makes this difficult to believe. The situation is a nightmare just to read about; it's even more of a nightmare to try to work within.

Jane Green, from Vixen Collective, the peer-only sex worker advocacy group in Victoria, ran me through just some of the hurdles that sex workers face while trying to earn their living there. 'There's a number of primary models of sex work regulation.

'Full criminalisation, which is probably the easiest to explain: it's illegal, we're not meant to do it, but obviously it still occurs. I worked the first ten years of my working life under full criminalisation. Criminalisation doesn't eradicate us, but it severely limits our rights, and, importantly, our safety. And also our access to services, because when you have a combative relationship with police, when the police view you as a criminal and see it as their job to arrest you and restrict your behaviour, then you're not treated in a way that allows you to access police assistance.'

Because Victoria requires private workers to register with the government, there is a list of registered sex workers that is accessible by police (without a warrant), council workers, Consumer

Affairs Victoria and the Business Licensing Authority—and which means, because of the stigma still attached to the work, that sex workers can be vulnerable to being extorted.

'Essentially,' says Jane, 'they're keeping a list of us all as if we're criminals, when we haven't done anything against the law.'

There is one place in Australia where sex workers are legally treated not as criminals of some degree but as workers subject to the same laws as every other industry: New South Wales. In 2018, it was the only state to have decriminalised sex work (although some restrictions still apply to street-based work). New South Wales was, in fact, the first place in the world to successfully legislate for decriminalisation, passing laws in 1995 after organisations like the Australian Prostitutes Collective lobbied throughout the 1980s, in one case famously calling for sex workers throughout the country to withhold services from any politicians until they were willing to negotiate. Full decriminalisation, which removes sex work–specific legislation in favour of applying the same regulations that are applied to any other business and its workers, is now the model espoused by the World Health Organization, Amnesty International and human rights organisations worldwide—and it was the collective activism of Australian sex workers that set that standard.

Sex worker collectives were also instrumental in creating Australia's world-renowned response to the AIDS crisis. In the 1980s, New South Wales sex worker peer-education efforts were instrumental in stymieing the spread of HIV in the sex worker population, including setting up needle exchanges and individually delivering free condoms to every brothel and street-based sex worker in the state. Condom use rose from 5 percent of female sex workers' clients in 1985 to 88 percent in 1988, and by 1991, surveys of broad segments of the industry found condom use at 98 per cent. This approach to preventing HIV among sex workers is considered exemplary on an international scale, and sex workers in Australia now enjoy the same—or better—sexual health statistics as the general population. There has never been a documented case of HIV transmittal from a sex worker in Australia.

The only other place in the world to have adopted decriminalisation so far is New Zealand. In 2003, the country passed the Prostitution Reform Act, repealing previous laws governing sex work and extending all the protections and regulations of existing labour laws to the sex industry. Extensive surveying in the years since the introduction of the law has found that New Zealand sex workers report feeling less stigmatised thanks to the legitimisation of their work, and more protected by workplace health and safety laws now that the legislation treats their form of labour like any other. Changing the law had a tangible effect on social stigma, improving the health and well-being of people involved in the sex industry in New Zealand more than any previous effort.

But for sex workers outside of New Zealand and New South Wales, life is more complicated. In Victoria, because there are no protections under the Equal Opportunity Act for discrimination based on occupation or trade, sex workers do not have full legal protection from being discriminated against because of their work. It's still legal in many parts of the country for landlords to evict sex workers without penalty; being outed as a sex worker can also impact your ability to get a home loan or take out life insurance. It was only in 2016 that the Victorian judges' sentencing manual was updated, after heavy lobbying by Vixen Collective, to remove advice to reduce sentences for people who raped sex workers (referred to in the relevant cases as 'unchaste women'). And still, if sex workers want to pursue legal avenues—such as pressing charges for sexual assault, or seeking compensation for lost wages—they risk opening themselves up to further discrimination and disadvantage, because reporting requires them to out themselves. For many workers in the sex industry, it's just not worth it. For many others, the notion that they might even be eligible for legal protection seems laughable.

•

Stripping exists in a nebulous area between the 'legitimate' entertainment industry and the realm of full-service sex work. Like other sectors of the industry, stripping regulations vary wildly from state to state. Stripping is also in the middle of an unusual cultural moment—it's in the process of being legitimised. Celebrities who are out and unashamed about their former lives as exotic dancers lend the job a sense of repute, and dancing can promise an easy way for young women to translate a healthy Instagram following into income. For clubs, this means a steady influx of new women to earn them money. For the dancers, however, the increasing competition means the industry seems to be getting more and more hostile, and ever less stable. In a job where the risks of injury are high and the responsibilities of the employer unclear, this seems both unsustainable and unethical.

I check in with a friend who dances at a club in Melbourne. The work is exhausting, but well paid; she'll keep stripping for another six months, she thinks, save a bunch of money, then go back to school to train in IT. I ask what happens if she injures herself on the job. Does she get workers compensation? I can sense her snorting derisively even over Facebook Messenger. 'Def not,' she writes.

I call the club I used to work at and ask the same question. The receptionist can't answer me, and asks that I email her so she can pass it on to the club manager. I call WorkSafe Queensland, where an extremely helpful representative explains to me that, at least in Queensland, the rules governing whether a person is an independent contractor or an employee in the eyes of the law (and therefore whether or not they are entitled to WorkCover payments in the case of an accident or injury sustained on the job) are pretty complicated. She directs me to the Australian Taxation Office's worker determination tool, where I answer a dozen questions about my hypothetical stripper contractors, and where I learn that, probably, those strippers do count as my employees for the purposes of workers' compensation. Which is a long-winded way of saying that none of this is clear at all— and it only becomes less clear when you cross state lines.

The needless complication of these laws means that many dancers are completely in the dark about their rights under existing labour legislation. Many of the women in the industry who I spoke to confirmed that there's also a common wisdom within strip clubs that you are 'on your own', and this is backed up by research on how stigma affects sex workers. Several studies have found that sex workers often come to believe that discrimination, violence and lack of support simply come with the territory. This internalisation is not conducive to demanding better work conditions; it does, however, tend to suit club owners very well.

I spoke with a representative for Salome's Circle, a peer-support group for strippers working in Victoria, about exactly this: the pervasive sense within the industry that the business you work for is not on your side should things ever go wrong. It's not just that strippers often don't know that they're entitled to compensation if they're injured at work (and they are, just as they are entitled to lodge unfair dismissal claims and receive certain employee benefits, regardless of their contractor status)—it's that they don't feel as though their workplaces have their backs. In an anonymous survey run within Salome's Circle, none of the respondents said that they were sure their place of work would support them if they were injured on the job. Only *one* person said they thought they'd receive support if they were assaulted. When asked if they would try to seek compensation in the event of an injury, all said no. One respondent replied: 'I do not believe my workplace would assist me, and instead would fire me.' Another said she once saw a co-worker fall off stage, badly injure herself, and be sent off to the hospital in a taxi without another word from management. No one said they were certain about what rights they had at work.

Stripping is a physically demanding and sometimes dangerous job. The thought that you could be climbing metal poles in eight-inch heels every night and not be absolutely certain that if you fell and dislocated your shoulder you'd still have an income is, frankly, chilling.

Like other industries with regulation that does not provide adequately for workers' safety, strip clubs rely in part on workers' lack of knowledge about their rights in order to get away with less-than-legal business practices, all in the name of squeezing out the most profit. Cultural myths within stripping communities continue to circulate because they benefit the club owners.

If you have always been told that you are an independent contractor, responsible for your own safety, and without recourse should you get sick or be injured, you are unlikely to even consider talking to the relevant government body about seeking workers' compensation. The fact that most strippers are paid in cash complicates wage and compensation claims. And because stripping is part of the sex industry, practices that would stir outrage were they to occur in hospitality or retail simply don't get traction at the level of mainstream conversation.

As always, it's members of the industry themselves who are doing the most to change this. Leigh Hopkinson, author of the book *Two Decades Naked*, brought up the example of the death of Stacey Tierney. Tierney, a British woman working as a stripper while travelling in Australia and saving to study nursing, died of a drug overdose at an 'after-party' at the Dreams Gentlemen's Club where she worked in Melbourne in 2016. Although a British coroner's inquest in 2018 revealed that neither of the men who were with her at the time called an ambulance or tried to help her after she lost consciousness, no charges will be laid over her death. Leigh told me that Stacey's death illuminated the intersection of industry-specific labour practices and a public indifferent to the lives of sex workers. As she put it, 'If Stacey's death had happened on a construction site, there's no way the industry would continue with business as usual without taking a long, hard look at themselves.'

Leigh also spoke about just how much the stripping scene had changed even in the past ten years. After being a dancer for twenty years, she left the industry in 2014, and says that towards the end of her time in the clubs, she'd already begun to see the effects of a changing culture.

'When I worked, there were fewer clubs and fewer women dancing. I never felt that my job was threatened—I could take time off and I always had a job to come back to. I found that I was really respected by the clubs. There's a lot more women dancing these days, a lot more clubs, and a lot more dancers rostered on to each shift. So whereas on a Saturday night we would once have had fifty dancers working, there's now a hundred.'

These inflated rosters are themselves a source of income to the clubs, thanks to the widespread practice of charging strippers a 'house fee' to work on the premises. Leigh says that when she began dancing, house fees were nonexistent. Now, she says, clubs charge women up to $120 a night to dance. It makes a precarious job even less secure.

'You've got dancers who are basically working in order to pay back the house, and not knowing whether they're going to walk out with any money or not,' she says.

On top of having to pay for the privilege of working, strippers are also often saddled with questionable fines—for being late to a stage show or a podium set, for example, or for missing a shift. For a no-show, dancers can be charged a $200 fine, putting them further in debt to the house. The legality of this practice is difficult to ascertain, though Leigh says preliminary research by Salome's Circle suggests that it's dubious at best.

The popularity of stripping, combined with the absence of fair work regulations, means that many dancers are too afraid of losing their jobs to take time off. Clubs might have minimum shift requirements, but they are also at liberty to roster dancers only on quiet nights, thus affecting how much they're able to earn, without having to provide a reason. On top of this, many clubs have a practice of 'full rostering' as a method of dismissal.

Rosters are usually organised by dancers texting in preferred shifts to club management at the start of each week, dreading, as Leigh explains, the reply, 'Sorry, the roster is full'—to which there is no recourse, despite the fact that that same club may still be advertising dancer vacancies. This job insecurity has serious effects—including on women's safety, as the desperation to earn a living and to stay on management's good side dissolves boundaries that dancers would have once enforced.

'It's really changed the dynamic in terms of how dancers are viewed by management and by club owners. Dancers are much hungrier to make money than they once would have been, and there's increasing pressure to do things in the workplace that maybe you wouldn't otherwise do in order to make money.'

Stacey Tierney's death has galvanised much of the Australian stripping community into demanding change in the way the media and police treat them. Sex worker–friendly platforms like Twitter, sex worker organisations, and online groups like Salome's Circle are enabling strippers to compare notes, organise legal advice, and attempt to stay one step ahead of clubs that seek to exploit their labour. Although popular conceptions of strippers might suggest that the industry would thrive upon pitting women against each other, many women, both in stripping and sex work in general, are organising to intentionally contradict the narrative, unite strippers, express solidarity with other sex workers, and provide an invaluable place of community in a world that can be hostile to women who earn a living from their bodies.

Most of the people I spoke to, including Leigh, cite this sense of community as one of their top reasons for staying in the work that they do.

'That's a really big part of the industry for me, to have found my people,' Leigh says. 'To be with this outrageous bunch of women who are pushing boundaries, who refuse to be typecast into traditional ways of how women should or shouldn't behave. There's just so many fabulously talented, brilliant, eccentric, groundbreaking women who choose to partake in this work, and I think that's a part of the industry that's not always recognised.

'People are smart, people who are working in that area— often the stereotype is that we're not. But some of the smartest people I've met have been working in those spaces.'

•

The challenges facing strippers are a great example of how social attitudes influence the resources available to workers in particular industries. Every industry has its injustices, has workers taken advantage of, has people in positions of power breaking the law. But unlike other industries, sex work is assumed to be founded upon injustice, power imbalance and crime, and as such is accompanied by a pervasive notion that no one wants to be a sex worker—and that those who do are morally corrupt in one way or another. (Of course, research has shown, over and over, that neither of these things are true.)

When news broke in mid-2018 of rampant wage theft in the hospitality industry, traditional media and its readers were outraged. *The Sydney Morning Herald* called it 'systematic exploitation of workers'. Withholding fair pay from workers, or denying them superannuation or penalty rates, was an affront to basic decency. We sympathised with the chefs, waitstaff and dishwashers who'd been stiffed by bosses they'd trusted. There were protests, and there was pressure on policymakers to crack down on greedy millionaire restaurateurs.

But when Stacey Tierney died at her place of work, media support was minimal. Sympathies for exploited workers aren't nearly so forthcoming when those workers are part of the sex industry. When Tierney's family set up a public donations page to send her body home to England, some members of the public made it their business to decry as deeply offensive the very notion of contributing to preserving the dead woman's dignity. The sister of the owner of Dreams Gentlemen's Club told the media: 'I know strip clubs and I know the type of girls who work there. They go get high on whatever drug, do their dancing and go home.' Consider the gulf of difference between the public response to Tierney's death and the response to deaths on worksites, in work for the dole programs, or in the mining industry. Stacey Tierney deserves our respect—and our anger at an industry that failed to protect her.

Internalised social attitudes towards sex workers, along with a well-founded fear of being prosecuted instead of assisted by police, can prevent sex workers from seeking out the legal protections to which they are, in spite of much misinformation, entitled. However, some sex workers in Australia are starting to demand access to their rights from the legal system as part of their ongoing push for full decriminalisation. In Queensland, a recent case of fraud garnered media attention for its unusual plaintiffs and its unusual outcome: two female sex workers successfully brought a case of fraud against a man who had on separate occasions engaged their services and then left without paying. It was the first time in Queensland that a man was convicted of fraud for failing to pay a sex worker; local advocacy organisation Respect told the media that while these women had experienced success in the courts, other sex workers who had brought complaints of a similar nature to police had been dismissed or threatened with arrest themselves. And the fact remains that current Queensland laws mean that sex workers can't legally work together, or even keep in touch via text messages—a practice that many in the industry say is vital to keeping each other safe. However, visibility is the first step to legislative change, and the win for those two women—who eventually received their agreed-upon price from the man upon his conviction—is another step in the march towards industrial equality.

•

So what of the arguments against decriminalising sex work? I keep coming back to this, over and over: I just do not get it. The more I read on sex work, and the realities many sex workers face during their working lives, the more incensed I become—not just as a feminist, but as a vocal supporter of unionisation and labour rights. Looking back at my own professional life, I'm quietly astonished at the number of things I did for money, whether I liked them or not: stacked DVD cases, smiled at shouting customers, scrubbed floors on my hands and knees, wore lingerie and carried drinks. I did them all, probably to a similar degree of excellence (poor) and with similar levels of enthusiasm (low), and all for exactly the same reason: I needed money. But the last one on that list is the only one that people will take issue with. That sex workers remain so marginalised in Australia is the very antithesis of giving everyone a fair go.

And, appallingly, a vocal portion of feminists are among

the ranks of those who'd take that fair go away. Researching late one night, I came across Andrea Dworkin's speech 'Prostitution and Male Supremacy', which she delivered at a university symposium in 1993. It is ghastly: condescending, outrageously reductive, and apparently completely oblivious to how alarmingly it resembles puritanical attitudes towards sex. Dworkin is convinced that to be a sex worker renders a woman irreparably broken: 'In prostitution, no woman stays whole. It is impossible to use a human body in the way women's bodies are used in prostitution and to have a whole human being at the end of it, or in the middle of it, or close to the beginning of it. It's impossible. And no woman gets whole again later, after.'

My jaw literally dropped as I read. Although Dworkin's stance was informed by her own experiences of intimate partner abuse and a brief period of working in the sex industry, her rhetoric sounds an awful lot like those virginity analogies popular in Catholic schools, where they stick a bit of tape to various things and then tell the girls that that's what happens to their bodies and souls when they have sex before marriage. Consensual sex does not—cannot—tear the fabric of your being asunder. I thought the whole point of feminism was to allow women all the rights, vitality, resilience and intelligence they've been denied for so long. Why, when it comes to sex, must we be relegated again to the role of the delicate, the easily bruised, the virginal?

Obviously Dworkin has not been a big name in contemporary feminist debate for some time, but the echoes of her legacy linger on. Even the notorious 'Swedish Model' (sometimes called the 'Nordic Model') approach to sex work answers in large part to Dworkin and feminist legal scholar Catharine MacKinnon's ordinance against porn, which attempted to conflate all pornography with violence against women. The Swedish Model operates on the assumption that there can be no sex work without damage to the workers, and is a conscious effort to suffocate the industry out of existence. Instead of criminalising the provision of commercial sex, however, the Swedish Model criminalises its purchase, as well as criminalising third parties and the activities surrounding sex work. The model is regularly hailed by anti–sex work feminists and undereducated members of the media as the best possible approach to sex work, but while this may appear to shift the weight of legal responsibility off the sex worker, in practice it puts her in just as precarious a position. Dealing with flighty clients who are keen to rush through terms of agreement, fearing that they'll be arrested at any minute, means the sex worker's bargaining power is significantly reduced. If a sex worker is unable to adequately screen her clients, she is more vulnerable to abuse, violence, theft and unsafe sex practices.

In the United States, recent and extremely high-profile policy changes were ostensibly designed to address the other major criticism of legitimised sex work: that it encourages human trafficking. But according to sex workers around the world, the laws, intended to protect the most vulnerable populations, are instead dragging the United States—and, by association, many other countries—further into the reactionary past. The Stop Enabling Sex Traffickers Act (SESTA) and Allow States and Victims to Fight Online Sex Trafficking Act (FOSTA), two bills that became law in the United States in 2018, were theoretically set up to protect victims of sex trafficking by making it illegal for websites to host advertising for sex work services. What they effectively do, however, is force all sex workers underground.

Disturbingly, these pieces of legislation are already making life harder and more dangerous for workers who are in the industry by choice.

Jane Green from Vixen Collective explains, 'When you make things illegal, when you restrict them in that way, they're not as detectable if things go wrong. When Backpage [a low-cost advertising site that was used by many sex workers] was still in place in the US, if there were cases of trafficking and they were on Backpage, it was easier for the police to find them. If you suddenly remove those avenues, you're not stopping it, you're just making it less visible, and less easy to find for law enforcement.'

Legislative changes that improve sex workers' rights, like decriminalisation, also make it much harder to hide labour abuses and illegal practices like trafficking. When sex workers know they are supported by the law, they are more likely to report suspicious activity to police, and the entire system becomes transparent to authorities, making it much more difficult for traffickers to hide. As the authors of a 2012 report on the ongoing success of decriminalisation in New South Wales put it, 'Prostitution laws are the greatest allies of the exploiters.' In effect, FOSTA and SESTA are doing exactly the opposite of what they intended to do—and harming innocent bystanders in the process. As Jane keeps telling me, this is what happens when sex workers are left out of discussions about sex work.

•

Like many representatives of marginalised populations, sex worker advocacy groups often follow the credo *Nothing about us without us*. This was my biggest misstep when I wrote about my time at the strip club—to write a whole story about working in a club and not include the people who made the club work. Like many outsiders, I thought I knew all I needed to know about sex work. Like many outsiders, I didn't.

I still don't know all I need to know about sex work, because the sex industry is as complex and multifaceted as the many people who work within it. What I do know is that sex worker collectives are, like so many of the groups of women I've been privileged enough to spend time with in the course of my research, agents of change. The changes they strive for benefit all women: their activism demands stricter sentencing for perpetrators of sexual assault, regardless of their victims' occupations; their community work prevents the transmission of HIV and supports those living with the condition; and they teach the rest of society how to separate our moral squeamishness from our respect for a worker's right to do their job.

For many of us, there is a lot to philosophically untangle when it comes to thinking about sex work: our lingering, puritanical shame about sex, our fear of women who are not controlled by arbiters of purity, our reflexive pearl-clutching when we separate sex from romance, procreation and state-sanctioned unions. We hold on to prudish ideas of feminine sexuality at the same time as we are rapidly shedding our sexual inhibitions. We are curious about the lives of people more sexually adventurous than us but afraid of what a commercially sexual woman might mean for society at large. We are made uncomfortable by the publicness of what we have been taught is an intensely private, even shameful, thing. At least part of our deeply confused reaction to sex work is a combination of fear and curiosity. People don't understand what sex workers actually do, so they imagine the worst—and are more fascinated by it because of those imaginings.

Sex work also represents a totally different way of understanding feminine sexuality. We haven't yet struggled out of the clutches of the virgin/whore dichotomy, or looked directly at the uncomfortable fact that our culture requires women to appear sexually alluring while remaining chaste. Even the language we use to discuss sex hints at deeply held presumptions: women give it up, men take it. Feminine sexuality is both valorised and dismissed, one of those fun doublethink moments the patriarchy is so good at. Sex remains something that is done to a woman, who must receive it willingly and passively. No wonder our brains practically explode when it comes to commercial sex, in which female sex workers are involved not only in the act itself but in the business of advertising and performing their services.

I haven't even touched upon the evergreen argument about 'empowerment'—but I don't think it matters. The most important thing I've learned from my time speaking with sex workers and engaging with this debate, the thing that's freeing and obvious and so common sense it hurts, is that all of these justifications and contradictions and moral dilemmas—they *don't matter*. That tangle is none of our business. What is up to us is either to support the workers in their pursuit of equal working rights, or let them get on with the job.

9

FARMERS

Turning the earth

I want to write about farmers, so I call my mother. She lives on twelve acres in a place called Woopen Creek, near Babinda, an hour south of Cairns. On the tropical northeast point of the continent, it's hot all year round, and the average rainfall can climb to six metres. She and my dad are tree changers from temperate climes, and they grow vanilla.

Vanilla, the world's only edible orchid and the second-most expensive spice, is native to Mexico. In its homeland it's pollinated by a particular kind of native bee. Everywhere else, including in Woopen Creek, it's pollinated by hand. This means that during flowering season my mum gets up at dawn to walk up and down the rows of the shade houses, gently handling every creamy-green flower, pressing a flattened toothpick onto the membrane in each that separates male and female organs and pinching them together.

Vanilla is also a vine, and in most places where it's grown, it's trained onto nursery trees. At Mum's farm, though, it's trained up old branches—cyclone debris—and over hose-covered wires instead, which are strung in long lines at eye height down the lengths of the many open shadehouses that dot the property. As the vine grows down the other side of the wire and onto the ground, Mum scoops it up and loops it back onto the branches. Where it touches the earth, roots grow. The oldest vines resemble nothing more than thick, sensuous, leathery green haystacks.

As I'm writing this, my parents are in the middle of a bumper harvest, their biggest one in the fifteen years they've been in Far North Queensland: about six hundred kilograms of fresh, green beans, which will eventually go for between $600 and $1,000 per kilo. Seven years ago, they were recovering from their second Category 5 cyclone. Yasi cost the state of Queensland $800 million, mostly in lost income from the devastated sugar cane and banana farms. My parents, who had seen the destruction from Cyclone Larry five years earlier when they were just starting to set up the vanilla, were not willing to let their precious crop go the way of the bananas: flattened into pulp on the ground, each row a new tragedy. As Yasi began to swell out over the Pacific, they cut the guide wires for the vanilla and laid the heavy bundles of vines on the ground. Then they covered them with shade cloth, weighted it down and hoped for the best.

They ended up winning an innovation award for it. All the vines survived; the rot and fungus they feared would take advantage of their long days prone on the ground never eventuated. It was an unmitigated success. My mother is modest about it, as she is about almost everything. But to me, her choice to take a gamble on change is continuing in a proud tradition of farming women before her, one rooted in the beginning of agriculture itself.

How can I explain the farm? I have such mixed feelings about it. I was a teenager by the time we moved there, still fuming over being uprooted from my suburban New Zealand paradise, sweating foully in the persistent heat and humidity. It took me a long time to see the beauty in the cinderblock house, the endless flat green of the cane fields on the plain down below, the river at the bottom of our property where lurked the crocodile that would eventually eat our dog. Now I know that it is breathtaking. My mum lets the weeds grow into the vanilla houses, covering the mulch at the bottom of the vines. She lets wood rot where it falls in the bottom paddock. The place is heavy quiet, the kind you only get four kilometres from the highway, all thick with whirring insects just at the edge of hearing, and the heat pressing down on you like a blanket. In the rainy season, you can hear the rain coming, watch it if you're lucky and the sun's at the right angle: the squalls roll in from down the river in a silver sheet, just like the movies.

My mother is part of a slowly growing movement, a migration of liberal city women into the conservative heart of the country, where they send down the deep taproots they never could in all that concrete. Along with the many others like her, my mother approaches agriculture in a completely non-traditional way. The weeds in the shadehouses and the rotting wood are part of a philosophy that is being taken up across agricultural industries: a gentler approach than beating the earth into submission with pesticides, fertilisers and heavy machinery; one that people call permaculture, or biological farming, or regenerative agriculture. It is the breaking crest of a wave of change in Australia's deeply traditional industrial farming culture, and it is largely the work of a sparse but strong web of women.

•

When I call Kaye, she's just come in from the blueberry patch. She says she is always waging one war or another in the blueberries; her current one is with the birds. There are birds everywhere. She's never seen so many, so close to the house, and such unusual varieties: king parrots, rosellas, crows and magpies all jostling for a bit of food. The drought, she thinks, is behind it. They've been digging up her sweet potatoes and nibbling on the carrot tops that peek above the soil. She doesn't mind, really. 'Go and eat my sweet potato,' she says, 'that's fine, help yourselves.'

The drought that gripped all of New South Wales and most of Queensland as I wrote this chapter was the worst in hundreds of years. Many farmers, particularly cattle farmers, were in full crisis mode. Kaye is a cattle farmer, but she does things completely differently to most: she raises Dexter cattle, a small, compact Irish breed that have a much smaller ecological footprint, and who fulfil the permaculture principle of playing at least two roles in the ecosystem Kaye has set up. In this case, the roles are providing meat and milk, both of an exceptional quality, and an ongoing supply of manure, which Kaye turns into rich, worm-filled compost.

Kaye grew up in a farming family in the southern coastal city of Adelaide, in cherry and apple orchards, and pursued horticulture as a career for much of her adult life. Convinced by her heritage that there was nothing 'hard or unusual' about growing things, she took TAFE (Technical and Further Education) courses to bolster her knowledge and fulfil her desire to be self-reliant—she learned to drive a tractor, use a chainsaw and back up a trailer with the best of them.

'It made me very hands-on,' she says, 'and it made me think that I could do anything that I wanted to do.'

As we talk, I'm struck by the similarities between Kaye and my mum. Both are physically capable, TAFE-educated women to whom the thought of failure never seems to occur. Both have partners who, while supportive, have played backup roles to the women's practical ambitions. And both are deeply concerned with caring for and regenerating the land on which they work.

Kaye came to permaculture—a method of agricultural design and planning that works with natural ecosystems rather than against them—after reading about peak oil.

'It scared me a little bit to think that we could be so vulnerable and reliant on oil and petrol, and perhaps we needed to look at other ways of doing things that weren't so reliant on one item. I thought, well, the best thing to do would be to have some land and become self-sufficient in every way that you can. Your own water, your own electricity and your own food. That's when I embarked on moving to Bellingen, and we found some land that was big enough to run some permaculture principles, which incorporates animal husbandry as well.'

She moved with her partner to Bellingen, on the Mid North Coast of New South Wales, a place with a long history of agriculture both traditional and innovative. It was there that she took her first permaculture design course and completely shifted her perspective on farming. She learned that humanity was taking from the land seven times what it could supply in return, that traditional farming methods were destroying the health of the soils and local ecosystems, and that current attitudes towards the land were wildly destructive. She did not want to continue to participate in that system.

'I want to be someone who is treading lightly on the earth, rather than just taking all of the goodness out of it,' she tells me, which is, after all, why she chose the Dexter cattle, who literally have a lighter step.

Interestingly, all the farmers she knows who run Dexters are also women, and are also heavily invested in the ongoing health of their land. Kaye tells me that in the permaculture course she did when she first moved to Bellingen, more than twenty out of the thirty students were women. Even in her mainstream horticulture courses, she says, there were more women than men—about a sixty-forty split. While there are a lot of women who want to be involved in permaculture in her area, they often find themselves stymied by the most practical, and most insurmountable, obstacle.

'It boils down to money,' she says. 'I'm lucky because I was given free rein and I could do what I wanted to [on the land]. Of the other women, not very many of them have land. Unless you've got the land, you can't really do much.'

•

Although Australian farming women contribute at least 48 percent of farm income through their work both on and off the farm, they own only a tiny fraction of agricultural land. This is a pattern that repeats globally, where women produce 80 percent of the world's food and own less than 20 percent of the land. In Australia, just over half of the country's landmass is devoted to agriculture, which produces 93 percent of the food the country consumes. The Australian agricultural industry also feeds forty million people worldwide every day via exports. This country has been farmed for many thousands of years, and women have always been a major part of that work. But, at least in post-colonial Australia, women's contributions—and their access to agricultural autonomy—have often been dismissed, avoided or intentionally silenced. After 1891, census protocol stopped referring to women who worked on farms as 'engaged in agricultural pursuits', in order to avoid giving the impression that 'women were in the habit of working in the fields'. This meant that women's work on farms simply wasn't recorded for the next hundred years. Until 1994, the official census description of farm women was 'sleeping partner, nonproductive'.

This clearly does not line up with the facts of Australian agriculture. Of the 134,000 farms in Australia, 99 percent are family-run, which means they have women involved in their operation on at least some level. While official stats say women make up 28 percent of the agricultural workforce, that's not even taking into account the fact that most women who live and work on farms are employed in a plethora of roles that don't fit traditional notions of what farm work may look like—but without which farms would simply cease to function.

•

Most of the media that urban Australia consumes about farming women comes in the form of those ABC News videos that pop up in my Facebook feed every now and then, profiling gung-ho cowgirls wrangling cattle from horseback on ranches the size of France. For most women on farms in Australia, life doesn't really look like that. In fact, a lot of the labour in the country, particularly among traditional agricultural families, still falls along heavily gendered lines. Men tend to work in the fields, and women tend to work in the home, doing the bookkeeping, the ordering, all the finances, the housework, the childcare, and, depending on how remote they're living, the homeschooling as well. It has been an uphill battle to get this work recognised as work.

The Invisible Farmer Project has been telling the stories of women on the land in order to have their contributions to agriculture recognised and valued. Among the many women featured are dairy farmers, winemakers, pig farmers and organic chicken farmers, and all of them participate in community programs, farmers' groups, local schools and initiatives like tourism, value-adding and farmstays. All of the women I spoke to for this chapter are similarly involved in their communities, and this seems to reflect something I've heard over and over in my research: rural women are the glue that holds their communities together. Let us not forget the ongoing legacy of the Country Women's Association; let's not ignore, either, the fact that most of the charities that have been formed to provide aid to drought-stricken farms are run by women.

I spoke to Tash Johnston from one of those charities, Drought Angels, which has been running for four and a half years. They work to provide not only financial and material support to drought-affected families, but also emotional support. Their main role, Tash says, is to show the farmers that people do care about them.

'All you can do is just keep trying to let these people know that they're not alone, people do care, they're not forgotten about,' she says.

When I ask why so many of these charities are run by women,

she's quick to point out that the men are doing a great job too. Still: 'Farmers are so proud. They're like, "Oh no, no, I don't need help, I don't need this." But when a couple of women jump out of a ute (utility vehicle) and give them a smile, and go, "Hey! How ya going? We've got some goodies for you!", they can't say no.'

The fundamental work Drought Angels does is emotional—providing compassion and care. Tash recognises that women regularly take on this kind of work during times of crisis, pointing to the many women in Brisbane who assisted relief efforts after the 2010–2011 Queensland floods by collecting clothing donations and cooking food for the people doing the hard work of clean-up.

'Physically we are a bit more limited, we are less physically strong, to be lifting shovels of mud through houses or whatever. What we can do is cook meals and help feed the people who are out there doing physical labour. I'm not a women's libber or any of that kind of rubbish. I just think we're more compassionate.'

I find this attitude fascinating—Tash's reluctance to identify as a women's libber points to a deep social conservatism that I've come to expect from many residents of rural and regional Australia, but is also totally paradoxical, considering she is describing just how valuable coded-feminine work really is to communities in times of crisis. In much of the literature that interviews women farmers and rural women, going back as far as the 1980s and '90s, interviewees indicate both a discomfort with identifying as feminist and a satisfaction with performing the gendered work that they do. Women in the country tend to do work that doesn't look like urban stereotypes of farm work, but their work is what repairs communities after disasters, prepares them for future crises, and insulates them against a largely indifferent general populace. Rural women—those people who are propelling the industry that every Australian needs to survive—do not need the gospel of gender preached to them. They tend to be busy getting on with things. What people tend to take issue with is a lack of recognition, and that's a problem that persists to this day. Whether it is in the fields or in the home office, whether it's gendered or not, the work women do in the Australian agricultural industry is clearly vital. Nevertheless, stories of sexism in the industry abound.

Particularly, it seems, when it comes to inheritance. Because most farms are family-run, most farms change hands from parent to child—almost always from father to son. According to Leonie Blumson, a PhD candidate at the University of South Australia studying women's inheritance in farming, just 10 percent of farm successors in Australia are daughters. Often patriarchs are more likely to sell the farm than pass it down to a female inheritor. My mum knows a woman in exactly this situation. She's about my mum's age, and is one of the very few women who are actively involved in cane farming, out in the fields. She loves cane farming, comes from a long line of cane farmers, is passionate about the work. She's also an only child, and gay, and without a man in the picture her father refuses to give her the family farm. She now leases her own land elsewhere.

·

The Invisible Farmer Project says that farming women are 'key agents of change and innovation', pointing particularly to their work in natural disaster recovery, food security and sustainability. This does seem to be supported by the stories of the women I've interviewed—they are all creating change with their work, many in the field of sustainable and regenerative farming. Why are women so much more involved in the cutting edge of agriculture than they are in traditional farming? It might be because women are still, despite all their hard work and contributions, outsiders in agriculture. If you already occupy a marginalised position, you have more freedom to do radical or subversive things, because you are necessarily already radical and subversive. For many farming women, this radical perspective can come from something as simple as being a primary caregiver for children.

Rachael Treasure is a Tasmanian author and farmer who's heavily invested in regenerative agriculture. Another victim of patrilineal succession—her father let her ex-husband stay on the farm after the divorce, while she was forced off—she has strong opinions about women's involvement in agriculture.

'It's my belief that women need to really start to take ownership of the food production system and the management of soil health, because we are the gender that primarily are nurturers. It's essential that at some point women say "no" to what is happening.'

Rachael is appalled at mainstream agriculture's overuse of chemicals, its apparent lack of interest in sustaining the land's fertility, and its lineage of warfare-related practices and tools (including industrial pesticides and fertilisers adapted from chemical weaponry). For her, what needs to change in Australian agriculture is nothing less than a complete one-eighty— a return to a time when all agricultural gods were feminine, and nutritional knowledge was the realm of women.

Of course, this conversation doesn't necessarily need to be

gendered. What Rachael calls a feminine approach to the land is one that's nurturing, holistic, concerned with food webs; one that she calls masculine is chemical-based, unconcerned with soil health or the species that naturally grow, rapacious. But the shorthand she uses makes a simple and very effective point: women are more inclined to view farming and agriculture in a regenerative or holistic way because they are brought up to see the connections. They see the links between garden and kitchen and food and their children's well-being. It's women's role as mothers that makes them ideal custodians for the land—not something innate, but something tended to and reared within us as we are pushed (gently or otherwise) into the mould of motherhood. It allows us other levels of expertise. It lets us in on big secrets—not just how to look after our own kids, but how to care for everyone's mother: the Earth. More than one woman has brought this up while talking to me, or to others, about their participation in farming. Because many women still do the bulk of the childcare in their families, they are confronted more materially with their family's health, and how it fluctuates depending on the food they eat, the activities they do. Our gendered roles allow us to see around corners that are otherwise blind.

It's not that women are naturally or inherently more connected to the land because of our gender, but that a series of conspiring pressures has created in many women a certain keenness of eye for the natural environment, and its future. It's clear that the different ways we cultivate boys and girls contribute to the different ways that they grow up and relate to the land. For a long time, farming has been men's domain. Now that women are getting involved in greater numbers, a new perspective is at play, and certain long-held beliefs and practices are starting to change.

•

There's a growing demographic of young women who are moving to the country, some with a partner, many of whom are documenting their journeys via social media. It's a slow trickle at the moment, but every drop counts. Rachael says it's a natural right of every human being to be able to put our hands in the soil. People in cities can go their whole lives without doing that. No wonder we feel like something's missing. It's tempting to talk about feminine intuition and Mother Earth and natural, nurturing instincts, but I don't want to essentialise when it comes to figuring out why so many young women want to get back to the land. We all have our reasons, and they likely have nothing to do with gender, really. Maybe it's just that more young women than ever are not tied down by marriage or children; that we're educated enough to feel unfulfilled; that we're paying enough attention to the news, to the climate, to our society, to want to make something better. Maybe it's also an alluring thought, spending your days in hard physical work and ending up with something tangible at the end of it: eggs or fruit or just your first mustard sprout.

Victoria Taylor is a Londoner, born and raised. Growing up, she never had a garden. Now, though, she's been working at The Falls Farm on Queensland's Sunshine Coast for more than a year as a farmhand all-rounder. She has the warmth and passion in her voice I have come to expect when I talk to women who work on the land. When I catch her, she's just come in from frantically planting out beds in the market garden before she takes off on her first holiday since she took the job. She says she still thinks it's magic: putting a tiny seed into the earth, and a few weeks later pulling up a ruby-red beetroot the size of a cricket ball. I think it's a lovely way to put it, and I think about the sense of patience and mindfulness you need to grow things, and how paying attention to the process of vegetables fattening in the earth does turn into a kind of magic.

The Falls Farm is representative of a new wave of Australian farming. Owned by a couple who live and work in Brisbane, the farm is run by Christine Ballinger, the mother of the husband of the couple. On eighteen acres of former scrub in Mapleton, the farm encompasses a thriving market garden that supplies unusual, rare and heirloom varieties of vegetables, citrus and fruit to chefs and foodies in the area, as well as large tracts where the family has focused on restoring the land to how it once was before colonial farming. They've created a haven for local wildlife, a richly repopulated area of native trees and plants, and incredibly fertile soil, thanks to biological farming and permaculture practices.

Victoria was drawn to work at The Falls Farm not just by romantic notions of getting her hands dirty but also a willingness to look at the industry as a viable business opportunity.

'I was desperate to take control of what I was eating—it's the most important thing—but I also was really interested in it as a business. I love permaculture principles, I wish that everyone could be a hippie farmer walking around with bare feet all day every day, but I feel like there should be a balance. I feel like we should be able to work in beautiful environments but also that it can be a strong business.'

The business at The Falls Farm incorporates farm-gate selling, participating in local farmers' markets, a successful veggie box subscription service and luxury tourism via Smith

House, the attached restored colonial-era Queenslander. Victoria talks about how much she learns every day, how farming is both extraordinarily scientific and deeply creative, and how she relishes the opportunity to think things through while she labours physically. Like many women I speak to, her priorities have shifted since she began working on the farm. She can't imagine going back to working an office job after spending her days in the sunshine, breathing in the air, moving her body, reaching into the earth. I mention how similar her words sound to what I have heard from some of the young women I've spoken to for this book who are abandoning the modern world to enter convents—young women searching for meaning in their lives, in their case turning to spirituality; in hers, to the soil. She immediately sees the parallel.

Once again, I don't want to falsely essentialise. There are many women in agriculture who happily follow traditional, conservative farming practices, who think it is the best way to do things and are very reluctant to change. But anecdotally and statistically, more women are involved in innovative agriculture, like that happening on The Falls Farm, than any other kind of agricultural practice in Australia. Women from all backgrounds are recognising a broken system of food supply, and possibly something broken in themselves as well, and are choosing to go back to the land to work it out.

The big difference between the women who come from traditional farming practices and those who are choosing to enter it with a more innovative approach is that those women tend to come from the cities to the country, bringing liberal city ideals with them. Already existing outside of traditional rural communities, without a vested interest in social standing in those communities or in upholding the status quo, they have the opportunity to do things differently without fear of societal reprimand or isolation. Victoria says that she does not have a strong permaculture community around her on the Sunshine Coast—unsurprisingly, considering Queensland's overall conservatism—but it doesn't bother her. For other women, though, who've been in farming all their lives, innovation often takes different, more subtle forms.

•

As historian Bruce Pascoe describes in his incredible book *Dark Emu*, Australia has been cultivated for at least sixty thousand years. The original inhabitants of the land managed to settle into a remarkably harmonious way of living on this unique country, using agricultural practices that worked with, rather than against, their environment. Early white settlers described the fertility of the soil around Sydney and Melbourne, so rich and friable that horse's hooves would sink up to the ankle: the product of generations of yam farmers improving the earth with their crops and careful tending.

As Pascoe explains, the problem with Australian agriculture now is that much of it ignores that early wisdom, along with the newest scientific knowledge, to continue farming in ways that actively deplete the soil, decrease biodiversity and create an ongoing uphill battle against the natural way of things in the earth. Trying to get traditional broadacre farmers to change their methods is monumentally difficult. These practices are ingrained in family dynasties as untouchable traditions, passed down from father to son along with the land itself. Although dozens of landcare and natural resource management groups exist specifically to try to introduce new ways of doing things to those in agriculture, progress is frustratingly slow.

I am no longer surprised to find that a lot of the people involved in hastening that progress are women. At my mum's day job, where she works in natural resource management, the team on her current project—focused on improving water quality running off farms and onto the Great Barrier Reef—is 90 percent women. Many of the leading figures in permaculture and regenerative agriculture are women. Everywhere I look, the people making the changes are women—or, at least, women are disproportionately represented among them in an industry that is still, despite recent changes, stubbornly male.

•

Sue Middleton is a generous woman. I call her at 9 a.m. my time, forgetting that she lives—and has always lived—in Western Australia, which is two hours behind Queensland. Of course she's awake—she's a farmer—but she's also immediately accommodating of my mistake, and willing to share the abundance of knowledge she's acquired over a lifetime of farming and rural advocacy at 7 a.m., an hour which tends to be unconducive to any kind of cohesive thought for most people.

She's also from a far more traditional farming background than any of the other women I've spoken to, including my mother. But her traditional upbringing and current enterprises—broadacre grains, plus pigs, sheep and citrus—do not preclude her from being just as convinced of rural women's power as agents of change as I am.

Sue's career is dazzling. Born and bred in country Western Australia, she completed university and then went straight back to the land at the age of 22 with the goal of making rural and regional Australia prosperous. She's served on dozens of advisory boards, including the first Regional Women's Advisory Council in 1997, travelled extensively, and in 2010 was named Rural Woman of the Year by the Rural Industries Research and Development Corporation. In her work since setting that goal in her early twenties, while focusing on community development, rural resilience, landcare and natural resource management, she has realised that rural and regional Australia's prosperity is directly linked to the success of its women.

'I'm not interested in women's work because I'm a woman,' she tells me. 'I'm interested in women's work because it's really going to matter for where we're heading as a nation, and for where agriculture as an industry is heading.'

The example she uses to illustrate her point is the 2011 live export debate. It's a touchy subject for many Australians: locally raised sheep and cattle were being sent overseas to South East Asia, kept in terrible conditions during transport and slaughtered inhumanely upon arrival. She says that many influential agricultural men's responses were to either wash their hands of it—'It's not our responsibility'—or to propose completely banning live trade.

'The people who came in who solved that problem, who shifted that, were women. They shifted it because they looked at Indonesian families and said, these people need live trade because they have no refrigeration at the other end.' A group of women from the West Australian beef industry, led by local farmer Catherine Marriott, toured Indonesia in order to meet the people at the other end of the supply chain.

'Off of the back of that came the changes, to make sure that those animals can be slaughtered humanely.' The women's hands-on, in-person connection not only to people in the industry in Indonesia but to Indonesian families made all the difference to changing value systems that would keep everyone along the supply chain happy.

'We can be responsible,' Sue says. 'Those are our animals. Just because they've left the country doesn't mean we can't take responsibility for them. In Indonesia, life's a whole lot different. Their values for animals are different to the way we value animals. So if you want to bring those value systems together, we've got to understand a bit about their life and their challenges, and the fact that they eat a beef ball in a soup, not a piece of fillet steak. The women changed the conversation.'

This seems to me like the most invisible of invisible farming work: the unquantifiable, the personal, the communal. As Sue puts it, 'Women have a different way of working, and their different way of working is going to be really important to make sure that we manage the next ten years of change.' The collaborative approach demonstrated by many rural women to their challenges is going to be vital for Australia's ongoing, cross-cultural engagement with the rest of the world through trade because, she says, when women are driving the trade conversations, everybody wins.

The international interconnectedness that Sue mentions is by no means a new phenomenon. In 1994, newly formed non-profit organisation Australian Women in Agriculture put together the first International Women in Agriculture Conference, attracting 850 women from 34 countries to the biggest agricultural conference Australia had ever seen. It was also in 1994 that the Rural Woman of the Year award was first launched. The Australian

Women in Agriculture group has always been 'committed to ensuring that women influence the agricultural agenda', and has continued since the 1990s to run workshops to equip women with new, diversified skills, to retrain women on the land, and to make concerted efforts to preserve and improve rural communities. With women like Sue Middleton emerging from its initiatives, it seems pretty clear that their hard work is bearing fruit.

•

I remember Cyclone Larry. I had just turned sixteen, and had left home to live in Cairns with a friend of a friend of my mother's so I could attend high school in the city. Cairns would miss the brunt of the cyclone (if a Category 5 had passed through the city, it would have been catastrophic), so my parents instructed me to stay put while they weathered the storm an hour south.

We had the day off school. It was wildly hot, in the way only the tropics can be, even at dawn, which is when the wind started to pick up. Jenna and her fourteen-year-old son and I stayed in the house, listening to the radio and drinking tea, watching the sky go green and the palm trees reel in the wind. The radio warned us not to go outside, as a pair of garage doors was whipping around the streets. We all knew not to be seduced outside during the eye of the cyclone, but it was almost impossible to resist—I think I stood briefly in the backyard, listening to the shocked quiet, staring at the milk-green sky and smelling the ozone. It's the bit after the eye that really does the damage, because everything that's been blown in one direction is now picked up and flung in the other, creating total havoc.

My parents and six-year-old sister had gone to a friend's house down the road from their farm, where they huddled in the bathroom, all five of them. Larry had been declared a disaster situation, and evacuations were in order all along the coast. The house they took refuge in was in the rainforest—they still don't know why they decided to move there rather than wait it out in their newly purchased, empty, treeless cinderblock house. At the neighbour's house, early in the storm, a tree toppled onto the roof, smashing the skylight above them. They put my sister in the cupboard with a mattress over her, and held on tight.

Outside, the devastation was absolute. Driving home from Cairns the next weekend beside my shaken mother, I saw the rainforest on the hillsides begin to disintegrate as we drove farther south. It was as though someone had dragged a rake through the canopy, tearing off branches like blades of grass. The scene was brown and desolate. I remember thinking, Why would anyone stay here after this?

Only one person died in Larry, and it was from a heart attack—a testament to rural resilience if ever there was one. But it took a long time for the region—and my family—to recover. After the cyclone came one hundred days of rain, and I think realistically that this was more traumatic for my parents, who'd just moved from New Zealand to escape the perma-drizzle, than the storm itself. Everything grew mouldy. Laundry hung on the line for days and would never dry. When I go home now, the phantom stink of wet, musty linen still fills my head. And there was so much to clean up. Photos from the time show my parents in khaki farm clothes and strained smiles, deep hollows under their eyes, dragging debris out of the vanilla shadehouses and clearing the slopes around the house.

Larry was a rural rite of passage of the most extreme kind. Unfortunately, in the country, that's pretty much the only kind they've got. Talking to my mum about it now, she says what got her through it was the community around her. One morning in the weeks after the storm, some of the local women organised a morning tea for the whole town, set up tables in the community centre, invited everyone in, just to take their minds off the enormous job ahead of them for a few hours. Something as simple as a cup of tea and a scone bolstered her, she said. In all her years in the city, she never felt a sense of connection—to her community, to her work, to the land—like what she has now. She knows she was right to stay.

MATRIARCHAL SOCIETIES

Imagining Themyscira

When the DC Comics cinematic universe's first female-fronted film, *Wonder Woman*, was released in 2017, a collective sigh of envy went rippling through the femmosphere. Sure, the movie was good, and yes, the World War I–era plot was absorbing, but most of us chose to linger in the film's first twenty minutes, in the world from which Diana Prince came: Themyscira, the island of warrior women. It seemed like a kind of paradise. A land without men? Where women not only called the shots but spent their days training in combat and athletics, or pursuing one another in exciting lesbian romances? Sounds good to me, was the collective assessment on Twitter.

Directed by a woman, Patty Jenkins, and self-consciously focused on creating a strong female character that would be more than a trope, the film would inevitably be dissected endlessly by scores of fans and critics, receiving both adoration and condemnation. Everything from its star's political background (Israeli) to the appropriateness of its warrior women's costumes (various, depending on who you talked to) was picked apart, argued about and bickered over. We are so starved for heroic roles for women, we couldn't help but demand the world of this heroine; she was always going to fail us.

But what didn't fail us—what delighted us, almost universally—were the Amazons. Led by a phenomenal Robin Wright and with ranks swelled by CrossFit athletes, boxers and professional stuntwomen, the warrior women of Greek myth galloped onto the screen in leather and brass armour, doing their own stunts and shooting a bunch of German soldiers with flaming arrows, and they never once told each other not to cry. (In the audience, with six of my girlfriends, I cried uncontrollably.)

My favourite moment in the film comes within the first ten minutes. Hippolyta, the Amazon queen (played by Connie Nielsen) is showing her daughter Diana the legendary sword, forged by Zeus, that she will one day end up wielding. As baby Diana stares longingly at the sword, Hippolyta puts her hands on her daughter's shoulders, and her hands look just like my mother's hands: tough, wrinkled, weathered, with short nails and thick knuckles. It is a shock to see hands like that in a Hollywood movie, on a character designed to inspire admiration and awe—a little glimpse of what it might be like to see women I recognise on screen.

•

Wonder Woman was the creation of 1940s American writer and psychologist William Moulton Marston, who drew on early feminists, and his own wife and their shared life partner, for inspiration. As such, Wonder Woman was surprisingly progressive for a comic book character who first appeared in 1941. A lasso-slinging, Axis-fighting World War II heroine, she regularly upended the common 'damsel in distress' tropes of contemporary comics, freeing herself from bondage in practically every escapade—the sexual connotations of which has not escaped the examination of fascinated readers ever since. And although early volumes focused on her exploits battling the Nazis, throughout her nearly eighty-year history her backstory has developed into a rich reimagining of classical mythology—focusing, of course, on the warrior women of Greek myth: the Amazons.

You can see why Marston imagined Wonder Woman as the princess of the warrior women. For a 1940s man, he lived a remarkably modern life, cohabiting with his wife, fellow psychologist Elizabeth, who is rumoured to have given him the idea of a female superhero, and their polyamorous partner, Olive Byrne, who similarly helped inspire Wonder Woman in her appearance. An outspoken feminist and unabashed S & M enthusiast, Marston was not shy about believing women should be in charge—a conviction encouraged by his work developing the technology that would become the polygraph machine, during which he decided that women were both more honest and more efficient than men.

But Marston's own personal matriarchy, and his wholehearted committal to it, is an unusual one. For most of recorded Western history, the spectre of the matriarchy has been terrifying to the men in whose imaginations it loomed.

•

Matriarchy anxiety has been around since at least the Ancient Greeks. The notion of the Amazons was a kind of bogeyman for them, first floated by Homer in the *Iliad* in the eighth century BC, and then enthusiastically integrated into Greek myth of all kinds over the next few hundred years. They existed as a kind of titillating cautionary tale of what might happen if women were ever given the opportunity to rule as men did: savage, fearsome horse-riding enemies who cut off or cauterised their right breasts in order to better wield a bow and arrow, an unconquerable force come to visit upon the Athenians the unthinkable—women doing to men what men had long been doing to women. Like all scintillating bogeymen, the Amazons enjoyed a surge of popularity in Ancient Greece, featuring in art and story from the fall of Troy to the trials of Hercules to the battle for the freedom of Athens, and came to symbolise the necessary subjugation of women as foundation for Greek democracy and civilisation.

The myth of the Amazons has persisted in popular culture despite their falling out of vogue with the Ancient Greeks after about the fifth century BC. (I'm thinking particularly of 1970s and '80s pulp, and the timeless *Futurama* episode featuring 'death by snu-snu'.) Most depictions of Amazons or similar tribes of warrior women are fundamentally eroticised, fusing the frisson of fear at being overpowered by a traditionally subjugated gender—perhaps hell-bent on revenge—with the alluring idea of a bunch of busty, sex-starved jungle women fighting one another for access to a Real Man. But in the nineteenth century, a different kind of matriarchy anxiety surfaced, this time with a veneer not of fear or eroticism but paternal superiority.

Swiss law professor and scholar Johann Jakob Bachofen appears to be the first to suggest, in 1861, that the Amazons were historical fact, not myth. His suggestion that humankind had been matriarchal for most of our history was taken up with excitement, as his argument was that the switch from primitive, goddess-worshipping matriarchy to enlightened patriarchy was what had brought about human civilisation. 'The triumph of patriarchy brings with it the liberation of the spirit from the manifestations of nature,' he wrote, capitulating again to that old idea that women are incorrigibly physical, bound to the earth and their bodies, while only men have access to loftier pursuits of intellect and spirituality. It was a historical theory enthusiastically received by social scientists and then by generations of feminists, both seduced for different reasons by the idea of a matriarchal prehistory only recently overturned. This despite the fact that, even now, only dubious shreds of evidence have been found for the existence of a prehistorical matriarchy like the one Bachofen describes.

The existence of any matriarchies at all remains a topic of hot debate among anthropologists, particularly, it seems, because the stubborn definition persists that describes matriarchy as simply a gender-swapped patriarchy. But the societies that still exist today that have come to be described as matriarchies do not follow this pattern. In fact, there haven't been any societies discovered to date in which women dominate in the same way men do in patriarchies. The markers of patriarchy are dominance, individualism, oppression, championing of individual success, rigid social roles and aggressive tribal allegiances. Matriarchies don't simply replace the major players in this system with women. They completely change the game.

According to pre-eminent matriarchy expert Peggy Reeves Sanday, matriarchies are 'women-centred societies founded on principles of gender balance and a gift-giving economy', forming a 'culture that seeks peace and stresses the importance of nurturing the young, the old, the sick, and the poor'. Sanday makes a distinction between domination, a common means of control in patriarchal societies, and what she calls conjugation, or coming together, which is often highly valued in matriarchal communities.

Unlike other academics, Sanday includes egalitarian and gender-equal communities under the term 'matriarchy', which allows her to point to several existing societies as examples of the social system, particularly Indonesia's Minangkabau. German anthropologist Heide Göttner-Abendroth is another proponent of this definition, rejecting the idea that a matriarchy must consist of 'rule by women' and its accompanying ideological distortions, and instead putting forward the idea that matriarchies are 'true gender-egalitarian societies'.

Göttner-Abendroth also accurately points out that much of the academic body of work devoted to studying matriarchies suffers from the same hang-ups as does any field that focuses on women: a dismissing, diminishing and devaluing of the subject matter. Along with Sanday and other social scientists like her, Göttner-Abendroth is at the forefront of a reimagining of matriarchal studies that encompasses a broad range of non-patriarchal societies. For this, we owe them a lot—because our fascination with these almost inconceivable ways of living goes back more than two thousand years. We're still—*I'm* still—intrigued by the idea of a woman-centred society. What are they like? How are they different? And what might matriarchy look like today, after two thousand years of most of the world's societies being run strictly by men?

•

The Mosuo are one of the world's best-studied matriarchies. They're so famous for their unusual social system that parts of their homeland, in the Himalayan region of China near the border of Tibet, have become tourist hotspots for people wanting to get a good look at 'China's last matriarchy' amid its stunning natural surroundings. The Mosuo, who also call themselves the Na, are matrilineal—property and family runs through the mother's side, and extended families all live within the same home under a ruling elderly matriarch. Famously, the Mosuo don't adhere to common notions of marriage. Instead, they have what's known as 'walking marriages'. In this system, women who have come of age and passed puberty have their own quarters—called 'flowering rooms'—with doors that face out of the family compound towards the rest of the world. To these doors may come suitors, after dark, who, with the woman's permission, may stay until dawn, upon which he must return to his family's home. These relationships are the product of mutual affection, not arrangements or political motivations. Any children the pair has together remain part of the mother's family; her brothers, who also live in the maternal house, will take on a significant role in rearing the child. The biological father (for which there's no word in the Mosuo language) has no obligations to his children, but may present gifts at the mother's house, and perform chores for her family, in order to keep close ties; at certain points of the year, he will be honoured by his children in special ceremonies. Because no one is formally married, there's no divorce; when a couple feels the spark die, they simply cease their meetings. Women and men are free to have multiple partners, although most modern Mosuo report having only a few throughout their lifetimes, serial monogamy-style (some older women, on the other hand, reminisce about their thirty or forty partners over their lives). Mosuo relationships tend to last, the women say, because if you don't spend all your time with a man, you don't have anything to fight about.

A 2016 Vice documentary on the Mosuo interviews some of the men in a Mosuo village near the Burmese border. They are idle, happy; they cheerfully explain that men in the village do almost nothing. The women are responsible not only for property and inheritance, but all the housework, cooking, weaving and agricultural work, as well as making all the family's business decisions. Men are theoretically responsible for taking care of politics, helping to raise children and slaughtering livestock—though from the documentary you'd be forgiven for thinking they are mostly responsible for sitting around. One male writer, Ricardo Coler, travelled from his native Argentina to spend two months with the Mosuo in the late 2000s, and in a 2009 interview declared that 'Men live better where women are in charge: you are responsible for almost nothing, you work much less and you spend the whole day with your friends. You're with a different woman every night. And on top of that, you can always live at your mother's house.'

Tourism and modernisation in the region have contributed to growing anxiety among elders about a loss of culture, both through pandering to domestic tourists' exoticisation (and eroticisation) of Mosuo society, and through migration—young Mosuo people are moving to the cities in larger and larger numbers, where they take modern jobs and often enter into traditional relationships. I understand their nervousness; although there are other matrilineal societies in the world, the Mosuo are the only remaining culture that practises something like walking marriage. Their way of life is totally unique.

•

Peggy Reeves Sanday, the anthropologist who's been so instrumental in redefining matriarchy and applying the term to existing cultures and communities, spent much of her fieldwork with the Minangkabau people on the Indonesian island of Sumatra. They're considered to be the world's most populous matrilineal society, with about 4.2 million people. Throughout Indonesia, the Minangkabau are known for their fluency in literature and language, their wide diaspora and their egalitarianism. Although the people follow Islam, they have also incorporated their traditional ways, known as adat, which place women firmly at the centre of things. Like the Mosuo, the Minangkabau are matrilineal and matrilocal, meaning property and wealth is passed down through the mother's line, and families live in extended family groups within one shared home. Author and educator Carol P. Christ explains that this is fairly par for the course when it comes to modern matriarchies; what's more complex, and what kept Sanday visiting the Minangkabau for the better part of two decades, are the many subtle ways in which women in the culture are honoured, and in which egotism and domination are punished.

Christ draws a connection between the Minangkabau's construction of gender, their focus on nature, and their agriculture-based philosophy, which pays special attention to the process of rice farming. Rice shoots are tender and vulnerable, the people say, and must be protected and carefully nurtured; so, too, must women and children be protected and nurtured. Sanday says that among the Minangkabau, it's not individualism or competition that's celebrated; it's that term she uses, conjugation—

a coming together—along with the wisdom required to keep communities in that state. She uses the word 'politesse' to describe a social system in which everyone is expected to protect the weak, and in which violence of any kind is not tolerated. In a culture like this, there's no need to use violence to prevent violence because politesse so strongly sanctions any occurring in the first place. Politesse means every member of Minangkabau society learns to always look for ways to promote harmony in their families and their communities. It is, in effect, the opposite of a patriarchy: instead of striving to dominate each other, the people seek to collaborate with one another; instead of violence and control, they valorise protection and nurturing. A matriarchy clearly doesn't have to be a system in which women hold all the power—indeed, the Minangkabau men are expected to take charge of integrating politics, Islam and their culture's traditions while governing—but it is so different in what parts of culture it privileges as to be almost unimaginable.

•

Not all modern matriarchies can trace their lineage back generations. Perhaps the closest living relative to the Amazons of *Wonder Woman* are the women of Umoja, a village in Kenya that was founded in 1990 by Samburu woman Rebecca Lolosoli. No men are allowed in Umoja. In the nearly thirty years since its creation, it has become a refuge for dozens of women fleeing gendered violence, forced marriages and rape.

Samburu women are traditionally held in a deeply subordinate position to men. The practice of marrying very young girls to old men is common, as is female genital mutilation (FGM). In the 1990s, more than a thousand Samburu women reported being raped by British military forces (although an investigation by the Royal Military Police did not result in any prosecutions); these women were often turned away from their homes by their husbands, who considered them to be defiled when they discovered what had happened. It was in this climate that Rebecca Lolosoli began to speak out for her rights and those of her fellow Samburu women. When she was severely beaten by men from her village in retaliation, and her husband refused to say or do anything to protect her, she chose to leave, starting the women-only Umoja, which means 'unity' in Swahili. In 2007 she told the magazine *Satya*, 'We formed a village so we could protect one another. The problem is Samburu women have no rights—no right to own livestock or land, to go to school, even to choose a husband. If a Samburu man kills his wife, no one cares—he paid the dowry, so he owns her.'

The women of Umoja are economically independent, having set up a thriving trade selling their beading craftwork to tourists. Close to the village is a safari camp site, and guides often bring tourists to visit Umoja (men are allowed to visit, but not to stay). They are charged a small fee for entry and are encouraged to buy the colourful and intricate bead jewellery made by the village's residents. It's this economic independence that has been most disconcerting to Samburu men in the region. According to Lolosoli, local men attempted to build their own village specifically to block the tourist trade to Umoja. The women responded by buying the land from underneath them.

Around fifty women live in Umoja, along with two hundred children. The village welcomes survivors of FGM, women and children with HIV, orphaned and abandoned children, and women fleeing domestic violence and forced marriage, and offers them economic and social independence and the support and care of an ever-strengthening community. They run a school for children from villages throughout the region, promoting education to all Samburu. Although no men are allowed to live in the village, many of the women still want to have children, so trysts or relationships with men outside are common. In a documentary, however, all of the women interviewed laughed at the idea of ever wanting to be married again.

Satellite villages following similar practices have started to pop up in the surrounding areas. In the YouTube comments underneath a documentary on the village, hundreds of women sound off—in jest or otherwise—about longing to move to a village just like it. A village of only women, surrounded by thorns and barbed wire, where every woman has equal status and gives just 10 percent of her income towards the running of the group, where Lolosoli has been democratically elected as chairperson for nearly thirty years—yeah, that sounds pretty good, actually.

•

I can see the appeal of these matriarchal communities. I'm not surprised that Western feminists have latched on to the idea, particularly considering many still subscribe—however romantically—to the exciting notion of a long, prehistoric matriarchal past. In the 1970s, there was a small but significant back-to-the-land movement among American lesbians, and to this day there are several flourishing (although, usually, ageing) women-only communities in rural parts of the United States. But I must be honest: as I read and watched, and absorbed these stories of matriarchies and matrilineal societies, often reported with such

wonder and awe, I felt uncomfortable. The truth is, this matriarchy stuff rubs me the wrong way at a very subtle level, like
fine-grit sandpaper, for reasons that author Cynthia Eller has
articulated better than I can. In the introduction to her book
*Gentlemen and Amazons: The myth of matriarchal prehistory, 1861–
1900*, she says, 'The gendered stereotypes upon which matriarchal myth rests persistently work to flatten out differences
among women; to exaggerate differences between women and
men; and to hand women an identity that is symbolic, timeless
and archetypal, instead of giving them the freedom to craft identities that suit their individual temperaments, skills, preferences,
and moral and political commitments.'

Yeah, I thought, totally surprised and totally in agreement as
I read it. There's the problem. Except for places like Umoja—
or Themyscira—where men are banned and women do everything, these communities don't look like the paragons of feminine
freedom I wanted to see. I love the idea of a matriarchy in
theory—but in practice it looks an awful lot like the same old
constrictive shit, designed to keep women in one lane and men in
another. All this stuff about nurturing life and putting children at
the centre of things felt alien and deeply discomforting to me, with
my profound lack of interest in childbearing and motherhood.
But I don't think the problem is necessarily solely with these
communities; the problem is that my personal tapestry is so shot
through with capitalism and patriarchy that it's impossible for me
to unpick. How do I know I wouldn't want kids if I was born a
Mosuo woman? How much of my sense of ambition and competi-
tiveness is the product of me, and how much of my culture?

I'm aware of my privilege—I often joke about how the only
way to make me *more* privileged would be to turn me into a man.

The truth of the matter is, I don't often feel oppressed by the patriarchy. Having aged out of street harassment, I now walk blithely through the streets of my town unbothered by car horns or shouts. I live the fairly cloistered life of your average inner-city 'creative', which means I often don't go out at night, into a world that's overtly hostile to women. I have the luxury of forgetting the patriarchy exists, forgetting that the deck is stacked against me, because realistically, in most ways—my class, my ethnicity, my sexuality—it's not.

But the patriarchy still gets its tendrils into me, unnervingly, making me itch. I read about matriarchies and I feel myself prickle at the thought of living in a 'child-centred' society, and then I am plunged into self-doubt. Why don't I want that? How much of my very being has been altered by living in a culture that actively denigrates motherhood, ignores children, glorifies personal achievement at the expense of others? How much can I blame on patriarchal capitalism, and how much is inherent within me? I watch the beginning of *Wonder Woman* again, and stop as soon as Diana leaves the island. Like many other women watching that film, I want to stay on Themyscira with the Amazons; I want to begin to learn myself again in the company of women. Of course, even Themyscira is the product of a patriarchy—originally the Athenian Greeks, and then the 1940s comic book industry, however progressive William Moulton Marston may have been. And even modern-day matriarchies still have male individuals. If I really wanted to learn myself in the company of women, I'd need to go live with the women of Umoja in Kenya. Or I'd need to continue the work of building my own community of women. As I wrote and researched this book, I felt the threads between us tighten; I felt our web strengthen. I am lucky—so lucky—that my work has brought me into the circles of these inspiring people. In my own community of women, I am supported and challenged, nurtured and reprimanded, reminded over and over not to confuse my own experience with others'. My friendships have deepened, my social sphere expanded; I feel apprenticed to the wealth of wisdom all my contacts have shared with me. I don't mean to leave men out of things—well, I sort of do. The point of this book was to address the fact that, for so long, I've felt like groups of women have existed at the margins of a society that privileges men in all their forms. I wanted to spend some time putting those women at the centre of things. I did not expect it to change me so much.

While writing this book, I tried to immerse myself in communities of women. Quickly it became clear to me that I already lived in a community of women—or mostly women. Nearly everyone on the team who will sell and publicise my book, almost all of my friends, my bosses and the people with whom I collaborate professionally are women. All of my fellow PhD students. My mother. My sister. How many of us live in what could be our own, self-constructed matriarchies? With our open-eyed friends, doing the hard work of pushing against the current of capitalism and patriarchy, actively loving one another, centring the group rather than the individual.

What would a matriarchy look like for Western women? Jessa Crispin's book *Why I Am Not a Feminist* touches on it a little when she turns her laser gaze to the shameful aping of patriarchal power systems done by white women in white woman–dominated industries. A matriarchy would not consist of women copying men down to the sneers and the power stances; it would consist of kicking the door open to those behind us, not kicking it shut. It might look like letting our children, boys, girls and others, cry when they felt the need to, wear what they wanted, love who they pleased (with their loved ones' permission). It wouldn't be a utopia—can you imagine the social anxiety that would come with living in a gift-based society, considering the drowning sensation I feel shopping for my family every Christmas?—but it would be something different, something, maybe, better. We would have to take down our greatest ambitions from the dusty, untouched shelves in our minds, and turn them over, looking for a maker's mark: did we come born with this, or was it put in there by those itching tendrils? Should we keep it, or should we put it aside?

Can we choose to build our own matriarchies, by choosing to turn away from what's expected of us as women? By resisting the tide that wants to push us apart, can we invoke politesse, and independence, and make our own islands of Themyscira, wherever they might be?

There is, obviously, a difference between the women-only paradise of the Amazons and the woman-centred co-ed culture of a matriarchy. It's unfair of me to conflate them. But it seems that in popular culture, we can't help it. The concept of an egalitarian or mother-focused society is so difficult to grasp that we have to remove men from the equation to bring it into focus.

•

There's still some resistance to the term 'patriarchy'. At this point in time, though, it feels beyond silly to try to refute it. For whatever reason (religious, political), most of the world's societies put men—patriarchs—at the top of the social pyramid. In the West, this means that traditionally male traits like ambition, aggression, dominance, egotism and physical strength are prized above others. It means women and girls are taught, sneakily, implicitly, to prioritise male attention and male approval. It means we must respect men in positions of power, let them do things to us, coddle and baby them, let them get away with murder. In practice, this looks like male-dominated industries, male-focused entertainment, persistent and demoralising objectification of women, the infuriating exhortations to women to simply be more like men, and the denigration and devaluing of traditionally feminine traits and pursuits, like motherhood, emotion, intimacy, gentleness and playfulness. Basically, it is a huge bummer. Combine patriarchy with capitalism and you've got an even bigger bummer: a system that exploits our rigid gender divide to make us unhappy, in order to keep us pumping money into the economy in a vain attempt to stem the flow of misery.

Individual men don't have to actively oppress women in order for patriarchy to continue to thrive. Patriarchy is the trellis upon which we train all our social interactions; it is at once common to all of us and bigger than any of us. And because of this, when I read about matriarchies, I can barely get my mind around them. Not because I can't believe they exist—I can—and not because they are difficult to understand—they're not—but because I cannot imagine how to practically apply their theories to the Western world. I find it near impossible to imagine my own culture as a matriarchy. The dream of a modern Themyscira is a fleeting, vaporous one. I can't catch hold of it.

11

NUNS

A radical order

Sister Maryanne has agreed to meet me in the café at St Vincent's Hospital in Darlinghurst, Sydney. I am very nervous. I have never met a nun before, but in the past few months I have become obsessed with them. She is running late, and I don't know what to expect, but when she appears, small and fine and dressed in a forget-me-not blue fleece vest, she hugs me straightaway, and I feel my nerves dissipate like smoke.

•

I first came to think about nuns through music. In 2017 the *Guardian* published an article by musicologist and conductor Laurie Stras, on a fascinating book of anonymous Renaissance-era motets that she had unearthed while flicking through a bibliography of sixteenth-century music prints. One of the motets was called 'Salve sponsa Dei'—bride of Christ. Stras deduced that the music—startling, ethereal, almost heretically dissonant in places, and written for five female voices—was the work of nuns. After a period of sleuthing, Stras came to believe that the book of motets was written by one nun in particular: Leonora d'Este, the youngest daughter of Lucrezia Borgia. I was hooked on the story: an Italian princess, raised by nuns after the death of her mother, commits herself to the abbey at age eight and becomes abbess by age eighteen, gracefully bowing out of the world of nobility that would have required her, more likely than not, to be married off to someone for her family's political gain. Instead, she lived out her days in the company of women, meditating, playing her instruments and composing the lush and gorgeous five-part polyphonies Laurie Stras rediscovered only a few years ago.

Since learning about Leonora, I have been unable to put away my romanticism about nuns. I am bewitched by stories of life in the convent. I read the Catholic literature and all the words sound like incantations to me: catechetical, ecclesiastic, liturgy, compline, canticle, charism. I say the syllables and I wonder. Sometimes I feel like my life is too busy—too much— to bear. I am trying to earn money. I am trying to make something of myself. I am trying to maintain a strong relationship with my partner, care for my sister and my friends, establish a career, navigate interpersonal conflict, decide what I want from my life, convince myself that I am doing the right thing. Now I find myself thinking covetously about stepping out of all that, like a dropped dress, and into religious life.

I imagine the breathtaking lightness that might come with letting go of pride, my favourite sin. You have to be humble to be a nun, don't you? I consider doing away with possessions, with personal ambition; I weigh up whether I would ever be able to stick to a vow of obedience. I think with relief, and then regret, and then relief again, of never having to wear make-up. The fact that I am not religious—that none of my family are, not parents or grandparents or distant aunts—does not even cross my mind.

·

In almost every major religion, you will find women who have devoted themselves to a monastic lifestyle of religious contemplation and service to their community. There are Buddhist nuns, Taoist nuns, Hindu nuns, Orthodox nuns, Protestant and Anglican nuns—but, of course, the nun figure in the popular consciousness is the Catholic nun, resplendent in black-and-white habit, preferably with a long rosary hung from her belt.

Christian religious women have been living in cloistered, sex-segregated conditions since at least 300 AD. These early nuns tended to be virgins or widows who devoted their lives to emulating Christ, and were the first to take up the veil as a symbol of their religious commitment. At the time, a veil was a garment worn only by married women; the nuns chose it to show that they were the brides of Christ. From early days, different groups of devoted women adopted different attitudes towards their ways of life: some remained secluded away from society in order to better devote their lives to prayer, while others went out into their surrounding community to perform charitable work, usually among the poor and ill. Over time, the vows of chastity, poverty and obedience were officially adopted. Chastity is fairly self-explanatory, though enforced to varying extents—some nuns today are still forbidden to even touch a man. Poverty means that nuns must forsake all worldly possessions, relying on their order for financial and material support, a vow that symbolises their trust in God to provide. Obedience requires nuns to respect the decisions of those superior to them, going where commanded and taking on responsibilities entrusted to them.

Technically, 'nun' is the term used in Catholicism to describe a woman religious who remains almost completely cut off from the rest of the world, in a closed convent along with her fellow nuns. These contemplative nuns do not interact with the outside world, except in very rare cases and only with permission from the bishop; some visitors are allowed, but only into a special room with a grille through which they may speak to the nuns, called the grated parlour. 'Sister' is the correct word for those most of us think of as nuns—religious women who participate in the community, usually in roles of education and healing. But realistically—and the Catholic Church will back me up on this—we can, and do, use the two terms interchangeably, and these days nuns, and their levels of engagement with the world, really exist along a spectrum from completely cloistered to actively pursuing demanding careers. Regardless of what you call them, these women share a devotion to God and the three vows (at a minimum—some orders require more vows, such as charity, devotion to life, or stability).

The vows are taken by almost all Catholic nuns even to this day, and it's modern Catholic nuns that I really want to focus on, particularly those who stuck around through and after the Second Vatican Council: the moment when everything changed.

•

I have to make a distinction between early modern nuns in Europe—those of the Middle Ages and the Renaissance—and modern ones, particularly those of the nineteenth century and onwards. But I desperately want to talk about those early nuns at least for a moment, because I am *fascinated* by them. I can't get into the nature of nuns, and particularly their feminist credentials, without also recognising the significant paradox the nuns of history pose. For some, the convent was a source of freedom and relief from relentless childbearing and gendered oppression. For others, it was nothing less than a prison.

This dichotomy seems to have fallen along lines of class, beauty and ability. Poor European families who could not afford wedding dowries for their daughters often sent them to convents, which required far more modest dowries than potential husbands did. Aristocratic women—like Leonora d'Este— were much more likely to be among those to choose a life in the convent, usually in order to avoid the unpleasantness of being a woman in the nobility. (The option of living out your days in the abbey was also made much more appealing by having a wealthy family willing to make frequent donations to ensure your comfort.) But even they were in the minority. Most aristocratic women in convents were forced into taking the veil—daughters who were too ugly to be married off, or those with disabilities, or simply those who would have bankrupted their families were they to be married to other members of the nobility.

In his book *Nuns Behaving Badly*, self-described archive mouse Craig Monson digs through hundreds of Vatican documents relating to convents of the period, and what he describes is closer to parody than piety: scores of aristocratic daughters sent off to the cloister with feather mattresses and embroidered curtains to decorate their cells, and male clergy running around exasperatedly after wayward nuns and their families who insisted on flouting church rules about contact with the outside world.

There are even stories of certain small-statured nuns sneaking into the ruota, a rotating barrel-like mechanism used for passing items from the outside world into the cloister, in order to take off on a jaunt outside convent walls.

With so many women involuntarily committed to the convents—in some parts of Europe they accounted for 14 percent of the female population—it's no surprise that there are several reports of nuns famously behaving badly. In the seventeenth century, one group of nuns burned down their convent in an attempt to be returned home; others, a hundred years earlier, were charged with performing magic and disciplined by the local clergy (I just cannot get enough of this). Nuns regularly proved a source of contention to the Church, either for this overtly unruly kind of behaviour, or for the more subtle rebellions like Leonora d'Este's, whose music was a point of much debate—some members of the Church believed the nuns' polyphony was angelic, but others considered it unbecoming of brides of Christ, arguing that it would entice the sisters to vanity thanks to its wild popularity with the layfolk of the late Middle Ages.

It appears that the convents have always presented something of a conundrum to the Church. Places designed to shunt women out of sight often end up fomenting some kind of thrilling discord or another, whether it's setting fire to your cell or writing celestial serenades. And nuns still present something of a conundrum, for the Church, for me, for all of us, I think: How do we slot the nun into our preconceptions of what a woman ought to be? Deliberately renouncing sexuality, marriage and motherhood, she neatly removes herself from being reduced to the level of her desirability or her sexual activity; her religious status affords her protection, a sense of the formidable, and deeply culturally ingrained respect. Her habit marks her as set aside from other women: the wimple replaces the hair, that most feminine attribute; the robe covers the sensuous form; the dress transforms the body, liberating the spirit from both her own flesh and others' desires. She gives up her possessions, leaves her family and devotes her life to her community, whether through prayer or action, and in this way is completely selfless—nuns are often spoken of as laying down their lives for the good of others. But she is also deeply devoted to herself, in ways not many other women can afford to be.

•

Sister Maryanne turned eighty in 2019, a year that also marked her sixtieth jubilee with the Sisters of Charity, an Australian order that has worked in education and health care since 1838. The order was founded by Irish nun Sister Mary Aikenhead, who devoted her life in Australia to service of the poor—a cause which is now the Sisters' fourth vow. This has manifested in the order's long history of aiding women on the margins of society, along with LGBTQ populations and HIV-positive people, including facilitating some of the first needle and syringe exchanges, during the HIV crisis in the 1980s—in other words, pretty radical stuff for an order of the Catholic Church.

Sister Maryanne seems to have recognised this vow of service to the poor as meaning much more than simply providing aid to those in financial distress. Forgive me—I know this sounds corny as hell—but talking with her at the wobbly table in the St Vincent's Hospital café makes me feel richer in spirit. And calmer. And at the same time like a tiny, ignorant baby bird.

Maryanne entered the convent in 1957, when she was

seventeen, as soon as she'd graduated from high school. She had been taught by Sisters of Charity, and says the choice to enter the convent was obvious to her: she wanted to be like them.

'We saw the women who were in the convent, and they were women who had a real sense of themselves, a sense of purpose. Women who had a vision. Women who led the Church in sort of this . . . underbelly way.'

The process of becoming a Catholic nun is not particularly straightforward. First, you have to become an aspirant; once both you and the order have agreed on your entering, you become a postulate, or an official candidate. Then you enter the novitiate stage, which can last several years—in Sister Maryanne's case, two and a half. Then you can take your vows, usually in two stages: first and final. The first are renewed on a year-by-year basis, and the final are, well, final.

Her father resisted her choice to join the order ('He said, "What have I done wrong for you to want to be a nun? Are you making up for the sins in my life?"'), and Maryanne herself worried that she'd never be allowed to eat chocolate ice cream again ('I was just a grown-up schoolgirl. I was—most of us were—naive, really naive.'), but once she was through the initial stages, and she began training, and then working, as a teacher, she began to settle in to life as a nun. And it has been a *life*.

With the support of her community, she has visited Bangladesh and India, China, South America and the United States, to carry out work with World Vision, local communities of women, and both Harvard and Boston universities. She assisted women's trade organisations in Peru during the 1980s, when the Shining Path was terrorising poor communities; some of her friends and fellow Sisters died during the civil unrest. She holds a Bachelor of Arts, a postgraduate degree from Harvard Graduate School of Education, and a PhD in theology from Boston College. She is a visiting professor at the School of Theology and Ministry at Boston College, where she taught every summer for thirty years; she is also a Professor of Practical Theology at the Jesuit College of Spirituality, Victoria, part of the Australian University of Divinity. She sits on the board of St Vincent's Health Australia. She is the author of numerous articles, chapters and books on spirituality, theology, feminism and priesthood. She says it's the support of her community that's allowed her to do it all—that the whole point of being a nun is exactly that.

'The essence of a religious life now, I would argue, is that you've got a community who share your vision of mission, who share your commitment to, for us, people on the margins of life. We will back that. We have got money to enable and support you in that. You're not working on your own. We're all in this together. That backing means the integral aspect for me of religious life now has gone from, "I wanted to be a nun like them," to "I want to live a life of real dedication, of real commitment." Because I really believe in my career.'

•

We can't talk about Sister Maryanne's career—we can't talk about the lives of any contemporary nuns—without talking about Vatican II. Officially called the Second Ecumenical Council of the Vatican, Vatican II was held from 1962 to 1965, and it completely upended almost everything about how the Catholic Church related to the common people, including the role of nuns. For the first time, the laity would be able to hear sermons spoken in their own language, rather than Latin; and for the first time, nuns were encouraged to shed their habits, adopting dress closer to that of the people in the communities around them. Pope John XXIII asked women religious to look again at the wisdom of their orders' founders to find inspiration for their missions. For many nuns, this meant leaving their cloistered life and going out into the world, working in their communities, attending universities and following innumerable paths towards fulfilling their vocations.

The Sisters of Charity began to move away from a monastic lifestyle—in which visits to family were curtailed, everyone wore habits made of thick black serge, and a strict schedule of prayers had to be followed, and towards a way of life in which they could freely pursue their true vocations, in the spirit of their fourth vow: service to the poor.

For Sister Maryanne, who had already been in her order almost ten years when the council closed, the changes represented the end of an extended childhood and the beginning of a spiritual maturity—not just in herself, but in the Church.

'In that period of time,' she says, 'we were like adolescents. But that's because we were emotionally adolescent, and we had to grow up, and we did. So, religious life itself has grown up, and the change of habit has become a change of habit.'

For the record, she hated wearing the habit, despite its figure-disguising qualities (she tells me she used to be a lot larger than she is now, and being hidden by the thick black serge was an added bonus of being a Sister). The heavy wool was completely impractical for Australian summers, and it was unhygienic, because there was no way you could wash it as often as you'd like. She felt de-feminised by the men's handkerchiefs they carried and the men's shoes they wore—though she remembers a certain way to wear your wimple, 'if you really were a bit keen on how you looked', with a gentle upward curve over the brow. She laughs. 'Vanity is vanity.'

•

When Sister Maryanne speaks, I am transfixed. The last time I felt like this, I was in Japan with my mother, at a Buddhist temple in the mountains near Nara, watching the only nun in the community put together the evening meal. There I felt the same sense of awe, the sense of being in the presence of a master, that I feel now with Sister Maryanne. I realise with a jolt halfway through our meeting that the reason I am transfixed is because she is a formidable philosopher and I have the privilege of listening to her hold forth. I feel like a student again, studying a subject I didn't know I would love. I wonder if this is how many women before me have felt upon joining a convent that promised to nurture their inquisitive natures, their curiosity into the mystery of all things.

Talking with friends about writing this chapter, we laugh about how obvious the choice would be to us, were we to have lived five hundred years ago. If you were a woman who was fascinated by maths, or history, or music, would you resign yourself to a life of laundry, a marriage of convenience or political advantage, a litany of children, the tyranny of childbirth (and possibly, if you didn't have the sense to shut up about your fascination with maths or history or music, being carted away to an insane asylum for impossible-to-repress women)? Or would you chuck it all in, cut your hair, and join a convent, where you could spend at least part of your day working away on whatever puzzle of the mind called to you, in between prayers and fasting and a spot of tending to the poor and the sick?

I'm quite sure life in a sixteenth-century convent was nowhere near as carefree as I'd like to imagine it—particularly if you were not, for example, a Ferrarese princess. (During the pre-modern period, there were actually two categories of nuns within the convents: those from noble backgrounds, who got to spend their time in prayer and reflection, and those from common families, who basically ran the places—cleaning, cooking and taking care of the business of keeping the convent afloat.) But nuns do still have something of the subversive about them, a sense of female conspiracy hiding in plain sight. Take up the habit and secrete yourself away in the heart of the most conservative institution available to you, and there, where no one would think to look, you may pursue your heart's true desires.

There is indeed a long history of women running away to the convent to escape whatever cruelty was about to be visited upon them—usually arranged or forced marriages. As Jo Piazza puts it in her delightful book documenting the lives of several fascinating modern nuns, *If Nuns Ruled the World*, many early nuns joined convents in order 'to escape being consigned to a life of procreation'. Even though orders from the Catholic Church required nuns to be cloistered up until the seventeenth century, able to accept visitors or go out into the world only with the bishop's permission, we can see from the wealth of historical evidence that these rules did not prevent many of the women in Middle Ages convents from living rich lives. Look at Leonora d'Este: her connections to her aristocratic family meant that her convent received gifts of grand organs, sheet music and song books, and invitations to meet and collaborate with other great musical minds of the era. She's not the only nun from the Middle Ages to contribute art and thought to the annals of history. Hildegard of Bingen, a nun who wrote during the twelfth century, appears to have been a bona fide genius, writing dramas, poetry, many pieces of music, possibly the first ever opera, and casually inventing her own language—all of which seems like it would be difficult to do were she busy raising a family. Mexican nun Juana Inés de la Cruz was a similar polymath who wrote poetry, theatre and prose, and whose seventeenth-century philosophical writings criticising misogyny and male hypocrisy earned a condemnation from the Bishop of Puebla; her poem, 'Primero Sueño' ('First Dream') is considered among the greatest contributions to poetic literature written in the Americas.

But with the rise of the women's movement, and the availability to women of more vocations than mother, wife or nun, the number of nuns in the world has been steadily declining since its peak in the 1960s. Curiously, though, in the past few years, there has been a resurgence in young women taking the veil. Even more curiously, most of these women are choosing to become contemplative rather than active nuns, and overwhelmingly join orders that still wear the habit and follow more conservative, traditional lifestyles. Online resources on nuns abound, including the very informative ANunsLife.org, and many orders, even cloistered ones, have lively online presences; commentators theorise that it's this, combined with an increasing sense of meaninglessness felt by young women who've grown up in a materialistic culture, that is drawing them towards the simpler ways of the contemplative, spiritual life.

•

Australian journalist Nancy Webb recently made headlines of her own after she declared her intention to join the Sisters of Life, an ultra-conservative Catholic order founded in New York in 1991, on the principle of preventing abortions. This presented something of a smudge on my rose-tinted nun-viewing glasses. Part of my bone-deep secularity means that I am firmly pro-choice, and the idea of a group of women devoting their entire lives to opposing a woman's right to choose—along with sterilisation, euthanasia and artificial contraception—made me feel a bit unwell. What was empowering about that? What kind of sisterhood could that be, that tried to force women to have children they might not want or be able to care for?

But reading more about the Sisters of Life allayed at least a little of my nausea. Unlike so many anti-abortion activist groups, their energies are not focused on shaming women for having sex or fearmongering about their eternal souls. Instead, they work to provide women with everything they might need to convince them that they are able to have and raise a child: food, cots, clothes, nappies, child care, emotional support—whatever they need. While I still cannot agree with any doctrine that privileges the rights of the just-conceived over the rights of the very much established personhood of the woman in question, this approach does seem to be rooted in the kind of compassion and practicality I've come to expect from nuns. For the record, not all nuns are anti-abortion; in fact, again and again during my reading, I came across stories of nuns doing things so un-Catholic that I got a frisson of second-hand excitement, the kind that comes with getting away with something wicked right under the nose of the school principal. For a group of people part of something as huge, complex and rule-obsessed as the Catholic Church, nuns do seem to be in the habit (sorry) of ignoring those rules as a matter of course—like the famously pro-choice Nuns on the Bus, who travelled the United States in 2012 campaigning against the ferociously Catholic and deeply conservative vice-presidential candidate Paul Ryan. That earned them a denunciation from the church for their 'radical feminist themes'. They were completely unbothered, of course.

In the mid-1990s, Sister Maryanne and several other women religious published a book collecting their writing on theology and feminism. The book is called *Freedom and Entrapment*, and I think that is so illustrative of the peculiar struggle of women religious in general: to be simultaneously trapped and freed by their religious institutions. I think all those women would turn towards spirituality and service regardless of what religion they belonged to; it's what some people, Jo Piazza included, call the God gene. And to a greater or lesser extent, all those women must wrestle with their overarching authorities on Earth for the right to do the work of something higher than all of them without inference.

•

There is an often retold story in my family about the time my dad punched a nun. The story goes that when he was about ten, he was receiving piano lessons from one of the nun-shaped monsters that inhabit the memories of so many of my parents' generation. She kept hitting him over the knuckles with a ruler when he made mistakes, so he told her, in a no-nonsense, ten-year-old manner, that if she did that again he would punch her. She did. He did. And he did not take any more piano lessons.

For most people around my dad's age, this story seems to jibe nicely with their pre-existing notions of nuns. When I talk to people twenty or thirty years older than me, they tell me a lot of horror stories about ruler-happy nuns with gimlet eyes, scanning the classroom like bewimpled Terminators seeking out wrong-doers. There are some fond memories, but mostly the nuns of their childhoods are slightly funny figures of fear, who, it seems, most would rather not think about much at all. For the rest of us, nuns appear as caricatures in *The Blues Brothers*, as fiends in horror films like *The Nun*, as Nazi-thwarting wise women in *The Sound of Music*, as foul-mouthed brats in *The Little Hours*. (And in porn. It was hard to do initial research on queer and lesbian nuns for this book, because Google was convinced I was looking for a particular kind of pornography. For the record, there are enough queer nuns to fill a book of their first-person stories, published in 1985, and just a few years ago a pair of nuns left their Italian convent in order to marry each other. The Pope was not impressed.)

But since I've been writing, and gleefully broadcasting my new nun knowledge on social media, a number of people I know have mentioned to me, in tones of faint surprise, that they know a nun. Their great-aunt, maybe, or a cousin, or a mother's friend. It's as though they intentionally slip from our memories—the better to get on with things, I suppose, un-slowed-down by scrutiny. I love the stories people have told me, though, always with the demeanour of recollecting a forgotten celebrity encounter: Great-Aunty Berenice is a Sister with a PhD in history from Oxford; Aunt Emma is an Ursuline nun with a sports obsession and its accompanying savage competi-tiveness, famous for organising family Olympics to coincide with the real-life summer ones; Sister Mary is a long-lost first cousin discovered by chance on the streets of West End, where she has become a legend.

Most nuns are humble by definition. We don't notice or think about them because we're not supposed to. (Vanity, you know.) But we owe them a lot. For a long time, it was nuns who took care of the sick, contributing not only their trained medical expertise but their spiritual reassurance and their emphasis on charity over profits well into the contemporary era. It's only now, with the dwindling numbers of nuns, that women religious are beginning to disappear from Catholic hospitals. We have a nun to thank for Alcoholics Anonymous, in fact: Dr Robert H. Smith, one of AA's cofounders, encountered Catholic nun Sister Mary Ignatia in a hospital in Ohio in the 1930s, where she convinced him that alcoholism was not a moral failing but a disease, and ought to be treated as such. This foundation of understanding continues to underpin AA's philosophy. A nun was instrumental in setting up the Mayo Clinic, and the mission of education shared by so many orders means that nuns are responsible for educating entire generations of children. When I think about nuns, it feels like there are these quiet, thoughtful, hardworking women all around me, in history and in the now, moving through the world creating as little disturbance as possible, but leaving great, surprising change in their wake.

•

In 1963, Dolores Hart, an up-and-coming Hollywood actress who'd had the honour of giving Elvis Presley his first on-screen kiss, shocked the press and her fans by giving up her film career to become a Benedictine nun. She had been pegged as the next Grace Kelly: blue-eyed, blonde, with one of those classic Hollywood smiles; instead, she turned her attention to God, and to connecting her chosen order to their local community through arts and theatre programs, publicised by her fame. Her story has puzzled people so much that she has been profiled and interviewed on and off ever since. In 2011, she was the focus of an Oscar-nominated documentary about her life, called *God is the Bigger Elvis*.

Just like spending time with Sister Maryanne, the short film instills in me a profound sense of peace—and a smaller sense of envy. Mother Dolores' abbey, the Benedictine Abbey of Regina Laudis in Bethlehem, Connecticut, is a self-sufficient and fully functioning farm, where the nuns produce a staggering array of food, cosmetics, clothing and other handmade objects. It's set in tranquil temperate forest, real storybook stuff: snow on the roof, hay in the meadows. Archival footage used in the documentary shows young nuns in the late 1960s and '70s running along a track through open woods, leading the abbey cow; cuddling with piglets and puppies; ploughing fields on a tractor; picking food while wearing broad-brimmed sunhats over their wimples. It's achingly sweet, the simplicity, the purity of it all.

And I wonder, is some of the appeal I'm feeling—and maybe the appeal to those other young women who are now joining convents—the allure of an eternal girlhood? In another story about American nuns, these ones contemplative nuns of the Dominican order in New Jersey, photographer Toni Greaves says that they all have the air of young girls in love for the first time. To be in love without any chance of falling out; to have your lover be God, and know he will never break your heart; to remain perpetually thirteen and full of joy as you grow and mature and put your mind and body to work . . . It's a heady thought.

In the documentary about her life, Mother Dolores also talks about how she broke off her engagement to architect Don Robinson in order to take her vows. She says it was impossible to explain to him why she chose to become a nun. It makes me think of all the women I know who feel that they need to, for want of a better word, 'settle'—that they *must* have a man, however average he might be, rather than live their lives alone, even if it means giving up what they really want in order to please or placate their partner. Do nuns, in choosing God, really choose themselves? Against this backdrop, it seems like the strongest, most admirable thing to put yourself first, to risk disappointing someone else, in order to follow what you feel is your true calling.

Robinson, who died in 2011, continued to visit Dolores at the abbey for forty-seven years. I cry when he reveals this while being interviewed. I think: That is true devotion. That's what real love looks like. Not possessive or demanding; just showing up. And I feel sad to think that many women in heterosexual relationships might need to take steps as drastic as joining a convent to make clear how serious their own desires are. How many women give up everything of themselves to the men in their lives—their careers, their dreams—to have children, to be wives? How many men would do the same? How many would it even occur to?

Even now, the division of labour along gender lines burdens women more heavily than men. How much mental energy is taken up by raising children? More importantly, how much is freed up by their absence? Nuns seem busy—depending on their order, they might spend their days toiling on their abbey's farm, or teaching, or out in their community helping the poor, or campaigning for the rights of the disenfranchised, or tending to the ill in hospitals (or, in certain memorable cases, breaking into nuclear weapon storage facilities)—but at night they go home to their own thoughts, their own quarters, their own chosen calling. I could get so much thinking done under those circumstances. If my days were structured around prayer and physical work, periods of silence, being up with the dawn, and always knowing that I was working in joyous pursuit of the one thing I truly wanted to devote my life to—I could get so much *done*. Instead, I am glued to my phone, scowling at Instagram, abandoning dirty dishes around the house, snapping at my partner and my sister. This is not, I confess, the life of feminist fulfilment I imagined for myself as a teenager discovering the movement. Whether nuns are feminist remains a topic of some debate. I can see it, though, in one way or another.

•

The Sisters of the Valley are one order who appear to have explicitly adopted nuns' subversively feminist leanings. They are a group of women who make their living growing cannabis by the cycles of the moon, and turning it into medicinal salves, tinctures and oils for customers seeking cannabidiol's anti-inflammatory, anti-anxiety, sleep-enhancing and pain-reducing qualities. They are also not religiously affiliated, beyond a certain Mother Earth–style spiritualism and an adherence to what they call 'ancient wisdom'; as one profile of the organisation tartly puts it, they are not *real* nuns.

But they wear a habit (white and blue), they take new names, they call each other Sister and, perhaps most importantly, they work in community with one another, at peace in their work on the land in Southern California. While their spiritual calling might be significantly more New Age-y than other, more established convents, their founder, Sister Kate, is convinced that the Sisters of the Valley are doing work in exactly the same traditions as their more mainstream religious counterparts. Well, maybe not *exactly* the same. The Sisters of the Valley are openly feminist, devoted to the empowerment of women through the financial success of their business (which reportedly took US$750,000 in 2017), and regularly share stories on their social media of the lives they have put behind them—full of ungrateful spouses, unfulfilling careers working for The Man, divorce, philandering, and subjugation under the patriarchy—in favour of their new enlightenment and sense of sisterhood. One Sister escaped sexual abuse in an oppressively religious upbringing; others talk about the relief of finally entering a space run by women after years struggling to thrive in male-dominated fields. On her blog, Sister Kate talks about following in the footsteps of the Beguines, a semi-religious but not ordained movement of women from (possibly) pre-history until the Middle Ages, who clustered their dwellings together in groups sometimes numbering in the thousands in order to put their efforts towards caring just for women.

Then there are the famous Sisters of Perpetual Indulgence, another order of nuns whose 'realness' is hotly contested. First appearing as high-camp drag characters on the streets of San Francisco in the 1970s, the organisation is now an international entity with orders throughout the Americas, Australia and Europe, all focused on charity and support for LGBTQ causes. They call themselves a leading-edge order of queer nuns, and have been active in campaigning for safer sex practices, sex positivity, and throughout the AIDS crisis. They also might be the only order not solely made up of women—and they're certainly not sanctioned by the Catholic Church. Nevertheless, they still seem to me to embody what's best about nuns: community, service, conviction in your beliefs. And the habit. People love a nun in a habit.

•

It seems crude to say it, but Sister Maryanne is a lot less godly than I expected her to be. When it comes to talking about God, she's careful, inclusive: it's mystery, she says, the unanswerable question, the unscratchable itch, the sense of divine love we all feel—she just calls that feeling God. She lives in what she terms a 'hub of hospitality', not a convent (and she says many more nuns live alone, or in small households, or even in caravans so they can travel and provide care wherever they are needed). She owns her clothes and her computer and her phone, and she has access to a car whenever she needs it. Her interpretation of the vow of poverty is less about having nothing and more about sharing everything. And she's pro-marriage equality. This seems emblematic of the nuns I've spent time reading about. They all seem concerned less with the specifics of dogma, or the specifics of what goes on in people's intimate relationships, than with acceptance, community, spiritual healing and that wonderful practicality of getting things done. In an interview, Mother Dolores Hart was once asked about the beret that she wears over her wimple; she replied that because Benedictine convention required her to keep her hair short underneath it, her head got cold, so she asked her superiors if she could wear a hat. She could, and she did, and she does. 'It's part of our tradition that what helps a nun to be herself can certainly be a part of our system,' she told the reporter, and I think, Of course it is.

•

Sister Maryanne is telling me about life in the convent pre–Vatican II. It doesn't sound so bad, but maybe it's just that she has a well-honed sense of humour about it. I regularly find myself guffawing, surprising myself as much as the other people near our table.

'When I entered', she tells me, 'we had a monastic model. We were up at five. We went through the day. At five o'clock in the evening, we said our prayers together. That meant you had to come off the basketball court or the tennis court, you're puffing and collapsing in the chapel, and you try to say some prayers.

'You were very grateful if it was rote prayers you said aloud, because sometimes we'd come in and we'd be expected to meditate. Well, we all fell asleep. Somebody once fell out of her preacher, the kneeler. Then she pretended she had fainted because she was so embarrassed about having slept'.

I love the idea of nuns falling asleep during meditation—a whole cohort of Marias from *The Sound of Music*, late to chapel, wearing curlers under their wimples. It's a scene that's likely to remain in the past, though, at least in Australia. The Sisters of Charity don't even have a convent anymore, let alone wimples to wear curlers underneath, and they haven't had a novitiate in a long time. But Maryanne does not see this as a pressing problem. 'We've never been about numbers. We have always been about service. When women have a cause they will work together at great costs. I don't think there will ever be great numbers the way there was in the past. But there will be a cohort of dedicated women, who can live a life of celibacy in order to witness to something.'

Ah, yes. Celibacy. She's the one who brings it up—'You haven't asked me about sex'—and proceeds to discuss at length the absurdity of the vow of celibacy, the pure nonsensical nature of it. And, of course, its necessity to doing the work that she does.

'We're not celibate because we don't have sexual feelings. We're celibate because this is a commitment.' There's a value in denial, she says, in favour of focusing on your true goal, and I confess that I sometimes think about how easy life might be if I never had to worry about sex, relationships, the emotional well-being of a particular other person. She asks me, What would be the loss if you were able to dedicate yourself completely to your writing? And I am not ready for that at all.

We talk about the habit some more instead, and she tells me the story of being bumped to the front of a line in a pharmacy in Boston because the man at the counter was Catholic and chose to serve the Sister first.

'I went up and I got my prescription filled before any of the poor people who were there, and I walked out and thought, Thank God I didn't have to wait. And then I went, Shit, Maryanne. You've lost the plot.' (Here she pauses, looks me in the eye, and says, '"Shit" is an acronym. It stands for Sacred Heart I Trust. Don't think that I'm swearing.') 'Not only were you glad that you were called first,' she continues, 'but you didn't even learn anything walking out. You didn't even look at those people. You just were glad to get out. What witness are you giving? You're privileged. A habit was never meant to be a privilege.'

These days she's happy to wear just her cross—a gift from her friends in the Columban order of nuns—and the Sisters of Charity pin, which she admits she sometimes hides if she doesn't feel like having hours-long conversations on aeroplanes. But it's more than just avoiding being confessed to; choosing not to wear a habit evens things out.

'One woman said to me, "Sister, why don't you wear your habit? I didn't know you were a nun." I said, "Well, if you did know I was a nun, how would you have spoken to me? Would you have spoken to me in the same way you're speaking to me now that you know me as Sister? Would you have talked to me about the things that really matter to you? Or would you have thought I'm too holy to be able to listen to it?"'

Maryanne doesn't want the unearned credit that comes with the habit, just as she doesn't want the undeserved holiness. She works with laypeople on all kinds of causes, in tandem and in harmony with her community. 'If you had two people in a habit,' she says, in a working situation like that, 'they'd be given the credibility of being the real energy source.'

For a moment I think about how humility looks a lot less difficult in real life, even for someone whose favourite sin is pride. Then Sister Maryanne tells me about going to a fundraiser where she got to sit in a Maserati, and I am laughing again, a lot, and loudly.

•

I don't mean to paint all nuns as saints. We know they're not. Throughout the history of the Catholic Church and its many cruelties against the poor, marginalised and vulnerable, nuns have been its handmaids—in the Magdalene laundries of Ireland, where unwed mothers and other 'undesirable' women laboured as slaves, in the schools where they beat the fear of God into their charges, and in the parishes where priests sexually abused thousands of children. It's hard to reconcile this knowledge with what I know of Sister Maryanne, of Hildegard of Bingen, of Sor Juana. Maybe all this reveals is that people seize what little power they can when it is made available to them, especially when they are otherwise powerless. To this day, no woman has been ordained by the Catholic Church. Catholic women religious are still pushed to the margins; it's there that they can choose to exercise what power they find in their communities, for good or ill.

Nuns do sometimes leave their orders. The reasons seem to be as varied as those for joining; the truth of it all seems to be that, just like any occupation, workplace or community, each individual unit is different. I find a message board, Phatmass, on which there are six pages of discussion between former nuns who left their vocations. The stories vary wildly. One left after overhearing her superiors loudly discussing how annoying they found her, which sent her into a spiral of depression lasting years. Several others say they were forced to leave in total secrecy, denied even the comfort of knowing that their former sisters would be praying for them. But still others say that their orders treated the change in vocation with grace and understanding, allowing them to come to their own decisions, say their goodbyes, and keep in touch.

It's not something I'd considered before I started writing about them: how nuns who left their orders, particularly those from a certain era or an order with a certain level of formality, would adjust to the outside world. Often, it seems, they were thrust out with no possessions, no money and, startlingly regularly, no practical skills—one woman on the message board described having to learn how to write a cheque for the first time. I can't imagine a bigger upheaval: to go from a community so closely knit as to do almost everything together, to being all on your own. Most of the women who shared their stories on Phatmass explained that they had to rely on another community of women to set them back on their feet: their mothers and grandmothers. I want very badly to believe that all nuns live as sweet and bucolic a life as depicted by Toni Greaves, who spent seven years on and off with the Dominican order in New Jersey. In her rosy photographs, the women chortle while eating together in a rough circle of shoved-together wooden tables, or play volleyball, or weed the garden. I want to think that everyone could enjoy the peace and certainty that Dolores Hart feels as prioress of her convent, or the sense of purpose that still drives Sister Maryanne. I want to believe it in the way I want to believe, in a vague sense, that everything will work out. But, even though I think nuns probably have a better handle on the whole serenity thing than the rest of us, it's more likely that they deal with just as many injustices, petty grievances and cruelties as we all do. Maybe the difference is only the radical nature of the choice they make, which sets them apart irretrievably, no matter how ordinary their lives may otherwise be.

And I do still think that nuns are, secretly, even if they're anti-abortion or cloistered or deeply conservative, also unavoidably feminist. A whole bunch of women hanging out together, doing secret spiritual things, thinking only of themselves, each other and their work? To me, still, even with my many treasured possessions and my beloved partner and my pride, it seems like some kind of paradise.

12

AUNTY DAWN DAYLIGHT

Dawn in Brisbane

With Aunty Dawn Daylight

I don't get to spend a lot of time with older women. My mother's mother died when I was seven. My paternal grandmother lives in a different city, and has since I was a child. Up until now, most of my professional mentors have been men. So getting to spend time with Aunty Dawn Daylight and Jagera and Turrabal elder was a rare treat. Not only did I get to hang out with an older lady and absorb some of her astounding wealth of knowledge and experience, I also got to discover a deeper connection to my own community because of her.

I lived in West End, an inner-city suburb of Brisbane, for five years. It's a suburb with a story common to inner-city areas all over the world: once the home of the poor or recently migrated, it's been gentrified by richer, whiter people (like me) attracted by lower rents and local charm, and it is changing almost unrecognisably. But even though brand-new apartment blocks are sprouting like cubist mushrooms on every corner, there is a core to West End that has not crumbled. There's still a sizeable population of first-generation immigrants, now in their seventies and eighties, who still meet in the same street-side cafés along the strip on Boundary Street. A number of people still sleep rough on the streets. And West End is where you'll find Musgrave Park, a millennia-old place of significance to the Turrbal and Jagera people, the Aboriginal people of the land from Moreton Bay to Toowoomba in what's now southeast Queensland. West End's history is there, if you choose to look.

Aunty Dawn is like a fibre-optic cable, connecting whoever is with her to that world at faster-than-light speeds. Sitting with her at a table on the footpath outside the Swiss delicatessen, I gape slightly as she warmly greets more than ten passers-by in the thirty minutes it takes for us to drink our coffee. They are older folk like her, or young Aboriginal people, or care workers, or blokes who've just gotten out of jail, or homeless people who live in the area, or local shopkeepers. They all know her name.

She takes me with her to give a talk at the Blind Eye Drop-In Centre, a daytime facility for the most vulnerable people in the city, who today are hosting about eighty kids from a local Catholic school. Aunty Dawn has brought her guitar, and will sing and tell her story to them. In the taxi on the way there, she gives the driver advice on keeping his mind sharp as he ages. When we arrive at the drop-in centre, she's greeted like a queen. Everyone tells me, 'We love this lady'. She knows every person in the place.

Aunty Dawn is the kind of person who's hard to get down accurately in words. She has a shock of white hair, stylishly cut. She wears bright colours. She's my friends' great-aunt, and sometimes when she's laughing she looks so much like them that my head spins a bit. She is entirely self-possessed, confident, educated and funny, completely free of false modesty and completely independent. She doesn't always answer her phone. Sometimes I think about what I want to be like when I'm older. I think being like Aunty Dawn would be pretty good. But I'm not doing her justice by giving you adjectives. I'm going to let her talk about herself in her own words.

Aunty Dawn and I met several times to talk about her life and her work in the community. The following is an edited version of those conversations. While talking with her, I didn't just find someone who has deep, resilient connections to the community of the place where I live; I found a role model, a friend, and a woman who has overcome incredible hardship to become a source of strength and wisdom to everyone around her. I think half of Brisbane must be lucky enough to call Aunty Dawn a friend. The other half probably just haven't met her yet.

•

My name is Dawn Daylight. They call me Aunty. I was born in 1947. I'm from Ipswich, I'm a Jagera and a Turrbal woman. My mother was born on the south side of the Brisbane River. You know how they classified Aboriginal people as being half-caste, quarter-caste, full-blood? I'm a bit of a mixer. My grandmother was of German descent. My father was quarter-caste Aboriginal. And my mother—well, the government wouldn't allow me to see my mother's records.

My mother and father were from the Purga mission. They had five boys and five girls. Out of those five girls, three girls—myself and my two sisters—were removed and put to work as domestic slaves at eleven and twelve and thirteen. The place I went to was a boarding school for girls, but I wasn't a schoolgirl. I was a slave, a domestic. I stayed there for a good number of years.

I went to university, I went and studied. I knew I was clever, I knew I was smart. I went to Griffith University, I did my arts degrees, I did a social work degree. I overcame those things, and I kind of put myself in a different place.

I have one child. My husband has passed away. My daughter is a schoolteacher, but she's also a counsellor. Whatever I've learned over the years, and the way I've kind of excelled and done different things, I've made a different life for my daughter.

I make myself busy, and I don't dwell on the past a lot. That past comes up for me every now and again. But, I think, music, poetry, painting—I'm a very good painter, I'm a very good storyteller— that's how I work through the pain and the stuff that I went through when I was a young girl.

Dawn was born in Churchill, a suburb of Ipswich that's now about an hour's drive from Brisbane. For the first eleven years of her life, she lived with her mother, Caroline, and nine siblings; her father, Reg, died when she was young. The Daylight family lived in their own house on a cattle property, where Caroline was caretaker and stockwoman in charge of two hundred head of cattle for the local abattoir—an unusual position of privilege for an Aboriginal woman of the time.

When I look at my mother, she was a very kind and giving person. She was born in 1902, a long time ago. She's passed now. I used to watch my mother—because my father had already died before I even knew him, basically, so I didn't know too much about him—my mother was always the breadwinner, the person who took care of us.

We grew up in a country sort of setting. We were very bushland. Mum was given a property to look after, and a house on the property, and she looked after the stock. She became a stockwoman. My five brothers were doing stock work and buckjumping, horseriding, all that kind of stuff. Mum was riding horses and fixing fences; plus, after she'd been out all day working, she'd come home and cook for us.

My mum did the best she could, the way she brought us up. When we did school stuff, Mum always had us dressed to a T, we had ribbons in our hair—she used to tie little pieces of rag in our hair to make curls, so we always had ringlets. And we had the best white dresses, and the most beautiful dress shoes and socks.

My brothers and my sisters, we all had the ethic of wanting to work. I think that's because my mother was a worker, a really known worker. If I was able to do a re-enactment, I could do it so well; I see all of those things in my mind, in my memory. It's something you never forget. All the Aboriginal people came to our place, my mother had a big pot on the stove, so all those people who were on the fringe would come and spend a lot of time with us. They had an outside area with a thing like a shanty, which was an old, dirt floor, makeshift little hut, and people would come and sit there day and night, and that's how they congregated. They'd always come over to our place.

Aunty Dawn's parents grew up on the Purga mission, a sixty-acre property set up in 1913 with help from the Salvation Army, who saw the new mission as a place to bring 'nomadic half-caste Aborigines' to Christian salvation. Purga was further from the 'temptations' of Ipswich than the previous Aboriginal mission, Deebing Creek; according to government documents from the time, the aim of Purga was to 'raise them [the Aboriginal residents] up another step on the social scale'.

Of course, the laws at the time made it difficult for Aboriginal people to access any kind of social mobility. Under the Queensland *Aboriginals Preservation and Protection Act 1939*,

Aboriginal people were severely restricted in their movement, their ability to marry, their work opportunities and their access to wages. But, once again, the Daylights were unusual: Dawn's father, Reg, managed with a lot of hard work and negotiation to get an exemption from the Act—meaning he was, in theory, to be treated by the law as a non-Aboriginal man.

My father was exempted from the [Aboriginal] Act in the 1940s. In some of the documents that I have been able to get, they said that my father was an Aboriginal person, but my father wasn't recognised as an Aboriginal person [at the time]. My mother was said to be of some other origin. There were no records really, when I think about it, that said that Mum was of other origin, which may have meant that she was Fijian. Her mother was German, my mother's mother was a white lady, and my father was said to be, I don't know whether they said quarter-caste, but not full-blood—but he was really dark. When they were trying to get declared exempt there were a lot of issues that they were having to go through, which the government put on people to be exempted: you weren't allowed to be associated with certain people, or be drinking, you had to be sober, you had to be able to manage your own money. But there were all these other things that were going on for both of them—for them to be able to get off the mission, there was really hard times for both of them. My father was only a young boy when he was removed and put on the mission outside of Ipswich.

Dawn describes her childhood as very happy. Although she suffered from several childhood illnesses, she has fond memories of her time at home with her mother and siblings, and of going to school at Churchill State School. But Dawn and her siblings were children during the 1950s, when government policies were overseeing the removal of thousands of Aboriginal children from their families.

Corey Green, a Melbourne community radio producer, put together a detailed radio story with Dawn about her experiences being removed by the state and put to work as an involuntary domestic worker—a slave—at All Hallows' Convent in Brisbane.

Dawn and her sisters Margaret and Carol were taken from their home without warning or explanation, and kept at All Hallows' in a part of the convent called the House of Mercy. Dawn was only eleven when she was taken away.

We called it the dungeon, All Hallows' Dungeon.

One day recently when I was coming home from Morningside College, somebody was sitting behind me. She came over and she tapped me and she said, 'Oh, I think I know you.' I said, Where from? She said, 'You were in All Hallows'.' I said, Yes. She said, 'You were the smallest Aboriginal girl. I pulled you off the fence.' It was that really strong cyclone fence, but up the top was barbed wire. Naturally you want to go home, because you don't belong to this place, in the compound. I don't think we were treated disrespectfully, even though it was child labour, forced labour, and we didn't get much money. We actually just got board and keep, which is, you know, a roof over your head and that's about it. So we never got any reparation and there was no money put in trust when we looked for it.

Somehow, I never really thought about the removal of kids, Aboriginal kids. I didn't really think that we were part of the Stolen Generation because the government's not saying that, the government's not even attempting to pay any compensation like a lot of the other Aboriginal older people who are my age have been allocated. You know, in the class action thing that's been taken up by lawyers now, we're not included, we're not entitled to any of that. My daughter used to work with DATSIP [the Department of Aboriginal and Torres Strait Islander Partnerships], where all the government records are supposed to be held. *They kept records of me too, but when I went to ask for them, they showed me a photograph of the 1974 floods and said that all the records had been destroyed. Probably ten years ago, I put an application in, my sister in Cairns, she put an application in—both rejected.*

When we went into that convent, I didn't even know that my sisters were already there. I hadn't even seen them. We were all basically in different parts. They separated us. So when I came home, when they let me go, after locking us up at night-time and then allowing us to come out in the morning and go to work and all that sort of stuff, it was really hard to make that reconnection to family. And I think when we all got married—Cathy got married, Margaret got married, Carol got married, I got married—out of the four girls who got married, we all got divorced. One of my sisters, she said she got married to get out of All Hallows'. She didn't want to stay there anymore. I had one daughter, and my other sisters had two. And I don't know whether that separation, and losing our family connection and trying to reconnect back to the family, does things to you, you know? You just can't settle down.

It was trauma. And people say, 'Oh, but you had a good time, didn't you? They looked after you.' How can you [say that about] slavery of children, when you don't even get to see it, or didn't even know at the time? What people don't know is that [there is] a generation of Aboriginal kids who are still hurting, who still don't have access to records, government records . . . Why is that so? I know they say evidence is gone and that's because of the floods in 1974, but prior to that I don't know. Why did they make it so difficult? I know it's all got to do with government policies and all that, but it would be nice for . . . I mean, you look at some of these people who are sleeping, lying around down here, they're lost souls. I suppose it's the same for them. The government tells them this and tells them that, and we go along and we believe it because we can't find out where things are. They're not made accessible to us.

So that's one thing: how that disempowers a people, disempowers us as Aboriginal people. We go through life feeling that emptiness, I suppose, because we just don't have the answers. And I'd like to know more about why we were put into All Hallows' to work when there's no records to tell us why. It'd be nice, just to know, for us, for my sisters, before we all die. I don't know whether there's a lot of hidden stuff that I don't really know about, that has never been spoken about. Sometimes it gets really emotional. I've been trying to work through all this stuff for a very long time.

•

Aunty Dawn's experiences at All Hallows' have continued to colour her life. The unanswered question of why she was taken away from a loving family is raised frequently when we talk. And Dawn has repeatedly come up against resistance from the government to have her and her sisters recognised as part of the Stolen Generations. According to Corey Green's radio documentary, this is compounded by the fact that All Hallows' has refused to acknowledge the existence of involuntary domestic workers in the convents.

As Green discovered in her research with Dawn, the Daylight girls should never have been removed from their family— not just because it's morally and ethically wrong, but because it was against the law at the time. They weren't being neglected at home and, furthermore, their father was exempted from the Aboriginal Act. The Daylight children were born free, and should never have been under the control of the state; there are legal documents from the time stating exactly that. But Dawn was a dark-skinned child at a time when the Director of Native Affairs was legally the guardian of every Aboriginal child under 21; he could, as Green says, move them about as he saw fit.

In Green's documentary, she discusses the role of the 'protector'—a local authority who controlled the Aboriginal people within a certain district. These protectors were in charge of where, when, if and for whom Aboriginal people could work, whether they could marry, who they could marry, and whether they could access their own money. The Aboriginal people themselves were largely left out of these processes, informed after the fact.

This is interesting to me considering Aunty Dawn's role today as a de facto protector of her community—not in the perverse sense of the Queensland government's 'protectors', but in the true sense of guardianship. An out lesbian woman, Dawn has made it her business to advocate for the rights of queer Indigenous people, joining groups like IndigiLez, an organisation for improving the lives of Indigenous lesbians in Australia, and travelling the country and abroad with the Pride Choir and the Gay Games. In 2018, she was honoured with an IndigiLez Leadership Award, and a Lifetime Achievement Award at the Queen's Ball, a Brisbane Pride event, for her work with the LGBTQ community.

I often do things for Pride because a lot of my sisters and a lot of my family are LGBTI community. I support them, and they support me too, being an older LGBTI person. At the Pride festival last year I sat down with the all the younger women, the IndigiLez women, and we made the banner and got right up at the front, right up at the top of the building where the parade went through.

Being in relationships with women, over time, there's just a natural instinct you have for [helping] people, I think. Every now and then, IndigiLez puts on retreats for women, for young and old, seniors and juniors. There are certain people on that committee of women, me included, who are able every now and then to attend conferences in Melbourne or Sydney, or if there's something going on of interest—whether it's suicide prevention, mental health, or just being in contact with community. That's something that's very prominent in our community: suicide prevention, helping people to see their way through—or just giving information or gathering information. I often get to go and speak at those conferences. I think it just helps us in our own self to be the best we can as LGBTI people.

We've got a lot of brotherboys and sistergirls that are in our community that people probably wouldn't even know. I have brotherboys and sistergirls round here in West End, and they have so much respect, and I have respect for them too because they're on their journeys and it's really hard sometimes for them to go it alone. And if I can be there, just to sit down and yarn with them, and they can come and give me a hug or something like that.

I think that people just need to appreciate who we are and let us live the life that we want to live. It's our choice, of who we choose to have as partners, and I think it's up to us. When I look at some of the younger women, I think, Hmm, they're having a hard time. So sometimes I try and talk to them in the street, I try and get them away from wherever they are or whatever they're doing and just sit down and have a coffee with them, or invite them to go out or something, or even to get involved, like we're trying to do with younger people, younger women. They really appreciate having older LGBTI community people. They have a lot of respect for me and I have a lot of respect for them because there are a lot of younger people who are still having problems. I think whatever I do, it just seems to be a natural instinct that I have, and a gift, I suppose, that some people have.

I wrote a bit of a chapter for a book that was launched here at Avid Reader [in West End]. David Hardy was the author of the book. It was just about me being an Indigenous lesbian woman who was as old as I am, and just finding a way in community, how people might see you, and how you identify or don't identify.

I don't use the word 'inspiration' to describe people very often, because it seems kind of cheap and overdone (and patronising). But I think Aunty Dawn is genuinely inspiring. She emerged from a deeply traumatic childhood with a drive to connect to the people around her, and she has devoted her life to her community. Health worker, educator, advocate for women in prison, musician, elder, LGBTQ role model: these are the roles Aunty Dawn has chosen to play. It's the choice that I find so inspiring, that I think about when I'm trying to imagine what I'll be like as I grow older: that I can choose to stay connected, to give back, to be someone vital to the people I care about.

I could have gone off the rails a long time ago, but I didn't. I chose a different path. And it was my choice, my choice to be who I want to be, and be the best I can be, basically. For me, all the things that I've said already, that's the journey, the path, that I think was meant for me. How I meet people out on the street, or how I meet people any-where, that was the road I had to take. And it's got nothing to do with Christianity, I'm not a Christian, even though I might go to church and sit down and have a meal with somebody, or talk to a minister or something like that. It's not Christianity-based, what I do, it's in my heart. It's like instinct.

My language is very bland and very simple. But I think there's a message anyway; it doesn't really matter whether you have the gift of the gab. And even though I've got those two awards I don't go and preach to these people on anything that I've done or anywhere I've been or anything like that. I made a choice to do something different, go a different path, and that's okay. They made a different choice, they're on their own journey, their own path. I'm not going to preach to our mob, our people.

I didn't have much education. I only had a domestic background, that was the only kind of work I was ever any good at. So when I got released from All Hallows', walked out of the gates, I didn't have any real skills. So I did domestic cleaning and floors and domestic work, meat works, bra factories, shoe factories, it was all factory work. That's probably the same for a lot of other Aboriginal people.

I went to Grade 7 in school but I came out of school with probably a Grade 4 education. I only got university qualifications when I was in my thirties and forties. When I came out of school I couldn't even sit down and write, I couldn't tell the time. I think it had a lot to do with my childhood illnesses and, I think, being removed from my family.

I went to Armidale to study. I had already done a course for Aboriginal and Torres Strait Islander people, it was called Aboriginal Studies, at Kangaroo Point. But because I was a health worker and an educator, I went to Armidale and did another Aboriginal Studies course through the College of Education. I did a cultural exchange and went over to Papua New Guinea with some of those students. There was about nine of us. And I was a health worker but I wasn't a nurse; we didn't have enough education to become a nurse or anything like that.

I worked in domestic violence in a women's shelter, and did work with Sisters Inside, musically, when Boggo Gaol still had the women's prison down the back. A couple of other women who I'm still in contact with, who are still working inside and outside of prison, got me involved in that. At the time I was working in Aboriginal health, but I was doing my placement at Women's House. So I got involved in that, because I've been a health worker myself, and because of having the background of how our family grew up, how we were sent away, and how all that sort of stuff really affected myself and my sisters.

I suppose I do a lot of stuff with other women because I make myself available. I mean, I don't wear anything that tells them very much about me, but I might see somebody and say, 'Oh, look, where are you from?' I make that connection. Where are you from, who's your mob? Even if they're just sitting by themselves, I just make myself open, friendly, to people who might be new to town, or from another country. And I think it's because I worked in Women's House, in the shelter, supporting women in not-so-good circumstances. And I did my certificate in community service and welfare. I think I've got that caring attitude where you can sense when somebody's not having a good time. And even myself, if I'm not having a good time, I'd like to think that I can reach out to people also. To not just be for other people, but seek the help that you need sometimes when you do need it.

I've been a muso, I do writing and I do storytelling, and I do a bit of poetry. I play ukulele, I play guitar, and I write and I sing my own songs. I worked at Woodford Folk Festival for maybe ten years or more. I did a performance on stage in the Murri venue, and started doing volunteering work, but it just got too much after a while. I used to play in this band with some other Aboriginal women. We went to the Woodford Folk Festival, we did a lot of things, just community events. And some of the songs we wrote ourselves. We used to practise up around the street just here past the radio station.

We also had the ukulele group going, and we had women from the West End area who were interested in just making that connection with other women. We started off as a coffee group at a coffee shop up here. I said, 'Why don't we do something again and keep going as a group.' But a lot of women didn't have a ukulele, a lot of them didn't play music, a lot of them couldn't read music, and a lot of them couldn't sing. I said, 'Doesn't matter, we can just tootle around with ukuleles.'

We had a beading group, so we used to go up to the place called Place of Belonging, up around the corner, and we did beading, and writing. Necklacing, Aboriginal colour beads. The thing is, too, with that kind of socialising, trying to get people together to do things, it's usually someone like me that instigates, starts things, tries to get something done. That sort of socialising and connecting with people, that's all you want to do, you want to make that connection. I think when you're getting older too, the company of people around is important. I mean, I can walk along the street here and it'd probably be every second person I pass that I'd know.

I just do what I do, and I just do it the best I can. I speak for my sisters too, Carol and them. I'd just like these kids to know, because sometimes they don't realise that there are people like me still around, and I tell them, that's a kind of healing. This place is a healing centre, and it even helps me heal as well. I come and I sit. I probably do a lot of dreaming here.

'Here' is the Blind Eye Drop-In Centre. We've been talking for three hours, moving through West End together, greeting every second person on the street. We've stopped at the weekly music group in the park where Dawn sometimes takes her guitar. We've swung past Coles to grab a spare battery so she can plug in for the performance she's about to give for the Catholic schoolkids. We've had a long, relaxed, freewheeling conversation with a friend at Blind Eye, who has her own stories of childhood atrocities, but who, right now, wants to talk about photography and where Dawn can get a camera like hers. Dawn's told me about her friend, a nurse, who's just discovered her own Aboriginal heritage, and how Dawn is helping her explore her ancestry, and I've promised to help get her guitar fixed—it keeps going out of tune, and I know someone who can repair it for free. I am feeling tired and alert, tingling with an unusual sense of connection. Being with Aunty Dawn is like touching a mild electric current: she makes me feel alive in a way I hadn't previously experienced. She's generous and patient, proud and independent, a fixture in this town, vital and ever-present. We are all lucky to know her.

13

WITCHES

The crone

There is a woman in my life for whom I don't have a title. She's just Joan. Old enough to be my grandmother, she's not related to me at all—she is, in fact, my mother's former schoolteacher, who took her in when she got kicked out of home and has remained a dear friend ever since. I guess the right term for her is 'family friend'. But for my whole life those words have felt inadequate to describe her, and the fullness of what she provided—provides—to my life. As a small child, I spent every afternoon after school with her, in the small garden outside her flat, where she would shuffle tulip bulbs around and I would arrange forget-me-not leaves into fairy beds. She took me to the local lake to feed the ducks, taught me about goslings and defended me from angry swans. She attended my music recitals and school graduations, she fed and housed me when my parents couldn't, and she indulged me in endless, sprawling games of make-believe, in which I was a mermaid or princess, and she was always a witch.

Joan never married or had children. As a child, it seemed to me that she existed purely for my benefit: to tell me stories from the olden days, to buy me books, to generously play the witch to my heroine. She was like my grandmother, but she was not a grandmother; she was a role model, a quiet, thoughtful, endlessly knowledgeable presence, whose experiences and understanding of the world were vastly different from my own.

'Grandmother' seems to be the only role we let older women play, but it is inadequate even for the grandmothers I know— my own and others'—with its reductive connotations of docility and bland kindness that don't even begin to touch on the real wealth an older woman can share with those younger than her. But there is, maybe, another role for old women—one we tend not to mention in polite society. Witch. More specifically: *crone*.

The witches in fairy stories are almost invariably old women. The crone—withered and malevolent—is what we grow up thinking of when we think 'witch'. What's so scary about an old woman? Why has she held on so tenaciously to her role as children-frightener that we still recognise that terror long into adulthood?

Maybe the same thing that made Joan perfect for the witch role in my make-believe is the same thing that made her so important in my life: her untethered wisdom. That Joan was unattached to a man always felt daring, somehow. Like Sister Maryanne, she has an aura of asexual freedom from the boring trappings of compulsory heterosexual courtship. For me, that's exhilarating; maybe for others it's a step too far outside of the narrow roles of femininity. Old women no longer have to contend with the vagaries of the desiring gaze, and without an inherent eroticism a woman is a creature even less knowable than before. Or maybe the monstrousness of the crone is that she's visible at all, when we prefer our old women to disappear completely.

Many post-menopausal women complain of becoming suddenly see-through, as people bump into them with shopping trolleys and ignore them in conversation. Maybe the crone, appearing at a christening to which she was conveniently not invited or materialising unpleasantly in the window of a candy house ripe for the snacking, is shocking just for making herself known.

Helen Garner's wonderful essay on growing old and doing away with the irritating trappings of decorum expected of women, 'The Insults of Age'—now this is a real crone tale. The glee with which she yanks an impertinent schoolgirl's ponytail, her brusque dismissal of simpering publicity agents, her cheerful but steely demands to be taken seriously are all classic witch behaviour. As is the popular poem 'Warning' by Jenny Joseph, which I'm sure my mum forwarded to me several times back in the days of luridly formatted chain emails. The promise of a gleeful, unencumbered old age is the promise of hard-earned cronehood. I'd like to think I see it on my horizon, too: a moment in my life where I cross the membrane into that realm of invisibility, and find myself somehow weightless and free.

Although the witches from fairytales might all be crones, current witch discourse remains obsessed with—and targeted at—youth. And the witch definitely is having something of a cultural moment, though it's by no means her first. Her popularity seems to experience a perennial revival alongside surges in women's rights: the revitalisation of Wicca in the 1970s, the boom in magic-adjacent popular culture in the 1990s, and now, the era of the digital witch, where many magically inclined young women find their communities in the ether of the internet. Vice is chock-full of witch-themed content, some of it fascinating, most of it self-consciously shallow. (The best features are about visiting renowned forest witch Susun Weed, who lives in Upstate New York, or about modern-day brujas engaging in the rituals of their ancestors after decades of colonial displacement from their own traditions. The mini-doco on Romanian witches who accept payment to cast love spells and predict the future is also a must-watch.) Sites like HelloGiggles, Zooey Deschanel and friends' foray into fluffy women's media, have articles called things like 'Witchcraft 101', with instructions on how to make a sufficiently mystical-looking grimoire. *Rookie* had a similar series on witchiness, with crystal guides and tips on how to set up an altar. And make-up giant Sephora recently courted controversy by advertising beginners' witchcraft kits, containing a bundle of sage, a rose quartz crystal and several mystical scents. (The kits were eventually pulled from production after an outcry from the witch community.)

The enduring figure of the teen witch is evidence enough of a youth-obsessed witch revival, as is the recent reboot of *Sabrina the Teenage Witch*, reimagined as *The Chilling Adventures of Sabrina* with a distinctly less bubbly and more Beelzebub-centred storyline. Focusing on the teen witch makes sense considering girls' historical association with uncanny events (Salem, Joan of Arc, the long tradition of pubescent girls attracting poltergeists and hauntings), and our continuing uneasiness over teenage girls' near-supernatural powers of change. But I'm no longer a teenager, and I won't be in Vice's target demographic forever. The appeal of identifying as a witch now, as I look into my future, is much more complex than when I was a thirteen-year-old first toying with Wicca.

•

We're at a cultural turning point where it feels like real change is at once within reach and about to be snatched away for good. Even as the #MeToo movement powers on, toppling predators from their thrones, the most powerful man in the world has made his predatory nature part of his brand and his platform. Women are spurred into solidarity with one another by the eerie plausibility of *The Handmaid's Tale* just as much as they are by the aspirational fantasy of *Wonder Woman*. The world, not just for women but for everyone, seems to have gone awry. Scientists tell us we have twelve years to undo a century of climate destruction. People are choosing to remain childless rather than bring new life into an uncertain world. Nazis are a thing again. A sense of unreality permeates everything, and for women, who have spent generations locked in a grim battle for rights—at our jobs, in our bedrooms, on the operating table—that other reality is a dark one. We teeter on this precipice; we could go either way; things are not in our control on any plane of the familiar. We're simultaneously the vectors of change and the bodies upon which it's wrought. It is a perilous place to be, in this uncharted terrain.

Being a witch promises us a lodestone: a legacy, a lineage of women, weird and wise, who came before us. It gives us a context in which to fit our suspicions, fears, superstitions and our new, unexpected lateral power. It provides meaning in an otherwise barren spiritual landscape, without demanding the sacrifice or cognitive dissonance of most mainstream religions. It suggests a connection to a broad, if invisible, network of other women practising the Craft. And it promises a compass with which to navigate the unknowable territory of growing older.

•

Humanity has a rich and enduring relationship with the super-natural, and in every culture there are people who commune with that realm by practising magic. Magic itself is a slippery term. In the West it occupies territory distinct both from science and religion; it's variously defined, depending on who you talk to, as controlling events through supernatural means, liaising with the Devil to cause harm to others, and/or ritualised actions to bring about change. For me, and I think for many witches, it's the ritual aspect that's most important. Magic and witchcraft ought to be distinguished from more general occultism and devil worship, which have the implications both of being more mas-culine and more closely aligned with standard religious styling, though many witches do consider their magical practice to be a form of religion or spiritualism. Importantly, not everyone who does magic is a witch; not all witches practise magic. Witches, like magic itself, are difficult to pin down.

But the big appeal of witchhood is surely its promise to women of a different way to be. Witches are mysterious, powerful, invul-nerable, unapologetic, demanding, spiteful, cruel, indulgent and independent—all things that seem pretty attractive alternatives to standard exemplars of femininity. There are so many ways to be a witch, from the glitter and rose quartz 'intention setting' of the fluffy bunny Wicca set, to the deeply unethical and defi-nitely illegal bone-collecting saga that scandalised Tumblr in 2015, to purely theoretical identity-claiming as a form of protest or dissention to the way things are. You can practise alone or in a coven. You can build a library of reference texts or make it up on the spot as you go. You can devote yourself to a single deity and perform elaborate rites for them, or you can call what you do a craft and keep gods out of it entirely.

Around the world, 'witch' means different things, and often carries with it heavier connotations than just fortune-telling or crystal healing. In Papua New Guinea, around one thousand witch-hunts take place every year, with many of their victims, usually poor or vulnerable women, tortured or murdered. In Tanzania, albino people are murdered and their body parts traded for use in witchcraft as charms to bring wealth or success. But what I know about is the Western, Anglo-European witch: a person who's both female and bad, who lies somewhere on the spectrum from creepily malicious to being in league with the Devil. These are the witches who populate our fairytales, who lure unsuspecting men to their dooms with glamours and magical disguises, who still loom close enough in the collective consciousness for the term to be deployed against any woman stepping out of line—a veiled reminder of the times we burned women like her. But for many women it's also a mark of strength, a choice to claim the marginal identity, and an avenue into a sisterhood that *feels* magical, regardless of whether it is or not.

•

I meet Brodie-Ann at her workplace, a red-walled shop in Brisbane's suburb West End suburb of Brisbane that's filled with tarot decks, books on the esoteric, and dead animals in parts or whole. She's exactly what I was hoping she'd be: pale and animated, with a lot of black curly hair and a red-lined cloak. She is a self-identified witch, and has been, she says, for her whole life. Even though many women identify as solitary witches— Brodie-Ann included—she recognises that part of the pull towards a witchcraft tradition is the promise of connection to other women. 'When women are together,' Brodie-Ann says, 'we raise power. We are something to be feared.'

I first came to witchcraft like most suburban white girls do: as a thirteen-year-old fantasy nerd with a flair for the dramatic. One of my friends' mothers was a druid and was happy to indulge our Celtic-inflected solstice parties and crystal collecting. My own mother, probably relieved that I wasn't spending my weekends getting drunk or having sex, bought me several bougie spell books—the kind you can get in chain bookstores—and helped me make my own broom to prop in the corner of my bedroom, collecting dust. I remember a lot of cheap essential oils, coloured candles and ribbons, and some hokey rhyming phrases designed to 'entice passion' or 'conjure confidence' into my life.

At the time it seemed like a real-life extension of everything I loved in literature: wonder, mysticism, magical girl protagonists. Ten years later, during my magical revival, the history of witchcraft and the women who practise it looked a lot darker, and a lot more complicated.

At first, when I made my early adulthood foray back into the realm of witchcraft, I found myself in familiar territory. My old patterns of magical thinking, neural pathways I recognised from my early adolescence, reignited, and I looked fervently for meaning—any meaning—in clouds, in the shapes of my cigarette smoke, in leaves dropped in my path from trees. In my early twenties, buffeted by unexpected crushes, jostling with former selves for some sense of identity, I was looking for something that offered a frame of control—and because I am not religious, and because I have always been a bit *woo*, the something was magic.

It was also extremely tongue-in-cheek. As I went headfirst

into my research, I'd surface every now and then to gleefully
report to friends on how to 'tie up a man's nature' using his
semen and a piece of cotton string, or to jokingly warn them
against starting new projects on the waning moon. But I still
found a lot of peace in the susurration of my watercolour pencils
in the Book of Shadows I started, a place to write flimsy rituals
and the magical uses of common herbs while listening to Kate
Bush and getting high with my velvet-draped friend Stephanie.
In witchcraft, even in the winking, self-parodying form I practised, I found that space to stretch my ego out fully that is so
often denied to girls and women. Brodie-Ann says magic is
about being 'self-governing', and that sounds about right. Magic
promises control to those who spend most of their time without
any, and it's also a site of luxurious self-indulgence. Doing
something like calling down the moon with a friend functions as
equal parts play, bonding exercise and testing the boundaries of
your beliefs—on your own terms, in your own time, with only
the pressure you want to exert upon yourself.

This is what captured me the most as I went deeper into
thinking about witches and everything they stand for: the glo-
rious, unfettered independence on offer, the clear-eyed com-
munion with other women around you, born out of your own
self-knowledge. Some of the appeal of being a witch, I think,
is the same appeal as being a nun: an opportunity to retain the
joyous wonder of girlhood, a time before sexualisation dulled
the edges of your interactions with the world. And, as well, tradition: the idea of sliding into place in a long line of witches—
outsider women, special women—is very appealing. It's fun and
fulfilling to imagine we are accessing some ancient ancestral
knowledge or wisdom.

There's also something deliciously corporeal about magic that maybe consciously plays into those old ideas about women being tragically Earth- and flesh-bound. I think about how I've always been fascinated by the bodily detritus we leave in our wake and how so much of that—hair, nail clippings, spit, semen, blood—is integral to making magic. All this is part of what I love about every black-lipstick-sporting fourteen-year-old and long-haired spinster aunt and old, irreverent wise woman. It's a defiance, almost childish, a leaning in to power. If you tell me I am just my flesh and blood, then I will make magic out of it. That enduring line from the art-house horror film *The Witch*: 'Wouldst thou like to live deliciously?' *Yes*, we say. *Yes, yes, yes*.

•

In the West, you can't talk about witches without discussing the so-called witch craze of the Middle Ages, during which an unknown number of women—some say in the thousands, some, dubiously, in the millions—were burned at the stake or hanged as witches. This era has almost passed into myth, becoming synonymous with society's punishment of independent or exceptional women. In truth, most of the women murdered for witchcraft were likely already outsiders: old, poor, without strong familial connections or social status, they were easy proxies onto which fearful and ignorant laypeople could project the incomprehensible terrors of medieval life. Failing crops, the death of infants and childbearing mothers, harsh winters, famines, poverty and impotence could all be blamed on a witch.

The Catholic Church was happy to oblige by torturing and murdering the accused. Ideas about women were becoming crueller, harsher and more deeply imbued with fear and loathing as the Church and its newly formed agencies sought to discredit feminine knowledge. Women, said the Church, were sex-crazed, naturally sinful, stupid, weak, superstitious; they were always just a few quick steps to falling into league with the Devil himself. On the wheel, accused witches confessed to flying on pigs or broomsticks to black Sabbaths, where they and their sisters would dance with Satan, learn his orders, and fly home to do his bidding. They stole children to eat or to offer up as gifts of souls to the Prince of Darkness. They turned milk sour in the goats' udders and caused married men to have lustful thoughts. At a time when sex was officially considered 'a necessary evil' (and bound by such strict rules as to where and when it could be performed, it's remarkable any further generations were conceived at all), any woman accused of inciting sin was at high risk of being branded a witch. Sex, death, domesticity—all the realms of women were also the realms of witchcraft. This is our magical heritage.

It pays to remember, however, that this heritage is an artificial one. Almost none of the women who were burned at the stake for practising witchcraft were actual witches, even in the permissive sense of the word today. They were almost universally unfairly maligned, God-fearing women, whose accidental proximity to natural disaster or death or poverty made them easy targets for the fear and anger of an ignorant and superstitious population. When we refer to the ashes of our foremothers, the conflagration is a false one, but it's so alluring as to be irresistible—and with the enduring construction of the witch as an amalgam of all things terrifying about the feminine, it's a small wonder so many women feel comfortable taking up the mantle now.

The most common magical practice for Western women these days has very little to do with what the witches of the Middle Ages were supposedly up to. Wicca, a new-age religion that purports to be based on ancient beliefs from the British Isles, in reality started to appear in its current iteration with Gerald Gardner in the mid-twentieth century, and shot to popularity during the New Age movement of the 1970s. This is the movement responsible for those big-box bookstore spell books I collected as a child, with titles like *The Goddess in the Office: A personal energy guide for the spiritual warrior at work* (by Zsuzsanna Budapest) and *To Ride a Silver Broomstick* (by Silver RavenWolf). Wicca emphasises a spiritual connectedness with the universe and the fertility-based God and Goddess, but its rules are fairly flexible, and it combines Celtic, Roma, Native American, Norse and Egyptian traditions and deities with little attention paid to accuracy or sensitivity. The gentle kind of 'spiritual manifestation' magic of Wicca, couched in terms of 'realisation of intent' or 'harnessing universal energy', promises no dalliances with the Devil, no flying, no milk-curdling and no influencing another's will. In fact, as Wiccan author Tudorbeth explains in the introduction to *Spells in the City*: 'Spells are like prayers, with the added kick of using nature to fuel them. They are always for good, for healing, and for giving and receiving that which we desire without bending the will of another.'

Brodie-Ann is not a Wiccan. She refers to herself as Pagan and practises a more hands-on, 'roots, stones and bones' kind of magic. This kind of folk magic has its origins in the spiritual traditions of historically disenfranchised populations—poor Irish and English folk, African practitioners displaced to America by the slave trade. It tends to deal with spit, semen, sex and spirits, along with blood, candles, graveyard dust, perfume, psalms and saints mixed up into rituals and charms that feel a whole lot more practical than prayers with an added kick.

'It's not meant to be going somewhere and getting your chakras aligned, and spending a hundred and fifty bucks. That's not magic, to me.' (I laugh. I know exactly what she's talking about.) 'There's a lot of sort of woo-woo business bullshit that goes on in this world at the moment. And it's not the old roots, stones and bones healing stuff. That's where I think my focus is, and I love that it's practical, and that it's powerful, and it's empowering magic. Again, it was created out of necessity by an oppressed people. And it survived, you know? And it was ancestral and hardcore.'

Ancestral and hardcore. Not a phrase that's commonly associated with women, I think. Brodie-Ann tells me something curious while we're talking: she says that the women who seek her services are almost always focused on improving themselves rather than influencing other people. They'll want to increase their chances of meeting someone to love, or boost the passion in their life. Men, on the other hand, are the only clients who'll ask her to do things she won't do: 'Like a love spell against a woman's conscience,' she says. 'When it comes to someone trying to manipulate or bend someone's will, I've only had men ask me to do that.'

I find this so interesting. It's only anecdotal, and while I'm sure there are plenty of women out there who've explicitly tried to use magic to influence the will of their object of desire, I think it's very telling that the women who see Brodie-Ann are choosing to use her powers generously rather than for specific personal manipulation. I don't want to make sweeping statements about the different fundamental natures of men and women—but how fascinating, that even in a space that's so decidedly feminine, women will contain or constrict their power so as not to unduly hurt someone, and men will abuse it. Some men. Sometimes.

·

I used to be afraid of getting older. As much as I wish I didn't, I place a fairly high importance on my physical appearance, and the thought of parting with my youth—slowly but surely— used to make me panic a little. This was coupled with the inconvenient fact that I don't want to have children. That old witch triad—maiden, mother, crone—it's so rooted in the reproductive that it feels like it falls apart when you take offspring out of the equation. I often felt like I didn't have a real rubric of how to be as an older woman. My grandmother's life revolved around her children; even Joan spent most of her time looking after her nieces and nephews, and their kids, and me. And I had swallowed the scorn we reserve for mothers and the child-adjacent just as I'd swallowed the imperative to be beautiful. I used to be very willing to entirely disqualify as role models women who'd had children. Which is absurd, because many of the women I've spoken to in the course of writing this book have children, and all of them appear to still be fully human, still have dreams and ambitions, still be rich and complex creatures with a wealth of knowledge and an intricate internal life. Surely something so steeped in blood magic as motherhood is enough to make a witch out of anyone.

These days I've shed my disdain for maternity, and I'm no longer so afraid of getting older (though I still don't want children). In a youth-obsessed culture, the witch—the crone—

presents an alternative to ageing into invisibility: an enviable, self-possessed woman at the height of her powers, who does what she chooses, who's beholden to no one. As I grow, the witches from the Disney films of my childhood start to look much more interesting than the heroines. Ursula from *The Little Mermaid* is a body-positive, ambitious loudmouth with fabulous make-up; the evil Queen from *Snow White and the Seven Dwarfs* is calculating, glamorous and talented as hell (if a little one-eyed about her stepdaughter), and she's willing to put her looks and her life on the line to get what she wants. Old women are revered as keepers of wisdom in lots of cultures. It took me a little while, and some adjusting of the terminology, to get my own ideas on track, too.

·

One of the things I've come to envy about older women is their connection to each other. Aunty Dawn and Sister Maryanne are great examples of this—they're both pivots around which their communities revolve, and they both have dozens of close female friends. I hear this often: that as women age, their friendships with one another deepen. It's happened to me already and I am greedy for more.

People send me stuff about witches all the time now. Although I no longer consider myself a practitioner of magic, I receive every link and book recommendation with profound gratitude. Every morsel passed along that shows another weird woman, alone or in a group, young or old, dressed in black or in a bright bandana, planting seeds or throwing bones, is an artefact of women's resilience, independence and joy in the face of despair. I love to be reminded of this worldwide coven, this network of wise women, whatever their creed. I love that a witch doesn't have to look one way or be one thing. I love witchcraft's non-committal nature, its self-directed learning, its entrepreneurial spirit, how welcoming it is to anyone with a streak of the mystical and a desire to do *something* to deal with a world that can feel incorrigible. I love the power it promises, and the pleasure it holds, and I love with all my crone-ish heart that it has always been and will always be the realm of women, together.

ACKNOWLEDGEMENTS

This book would not have been possible without the time, generosity and patience of so many kind, beautiful people. My deepest gratitude goes to my editor, Kathryn Knight, whose good-humoured tolerance of my disregard for deadlines should earn her some kind of award, and to Meredith Curnow, my publisher at Penguin Random House, for always being game to field a frantic phone call about my many insecurities and for always knowing exactly what to say to assuage them. My very sincere thanks as well to Lex Hirst, former commissioning editor at Penguin Random House, and to Sam Twyford-Moore and Brigid Mullane, without whom I would never have written the book in the first place; thank you all for taking a chance on me.

Witches is about women working together, and it makes me unutterably happy that it's the result of women working together, too. To every astounding woman I interviewed for this book, to Jane Green, the Vixen Collective, and the women of Salome's Circle, to my magnificent co-authors Liz Duck-Chong and Aunty Dawn Daylight, to my rigorous PhD supervisors Dr Hannah Stark and Dr Danielle Wood, to my brilliant mother, Fiona, to Joan, and to my dear friends who let me rant and cry about whichever chapter was kicking my arse at the time—Sally Edwards, Madeleine Laing, Stephanie Vidot, Joanna Ling and Emma Doolan, especially—for all your empathy, wisdom and support, thank you, thank you, thank you.

There were a couple of men, too, without whom I probably wouldn't have made it to the end of a book. I want to thank my dad for teaching me to read critically, research efficiently, and write like a human being. And to Donnie: thank you. I love you. I owe you big time.

About the Author

SAM GEORGE-ALLEN is an Australian writer and musician. Her essays, memoir, and cultural criticism have been published in *The Guardian*, the *Griffith Review*, the *Lifted Brow*, LitHub, and *Overland*. She lives in a haunted village in the south of Tasmania with her partner, a dog, a cat and five chickens. *Witches* is her first book.